Collaborative Governance for Local Economic Development

Although collaborations for local and regional economic development have been popular in recent years, it is not yet wholly clear when or how such efforts bring successful outcomes. Using an integrative conceptual framework for collaborative governance, this innovative collection provides a systematic and interdisciplinary analysis of real-world collaborative networks for local and regional economic development.

Focusing on a wide range of collaborative economic development in diverse cities and regions in the U.S.A, Canada, Germany, India, Italy, and South Korea, the chapters explore what forces motivate the emergence of collaborative economic development efforts. Each chapter explores the factors which contribute to or hinder collaborative governance efforts for economic development and identifies lessons for overcoming challenges to creating communities that are economically resilient, environmentally sustainable, and politically engaged in the era of globalization.

By focusing on collaborative governance and its implications for the ability of policies to meet the challenges of the 21st century, it provides lessons for researchers in public management, urban planning/development, public policy, and political science, as well as practitioners interested in promoting local economic development.

Denita Cepiku is Associate Professor in Public Management at the University of Rome "Tor Vergata," where she teaches Business Administration and Global Public Management and serves as the coordinator of the PhD program track in Public Management and Governance.

So Hee Jeon is Associate Professor and undergraduate director of the Public and Nonprofit Administration program in the Department of Political Science and Public Administration at Central Michigan University.

David K. Jesuit is Professor in the Department of Political Science and Public Administration at Central Michigan University and Chair of his Department.

Routledge Critical Studies in Public Management
Series editor: Stephen Osborne

The study and practice of public management has undergone profound changes across the world. Over the last quarter century, we have seen

- increasing criticism of public administration as the over-arching framework for the provision of public services,
- the rise (and critical appraisal) of the "New Public Management" as an emergent paradigm for the provision of public services,
- the transformation of the "public sector" into the cross-sectoral provision of public services, and
- the growth of the governance of inter-organizational relationship as an essential element in the provision of public services.

In reality, these trends have not so much replaced each other as elided or coexisted together – the public policy processes have not gone away as a legitimate topic of study, intra-organizational management continues to be essential to the efficient provision of public services, whilst the governance of inter-organizational and inter-sectoral relationships is now essential to the effective provision of these services.

Further, whilst the study of public management has been enriched by the contribution of a range of insights from the "mainstream" management literature, it has also contributed to this literature in such areas as networks and inter-organizational collaboration, innovation, and stakeholder theory.

This series is dedicated to presenting and critiquing this important body of theory and empirical study. It will publish books that both explore and evaluate the emergent and developing nature of public administration, management, and governance (in theory and practice) and examine the relationship with and contribution to the over-arching disciplines of management and organizational sociology.

Books in the series will be of interest to academics and researchers in this field, students undertaking advanced studies of it as part of their undergraduate or postgraduate degree and reflective policymakers and practitioners.

Crossing Boundaries in Public Policy and Management
Tackling the Critical Challenges
Edited by Luke Craven, Helen Dickinson and Gemma Carey

Public Administration Reformation
Market Demand from Public Organizations
Yogesh K. Dwivedi, Mahmud Shareef, Sanjay K Pandey and Vinod Kumar

The Projectification of the Public Sector
Edited by Damian Hodgson, Mats Fred, Simon Bailey, and Patrik Hall

Ethics Management in the Public Service
A Sensory-based Strategy
Liz Ireni-Saban and Galit Berdugo

Critical Perspectives on the Management and Organization of Emergency Services
Edited by Paresh Wankhade, Leo McCann, and Pete Murphy

Public Service Management and Asylum
Co-production, Inclusion and Citizenship
Kirsty Strokosch

Networks and Collaboration in the Public Sector
Essential research approaches, methodologies and analytic tools
Edited by Joris Voets, Robyn Keast and Christopher Koliba

Collaborative Governance for Local Economic Development
Lessons from Countries around the World
Edited by Denita Cepiku, So Hee Jeon, and David K. Jesuit

For more information about this series, please visit: www.routledge.com/Routledge-Critical-Studies-in-Public-Management/book-series/RSPM

Collaborative Governance for Local Economic Development

Lessons from Countries around the World

Edited by Denita Cepiku, So Hee Jeon, and David K. Jesuit

Routledge
Taylor & Francis Group
LONDON AND NEW YORK

First published 2020
by Routledge
2 Park Square, Milton Park, Abingdon, Oxon OX14 4RN

and by Routledge
605 Third Avenue, New York, NY 10017

First issued in paperback 2021

Routledge is an imprint of the Taylor & Francis Group, an informa business

Publisher's Note
The publisher has gone to great lengths to ensure the quality of this reprint but points out that some imperfections in the original copies may be apparent.

British Library Cataloguing-in-Publication Data
A catalogue record for this book is available from the British Library

Library of Congress Cataloging-in-Publication Data
A catalog record for this book has been requested

Typeset in Sabon
by Apex CoVantage, LLC

ISBN 13: 978-1-03-208627-9 (pbk)
ISBN 13: 978-1-138-49096-3 (hbk)

Contents

Preface

This volume represents the continued intellectual collaboration of scholars and practitioners under the auspices of the Transnational Initiative on Governance Research and Education Network, or "TIGRE Net." This international group of scholars, students, and field specialists is dedicated to identifying the opportunities and challenges public managers confront in the global economy and to providing them with the strategies and skills necessary to overcome obstacles to domestic, cross-border, and international coordination. Outputs from the TIGRE Net include several academic conferences and workshops, which have been supported by a grant from the Canadian Social Science and Humanities Research Council (SSHRC) and academic partners in the U.S., Italy, and Canada. Research from these events has been published in a number of academic outlets, including several edited collections. The most recent edited volume resulting from TIGRE Net collaboration is entitled *Public Policy, Governance and Polarization: Making Governance Work*, published by Routledge (2017). Previous volumes include *Governance and Public Management: Strategic Foundations for Volatile Times* (2014), also published by Routledge, and *Making Multilevel Governance Work: Lessons from Europe and North America* (2012), published by CRC Press. Outcomes from TIGRE Net have also been published in journals such as the *International Journal of Public Administration* (IJPA) and the *International Journal of Public Sector Management* (IJPSM). Core partners of TIGRE Net include universities in the U.S. (Central Michigan University & California State–Long Beach), Italy (the University of Rome "Tor Vergata" & the University of Macerata), and Canada (Memorial University [St. Johns], York University [Toronto], and Brock University [St. Catharines]).

Foreword: overcoming adversity through collaborative efforts

"Cities have the capability of providing something for everybody, only because, and only when, they are created by everybody."

– Jane Jacobs

Imagine sitting on your front porch and looking around your neighborhood, only to see that the homes next to yours are abandoned and dilapidated. Imagine having to call the fire department in an emergency, only for it to take hours for someone to show up, if they show up at all. Imagine turning on the tap and not being able to trust the water for drinking, cooking, or bathing.

For many, this may seem like make-believe imagery. But for many living in my hometown of Flint, Michigan, this is their daily reality. And for millions of people living in older, industrial communities, countless other families face similar challenges because they live in places that continue to experience significant economic stress.

My hometown of Flint has captured many newspaper headlines in recent years due to the water crisis. But even before this human-made tragedy, Flint faced obstacles seen in many older, industrial cities and towns: population loss, the outsourcing of jobs, and rampant blight. While some have dismissed these challenges as unique to Flint, what is happening to my hometown isn't some anomaly. Rather, Flint is a warning.

There are dozens of communities in every region of the country – Youngstown, Ohio; Gary, Indiana; Buffalo, New York – that face economic stress so great that it threatens their solvency. Unfortunately, many of these places have been left behind by current public policy, completely lost in the national conversation. Despite lower unemployment and job creation across the U.S., many of these cities and towns are still struggling with the transition from the old to the new economy. And current public policy – or lack thereof – makes it nearly impossible for these older, industrial communities to compete in today's economy. Many of these places struggle with the basic elements of a civilized society: tackling blight, maintaining police and fire, and managing aging water systems that are one mistake away from catastrophe.

When I was first elected to Congress, I hoped that if I worked hard, I could eventually get a seat at the table with those working on behalf of these older, industrial communities. But after I arrived in Washington, I realized there were very few actual conversations happening amongst Members of Congress, and no comprehensive legislation to address the unique needs of America's cities and towns.

Right now, there are only a few existing community development programs at the federal level. Those that do exist – like the U.S. Department of Housing and Urban Development's Community Development Block Grant program (CDBG) – have consistently been cut over the last decade, by almost 40%. These steep cuts have coincided with increased demand for the program. In 2003, around 1,000 communities received CDBG funding. By 2017, that number had risen to over 1,200. Despite a 20% increase in outlays, the federal government cut CDBG funding by 39%, meaning America's cities and towns have been forced to do more with less.

At the same time, many states also cut support for basic municipal services. Since 2001, the state of Michigan cut revenue sharing to local communities by over $6 billion, according to the nonpartisan Michigan Municipal League. In Flint alone, state revenue sharing was cut by $54.9 million by the end of 2014. That amount of investment could have paid Flint's entire deficit and bond debts while still leaving millions in surplus.

It cannot be overstated how much of an impact this reduced funding has had at the local level. Because of budget cuts and extreme austerity measures, a whole subset of America's cities and towns are struggling to provide basic public services to their residents, including police, fire, and trash pick-up.

In the face of such extreme budget cuts, foundations, nonprofits, and the private sector have attempted to step up and fill the void. Their efforts have helped, but with direct state and federal support to cities and towns at its lowest levels in decades, philanthropy can't come close to replacing these investments in basic services.

America's cities and towns are worth supporting, for the sake of the people who live there and for our society as a whole. These are unique places where millions of people work, live, and raise a family. Across America, cities are places that are creative, inventive, and ingenious. That ingenuity connects and creates incredible, great big ideas.

Going forward, we must rethink the way we support America's cities and towns. We need to change the way policymakers approach, think about, and ultimately invest in these places. We must have an honest national conversation around communities like Flint and many others to ensure that policymakers understand what is at stake. We need a new "Marshall Plan" for these communities to inject new economic redevelopment into these places, including through more collaboration across all levels of government and the private sector.

At the state and federal level, we need a coherent and intentional policy that supports increased opportunity, promotes growth, and recognizes that our national interest includes strong, vibrant cities and towns. This includes making necessary changes to existing community development programs like CDBG while also targeting new investments in these older, industrial communities. Because of its potential size and scale, a nationwide infrastructure project has the immediate potential to inject new capital, economic growth, and jobs into these places, and we must approach such public policy with a focus on these fiscally stressed communities.

Additional collaboration between government, communities, nonprofits, and private entities will also be an important factor. Indeed, we have already seen the benefits of such projects in my district. The redevelopment of Bay City's downtown is a prime example of the good that can be accomplished through collaborative public-private partnerships between business owners and government. The storefronts are full, the historic buildings are being redeveloped for mixed use, and people are moving back into the city. Through the power of gathering resources and cooperating to breathe new life into the community, Bay City is just one of many success stories throughout the state.

While the water crisis has dominated Flint headlines over the past few years, the city has also been the beneficiary of successful public-private partnerships. The Genesee County Land Bank, which serves Flint, came out of collaboration between local and state governments, turning vacant and abandoned properties into vibrant places. Since the 1970s, Flint had lost nearly half of its population and much of its manufacturing base, leaving behind a significant number of vacant and foreclosed properties. But the tax foreclosure system intended to find new uses for abandoned properties was too complex and took far too long to efficiently deal with them, instead leaving them dormant and targets of speculators.

By creating the Genesee County Land Bank – a public-private partnership, the first of its kind – policymakers created an efficient way to allow Flint to move foreclosed properties to productive use. The land bank is responsible for tens of millions of dollars in redevelopment in Flint. It has also served as a model for over 120 other land banks across the nation, according to the Center for Community Progress. The city of Flint has made blight removal a key part of its Master Plan, and with the infusion of new federal capital, the Land Bank has removed thousands of vacant and abandoned properties in recent years.

These examples of new investment and collaboration are just some of the ways that reinvestment and redevelopment are happening in Michigan's communities. It is a roadmap of success concerning the work that remains.

What we cannot do, however, is simply take a balance-sheet approach to trying to "fix" America's cities and towns. Some benefits never appear on a balance sheet. For example, removing a vacant structure in a neighborhood is a proven way to raise property values for surrounding homeowners. But getting rid of blight will also have a profound impact on the future of a child who sits on their front porch and no longer sees a vacant building across from their house.

Instead, let's have a much more thoughtful, intentional, and holistic approach to revitalization. Ultimately, improving the quality of life for people is what matters when we address the challenges of America's older, industrial communities.

Our challenge is to find ways to revitalize these communities and tap into the potential of every family, of every neighborhood, of every community. The challenge is large, and the solution will be multifaceted, and will succeed only if it involves collaboration across government, nonprofits, and the private sector to help spur redevelopment and bring life back to America's great older cities and towns.

Dan Kildee

Introduction

This book explores collaborative governance efforts in various regions around the world to identify lessons for overcoming challenges to creating economically resilient communities in the era of globalization. Thus, the two core concepts that run through every chapter of this book and constitute a theme for the book are: collaborative governance, and local and regional economic development. Traditionally these two concepts have been perceived as not very relevant to each other. It was competition and winning, not collaboration and cooperation, that have traditionally been emphasized as essential for economic prosperity in a city or a region. Local governments have approached economic development as a zero-sum game where they should compete with one another to attract and promote businesses in their own jurisdictions (Lee, Feiock, & Lee, 2012). However, such a competition-driven approach does not help address issues associated with economic development, such as economies of scale and spillovers (Im, Jeon, & Kim, 2017). With the recognition that these issues can be better handled through collaborative efforts, an increasing number of cities and regions in countries around the world have cultivated and become involved with collaborative networks for economic development.

Scholars have also recognized the usefulness of collaborative governance for addressing complex problems, including local and regional economic development (Fleischmann, 2000; Im et al., 2017; Lee et al., 2012). Although collaborative efforts for local and regional economic development have been popular in recent years, it is not yet very clear when government entities initiate or are involved in such collaborative efforts and, more importantly, when such efforts bring successful outcomes for economic development. Recognizing this gap in knowledge, this book aims to advance our understanding of successful collaboration networks for local and regional economic development. Why or when are government entities and private actors involved in collaborative economic development efforts? How can such collaborative efforts be better facilitated? What are the preconditions for collaborative governance to lead to successful economic development? This book analyzes diverse cases of local and economic development from around the world in order to address these questions. By so doing, this book aims to promote improved collaborative governance arrangements to foster community development and redevelopment.

Below, we review existing literature on collaborative governance and introduce the integrative framework that every chapter of this volume uses to analyze real-world cases of collaborative governance for economic development. We discuss why the particular framework has been selected as the theoretical basis to analyze various cases and briefly describe the framework. Finally, we introduce the main themes of each chapter of the book.

Collaborative governance

Collaborative governance is defined as "the processes and structures of public policy decision making and management that engage people constructively across the boundaries of public agencies, levels of government, and/or the public, private and civic spheres in order to carry out a public purpose that could not otherwise be accomplished" (Emerson, Nabatchi, & Balogh, 2012, p. 2). Thus, collaborative governance involves a relationship intended to increase public value through reciprocity and working together with the public (Agranoff & McGuire, 2004, p. 4; Bardach, 1998, p. 8; Huxham, 1996). It is a hybrid mode of decision-making and service provision in which a public agency deliberately and directly engages non-state entities in a formal, consensual, and collective decision-making process to manage programs and to solve problems that cannot be easily or at all solved by single organizations (Agranoff & McGuire, 2004; Ansell & Gash, 2008, p. 544).

Wicked problems and interdependency are two main concepts in collaborative governance theory. Collaborative settings are established when wicked problems exist and the several actors involved are aware of interdependency and recognize a certain value of working with other partners (Kickert, Klijn, & Koppenjan, 1997, p. 6). Wicked problems are unstructured and continually evolving, crosscutting multiple policy domains, levels of government and jurisdictions and, consequently, involving the different views, culture, values, and political background of several stakeholders (Weber & Khademian, 2008). If not managed properly, this multiplicity will easily transform into conflict. Collaboration could be an instrument for achieving broader effects, such as enhanced social capital through cohesive communities, shared values, and trust. Meanwhile, interdependency is created when no single actor, being it public, private, or third sector entity, has all the knowledge and sufficient overview of information, or power required to solve complex, dynamic, and diversified problems. Therefore, no single actor could dominate unilaterally in a particular governing model (Kooiman, 1993, p. 4). Mutual trust and active citizenship are encouraged through collaborative arrangement values (Cepiku, 2017). It can be a means for strengthening and revitalizing democracy as it develops new relationships between citizens and state based on trust, ethical standards, and accountability (Alford, 2014; Cahn & Gray, 2012; Pestoff, 2006; Ostrom, Parks, Whitaker, & Percy, 1978).

Many collaborative forms exist, each demanding specific management issues (Huxham, 2000, p. 341). Collaborative organizations can be isolated, which have a short life if they are not inserted in an institutional framework, or institutional, existing among other organizations. One of the most important features of collaborative arrangements is that there is neither hierarchical authority nor formal subordination. Interaction is based on expertise, trust, and legitimacy. Collaboration is voluntary and members could step out at any time if they are not satisfied or aware of the value produced from collaboration (Hill & Lynn 2003, p. 65), allowing collaborative interactions to exchange resources and negotiate shared purposes, rooted in trust and regulated by shared rules.

Collaborative governance is a term that is loaded with ambiguity, and several normative and positive definitions are found in literature (Cepiku, 2013; Frederickson, 2005). Bretschneider, Choi, Nabatchi, and O'Leary (2012) identify three approaches to collaborative governance: 1) theories of organizational behavior that mainly refer to resource dependent theory, which suggests that individual organizations do not have enough resources to achieve their goals (Pfeffer & Salancik, 1978); 2) public value theory, according to which managers give away their autonomy if public value will be created easily through collaborative governance. If properly implemented, agencies in collaboration with the private sector will achieve public goals becoming a powerful lever for creating public value (Donahue & Zeckhauser, 2011); and 3) the availability of performance information, which could be useful for sharing or reallocating resources among organizations. Performance information could also be used to inform partners on the convenience of collaborative arrangements, aiming to strengthen their commitment and willingness to collaborate with others, thus having an advantage compared to other organizational forms (Bretschneider et al., 2012; McGuire & Agranoff, 2007, p. 21).

Some of the reasons that motivate citizens to collaborate with the public sector are material self-interest and intrinsic rewards, such as sense of belonging and the need to feel competent (Alford, 2014). Citizens are willing to collaborate or co-produce based on their personal features, on the kind and salience of the service provided, on transaction costs that make voice more relevant than exit, and the ease of involvement, among others. Collaboration between citizens and civil service organizations is motivated by the fact that it achieves strong user and citizens' engagement, and also due to governance drivers, such as low administrative capacity of the public sector, and logistical drivers, deriving from the intrinsic nature of the specific public service (Bovaird, 2007; Joshi & Moore, 2004, p. 855; OECD, 2011, p. 48). Hence, the successful implementation of collaborative governance will depend on the social capacities of secondary associations and the ties between local and central government officials, which are crucial to how well decentralized governance institutions function (Culpepper, 2003). Despite its positive effects, citizens' participation faces several challenges

(Frieling, Lindenberg, & Stokman, 2014), such as: 1) the dilemma of size; 2) the dilemma of excluded or oppressed groups; 3) the dilemma of time and crisis; 4) the dilemma of technology and expertise; 5) the dilemma of common good; and finally 6) the dilemma of sustainable cooperation.

Two main arrangements of collaborative governance are inter-institutional networks and co-production (Cepiku, 2017). Networks include multiple organizations, linked by some form of structural interdependence, in which one organization is not the subordinate of others; are shaped around policy problems and programs; and are reproduced and changed by the interactions of different actors (Kickert et al., 1997; O'Toole, 1997, p. 45). Their system is mainly based on members' expertise rather than hierarchical positions (Agranoff, 2003, p. 11). Intergovernmental and intersectoral networks are fundamentally changing the nature of public policy and administration at all levels of government (Collaborative Democracy Network, 2006).

Three forms of network governance identified are: self-governance networks, lead-organizational networks, and administrative-organization networks (Kenis & Provan, 2009; Provan & Milward, 1995). The critical point of collaboration sustainability is to choose the appropriate institutional design and then implement it. When only few actors are involved, it may be appropriate working as a self-governed network, while in a lead organization network, one member bears the responsibility for network management. Both types have their pros and cons. Self-governed networks may be inefficient with frequent meetings and difficulty in reaching consensus, but partners do not fear a loss of control. To the contrary, while a lead-organization network may be efficient and sustainable, it may produce a lack of commitment by the partners (Cepiku, 2017).

Co-production is first studied in the late 1970s by Ostrom et al. (1978) and Parks, Baker, Kiser, Oakerson, and Ostrom (1981). It is defined as the combination of activities that both citizens, contributing based on voluntary efforts, and public service agents, involved as professionals, contribute to the provision of public services (Parks et al., 1981). Co-production enables the user to take more control and ownership, transforming the relationship between service providers and users. It could lead to better outcomes as results will be aligned to citizens' needs. An interesting form of co-production is user innovation, whose main characteristic is the involvement of users in the innovation process, making evident users' needs by using assets of other organizations and individuals to discover, develop, and implement ideas within and outside boundaries (Bommert, 2010; Eggers & Singh, 2009, p. 98; Wise & Høgenhaven, 2008). It increases citizens' trust in government, improves awareness of social problems, and delivers effective practices based on citizen experience (Cepiku, 2017). User innovation conditions can be found at the macro level, including country traditions and public policies, at the meso level, that includes legal and institutional conditions, and at the micro or organizational level, that includes past experiences, incentives, and power resource asymmetries (Sørensen & Torfing,

2011, p. 860). User innovation has an impact on organizational structures and behaviors and requires a focus on expertise, rather than on position (Meijer, 2014, p. 213). A disadvantage of co-production is that it can be accessible only to specific social groups, worsening the gap between different social classes (Bovaird & Downe, 2008; Brandsen & Helderman, 2012).

Managing a network or a co-production project is complex, as it includes management in a situation of interdependencies. It requires an appropriate institutional design, development of proper management mechanisms, implementation of performance management systems, and effective leadership. The voluntary nature of collaborative governance increases the importance of measurement and performance information at multiple levels, especially when community-based arrangements are composed of both public and private actors (Cepiku, 2017).

The conceptual framework of performance collaborative settings was first developed by Provan and Milward in 1995 and was further developed by Klijn, Steijn, and Edelenbos (2010) and Cepiku (2014). According to these scholars, collaborative settings include: 1) intermediate outcomes in terms of quality of collaboration management; 2) outcomes produced for the benefit of each partner (or organizational-level performance); and 3) outcomes achieved for the community at large.

The quality of collaboration can be evaluated by measuring conflict resolution; the productive use and reconciliation of differences in perspectives; the extent to which the collaborative process has encountered stagnations or deadlocks; administrative efficiency; stability and flexibility of rules and of the organizational form; inclusiveness of decision-making; and satisfaction of the participants with network management (Klijn et al., 2010; Mandell & Keast, 2008).

The outcomes of collaboration can be divided into two levels: single-partner level and community level. The outcomes at the single-partner level refer to the satisfaction of each member with both the results delivered by collaboration arrangements and the management of interaction (Crosby & Bryson, 2010, p. 226). To the contrary, the outcomes at the environmental or community level include the overall benefits delivered to the community that go beyond partner-increased well-being. However, costs to the community, the social capital created, and public perceptions that problems are being solved are just some of positive and negative externalities that emerge from collaborative settings (Provan & Milward, 1995). Furthermore, particular attention must be paid to negative and unforeseen effects in terms of equity and external accountability and to longer-term impacts (Cepiku, 2017).

The context in which collaboration takes place is a relevant determinant of both the quality of interaction and the final outcome produced for the partners and the community. Collaboration settings get affected by exogenous and endogenous determinants. Endogenous factors can be managed by collaborative leaders and include the organizational structure, the management, and the leadership style. These factors are considered to be the most important determinants of success or failure (McGuire & Agranoff, 2007, p. 23). Exogenous determinants include those factors that cannot be controlled by collaboration managers or partners. Some of these elements are resource munificence and cohesion, system stability, goal consensus among partners prior to collaboration, the number of partners and their geographic location, competing institutional logics and complementarity of partners, trust and previous collaboration history, external legitimation (support from public opinion, community, and other stakeholders at inception), purpose of the collaborative arrangement, nature of tasks and severity of the problem, environmental shocks, and number and kind of constituencies, among others (Kenis & Provan, 2009; Provan & Milward, 1995). The presence and relative relevance of these elements changes from case to case and from one policy sector to another.

Institutional design choices affect the way collaborative agendas are formed and implemented and have consequences for what can actually be achieved (Baker & Faulkner, 1993; Cross, Parker, & Borgatti, 2002; Huxham & Vangen, 2000; Kenis & Provan, 2009; Provan & Milward, 1995). It includes designing the division of resources and actor positions of the lead organization, rules of entry, the boundaries of collaboration, values, norms, and perceptions (Cepiku, 2017). Identifying, motivating, and activating the parties necessary for tackling a particular problem may require an analysis of previous strategies (Kickert et al., 1997). The management process of collaborative agreements includes a wide range of functions, such as active collaboration, arrangement of interaction, brokerage, mediation and arbitration, and legitimacy building. Mechanisms able to arrange interaction, such as formal agreements and conflict-regulating mechanisms, avoid free rider behavior and manage accountability and premature exiting behavior. This is done by ensuring that times and meeting places are agreed upon, notes and minutes are kept, and the quality of the dialogue is monitored (Milward & Provan, 2006, p. 18). In the meantime, brokerage consists of matching problems, solutions, and partners. If conflicts arise, mediation and arbitration will be implemented ensuring that relations are maintained and confronting the parties with the perceptions and interests of the "outside world" (Cepiku, 2017).

In addition, both arrangements require adjusting the behaviors of actors with different ambitions and objectives; coordinating the strategies of actors with different goals and preferences with regard to a certain problem; initiating and facilitating interaction processes; and creating and changing institutional arrangements for better coordination (Friend, Power, & Yewlett, 1974; Kickert et al., 1997, p. 10, pp. 43–4). Building and maintaining legitimacy on collaborative governance arrangements is critical due to its voluntary nature (Milward & Provan, 2006, p. 19).

The resulting impact from collaborative initiatives can be physical, environmental, social, economic, and/or political (Emerson et al., 2012, p. 18). Innes and Booher (1999, p. 419) provide an exhaustive list of potential impacts that may emerge from a collaborative initiative. Some outcomes will be direct effects immediately identifiable at the end of the project. They refer to them as first order effects: social capital (trust, relationships), intellectual capital (mutual understanding, shared problem frames, agreed upon data); and political capital (ability to work together for agreed ends, high-quality agreements; innovative strategies). Second order effects will occur while the project is underway, but outside the boundaries of the project or even after it is completed. These include new partnerships; coordination and joint action; joint learning extensions into the community; implementation of agreements; changes in practices; and changes in perceptions. Others will be third order effects, which may be evident at a later time: new collaborations; more coevolution, less destructive conflict; results on the ground (adaptation of cities, regions, resources, services); new institutions; new norms and heuristics; and new discourses.

Theoretical framework for case analysis: Emerson and Nabatchi's (2015) integrative framework for collaborative governance

As discussed above, the existing literature on collaborative governance has explored various aspects, ranging from its purposes, to the forms of collaborative networks, to conditions for successful implementation of collaborative networks, to the effects of collaborative networks, and to the evaluation of collaboration quality and outcomes. Recently, Emerson and Nabatchi (2015) conducted an extensive review and synthesis of such literature on collaborative governance. Based on the review and synthesis, Emerson and Nabatchi (2015) developed an integrative framework.

While there are other frameworks for collaborative governance, Emerson and Nabatchi's (2015) integrative framework synthesizes a wide range of literature on collaborative governance and relevant conceptual frameworks, and considers a comprehensive set of factors that could affect collaborative outcomes. As Emerson and Nabatchi (2015) suggest, their framework also arranges different components in a way that postulates a causal relationship between the components. Accordingly, Emerson and Nabatchi's (2015) integrative framework serves as a particularly useful tool to test theories and find ways to improve practices. As such, we chose Emerson and Nabatchi's (2015) integrative framework as the theoretical basis for every chapter to use so that each chapter can examine real-world cases of collaborative governance for economic development in a systematic manner.

Before introducing the main themes of each chapter, below, we provide a brief description of Emerson and Nabatchi's (2015) integrative framework for collaborative governance, which consists of three dimensions: the system context, the collaborative governance regime (CGR), and its collaboration dynamics and collaborative actions. The system context is the external environments that influence and are influenced by the CGR, and it includes such factors as legal framework, political dynamics, socioeconomic characteristics, and so on. The CGR, which is the central feature of the framework, is defined as "a system in which cross-boundary collaboration represents the predominate mode for conduct, decision making, and activity" (Emerson et al., 2012, p. 10). Finally, the collaboration dynamics and subsequent collaborative actions over time are what constitute a CGR (Emerson & Nabatchi, 2015).

According to Emerson and Nabatchi's (2015, p. 44) integrative framework, the emergence of a CGR can be explained by four *drivers*, which emerge from the system context: uncertainty, interdependence, consequential incentives, and initiating leadership. Once the CGR is formed, collaborative governance operates based on participating actors' interactions, where collaboration dynamics come into play. The *collaboration dynamics*, composed of "three interacting components" of principle engagement, shared motivation, and the capacity for joint action (Emerson & Nabatchi, 2015, p. 28), lead to *collaborative actions*, which in turn produce collaborative *outcomes* or *impacts*. Finally, responding to the nature and level of the collaborative outcomes, the CGR itself may experience *adaptations*.

Plan of the book

As noted by Congressman Dan Kildee in the Foreword of this edited volume, collaborative governance approaches to economic [re]development in regions devastated by deindustrialization, such as Flint, Michigan, have already resulted in some success stories. Indeed, he emphatically calls for more of this style of governance in order to promote urban renewal. As we will see, his optimism is supported by several cases examined in this volume. However, the chapters also highlight challenges to collaborative governance and failures.

Chapters 1 and 2 of the volume focus on cases in Representative Kildee's geographic area, namely the North American regional hub of automobile manufacturing that experienced substantial deindustrialization over the last several decades. Specifically, Greitens and Quarles examine Detroit's renaissance as a Midwestern cultural center in Chapter 1. They discuss the competitive paradigm that dominated approaches to economic development in Detroit and the surrounding area for decades, which, despite some accomplishments, fostered a climate of distrust in a zero-sum game climate. This distrust between leaders in different localities, especially Detroit and everyone else, still exists. In this context, they examine the rather remarkable case of the Detroit Institute of Arts (DIA), whose renaissance ushered in a transformative decade of collaborative governance approaches. They find that the collaborative relationships that were developed to rescue this cultural treasure were primarily fostered by an exogenous variable, namely the shift towards Richard Florida's (2014) concept of economic development rooted in "cool cities." They conclude on a cautionary note, however, raising concerns about the decreasing capacity of local actors to engage in such collaborative partnerships due to shrinking public budgets.

Chapter 2, by Robert Heuton, examines the Canadian city of Windsor, which is just across the Detroit River from Detroit and is also part of the North American automobile manufacturing hub. Unlike Detroit, however, Windsor has not successfully embraced collaborative governance, and economic development efforts are therefore more limited than their U.S. neighbor. Indeed, Heuton finds that this border constitutes a barrier to collaborative regional governance and notes the efforts that have been made, mostly unsuccessful, such as in the case of the Detroit-Windsor bid to host Amazon Headquarters Two, to overcome this obstacle. Despite this recent failure to attract Amazon, he concludes that the Windsor-Detroit region is in a strategic location and that new collaborative approaches are needed to help the area realize its potential. In short, collaborative governance does not happen without effort, resources, and commitment by local elites.

While Emma Powell's case studies remain North American, in Chapter 3 she examines a relatively new tool for economic development that has been applied in different countries and contexts: Social Impact Bonds (SIBs). SIBs represent an extension of traditional public-private partnerships and represent a market-driven approach to growing revenues and increasing outputs. New York City's *ABLE Project for Incarcerated Youth* and Michigan's 2016 *Strong Beginning's Project* are the specific SIB cases she examines, determining that such approaches clearly demonstrate a collaborative governance model of policymaking. She concludes that these tools require trust in order to yield successful outcomes and may be applied to a broad range of issues.

This type of trust-based collaborative mechanism is also examined by Arindam Biswas and Mohit Dev in Chapter 4. In their contribution, however, they focus on the informal sector in the Indian urban transportation system. Specifically, they provide us with an insightful overview of the informal networks that have evolved alongside formal institutions in the rapidly growing urban transport sector in India. While they are not definitive and provide some stipulations, they assert that studying the process of collaborative governance in this sector enables us to see how, in fact, informal networks may be more accurately described as formal institutions. This is a contentious claim that merits further investigation and discussion in a different venue. Regardless of the outcome of this theoretical debate, they envision that the collaborative processes within the Indian urban transportation sector will endure for the foreseeable future.

Next, in Chapter 5 Eunok Im and So Hee Jeon study collaborative governance in the Republic of Korea (ROK). They provide a very useful example of how a central government can promote and facilitate collaborative governance processes between subnational government structures in order to promote regional economic development. Focusing on the mega-economic regions (MERs) initiative, a regionally based governance introduced in Korea in 2009, they analyze the context, drivers, operation, and outcomes of the

MERs. There are a total of seven MERs in the ROK, each defined according to an area's economic specialization. One of the main purposes of the MERs was to promote collaborative governance among the local governments within each territory, primarily provinces and municipalities. With powerful incentives provided by the central government, it is not surprising that Im and Jeon find strong evidence of a collaborative style of governance. However, this collaboration did not just result from financial incentives; factors such as uncertainty and economic interdependence among local government actors, and proactive leadership from the central government also fostered collaborative governance. Finally, they conclude that the spatial model of economic development implemented in the ROK could be emulated with success in other countries, such as France or Japan.

Chapter 6, by Nebojša Čamprag, examines Germany, with a focus on economic development strategies implemented in the lander (states) that comprised the former German Democratic Republic (GDR). Similar to Chapter 2 focusing on the case of Windsor, Canada, this chapter finds that there have been many obstacles to implementing collaborative governance in Germany. Notably, the smaller municipalities have lacked sufficient resources, including human capital, to manage complex collaborative arrangements, echoing a concern raised in the conclusion of the first chapter by Greitens and Quarles. Moreover, resource disparities between local partners presented similar obstacles to collaborative governance, limiting even the ability of more prosperous localities to engage in collaboration. Finally, the centralized planning in which local governments had no role in economic development planning that characterized the former GDR created a powerful path dependency that presents a barrier to initiating any planning for economic development. They note that even the relative success of collaborative governance approaches in the cities of Dresden and Leipzig that were identified were highly contingent on distinctive attributes within these cities.

Denita Cepiku and her colleagues offer our final case studies in Chapter 7. Drawn from Italian municipalities, they explicitly seek cases that represent "best" and "worst" practices in collaborative governance. Italy provides a particularly fertile ground for case studies since it has enacted a number of reforms that seek to promote collaboration in response to the global financial crisis of 2008. Among the five cases they examine, they find three successes, with the other two being considered failures, or at least not successful. They conclude that the factors that determine whether a collaborative governance approach succeeds or not include, among other things: the nature of the problem, the type of organizational arrangements among the local actors, the relative power of local partners, a reluctance on the part of public sector actors in losing autonomy, a failure to provide incentives and rewards, and a varied commitment to common goals between the partners. Perhaps most importantly, they urge practitioners to lay stronger foundations among citizens by seeking to build community ties prior to launching collaborative projects and to acknowledge at the outset the risks entailed with collaborative governance. In short, not all efforts will succeed, and managers need to adapt to this reality and overcome their risk-averse predispositions.

We invited Rick S. Kurtz to draft a conclusion for us in the final chapter. In addition to a worthwhile overview of the chapters we have just described, Kurtz presents one additional approach to economic development that practitioners should consider. The "lean startup–fail fast" business model is, Kurtz admits, a difficult model to sell to citizens and risk-averse public managers. However, he argues that this method, which is premised on starting small with a minimally viable product, might be akin to "incrementalism with a 21st century twist." In other words, start small and, if successful, scale-up. Regardless of what one considers the merits of this approach, Kurtz echoes Representative Kildee in the Foreword and ends with a call for collaboration across all sectors. Indeed, we hope that the following contributions inform and equip readers and ultimately inspire effective actions by practitioners and citizens to promote prosperity in their communities in the era of globalization.

References

Agranoff, R. (2003). *Understanding networks: A guide for public managers*. Bloomington: School of Public and Environmental Affairs, Indiana University.

Agranoff, R., & McGuire, M. (2004). *Collaborative public management: New strategies for local governments*. Washington, DC: Georgetown University Press.

Alford, J. (2014). The multiple facets of co-production: Building on the work of Elinor Ostrom. *Public Management Review*, 16(3), 299–316.

Ansell, C., & Gash, A. (2008). Collaborative governance in theory and practice. *Journal of Public Administration Research and Theory*, 18(4), 543–571.

Baker, W. E., & Faulkner, R. R. (1993). The social organization of conspiracy: Illegal networks in the heavy electrical equipment industry. *American Sociological Review*, 58(6), 837–860.

Bardach, E. (1998). *Getting agencies to work together: The practice and theory of managerial craftsmanship*. Washington, DC: Brookings Institution Press.

Bommert, B. (2010). Collaborative innovation in the public sector. *International Public Management Review*, 11(1), 15–33.

Bovaird, T. (2007). Beyond engagement and participation: User and community coproduction of public services. *Public Administration Review*, 67(5), 846–860.

Bovaird, T., & Downe, J. (2008). Innovation in public engagement and co-production of services. In *Policy paper to department of communities and local government*. Cardiff: Cardiff Business School.

Brandsen, T., & Helderman, J. (2012). The conditions for successful co-production in housing: A case study of German housing cooperatives. In V. Pestoff, T. Brandsen, & B. Verschuere (Eds.), *New Public Governance, the third sector and co-production*. New York: Routledge.

Bretschneider, B., Choi, Y., Nabatchi, T., & O'Leary, R. (2012). *Does public value matter for collaboration? Evidence from an experimental analysis*. Paper presented at the Creating Public Value Conference, University of Minnesota, Minneapolis, September 20–22.

Cahn, E., & Gray, C. (2012). Co-production from a normative perspective. In V. Pestoff, T. Brandsen, & B. Verschuere (Eds.), *New Public Governance, the third sector and co-production*. New York: Routledge.
Cepiku, D. (2013). Unraveling the concept of public governance: A literature review of different traditions. In L. Gnan, A. Hinna, & F. Monteduro (Eds.), *Conceptualizing and researching governance in public and non-profit organizations: Studies in public and non-profit governance* (pp. 3–32). Bingley: Emerald Group Publishing.
Cepiku, D. (2014). Network performance: Toward a dynamic multidimensional model. In R. Keast, M. P. Mandell, & R. Agranoff (Eds.), *Network theory in the public sector: Building new theoretical frameworks*. New York: Routledge.
Cepiku, D. (2017). Collaborative governance. In T. Klassen, D. Cepiku, T. J. Lah (Eds.), *Handbook of global public policy and administration*. London: Routledge.
Collaborative Democracy Network. (2006). A call to scholars and teachers of public administration, public policy, planning, political science, and related fields. *Public Administration Review*, 66(s1), 168–170.
Crosby, B. C., & Bryson, J. M. (2010). Integrative leadership and the creation and maintenance of cross-sector collaborations. *Leadership Quarterly*, 21(2), 211–230.
Cross, R., Parker, A., & Borgatti, S. (2002). *A bird's-eye view: Using social network analysis to improve knowledge creation and sharing*. Somers, NY: IBM Corporation.
Culpepper, P. D. (2003). "Institutional rules, social capacity, and the stuff of politics: Experiments in collaborative governance in France and Italy." Working Paper Series rwp03–029, Harvard University, John F. Kennedy School of Government.
Donahue, J. D., & Zeckhauser, R. J. (2011). *Collaborative governance: Private roles for public goals in turbulent times*. Princeton; Oxford: Princeton University Press.
Eggers, W. D., & Singh, K. S. (2009). *The public innovator's playbook: Nurturing bold ideas in government*. Washington, DC: Deloitte Research and Ash Institute for Democratic Governance at the Harvard Kennedy School of Government.
Emerson, K., & Nabatchi, T. (2015). *Collaborative governance regimes*. Washington, DC: Georgetown University Press.
Emerson, K., Nabatchi, T., & Balogh, S. (2012). An integrative framework for collaborative governance. *Journal of Public Administration Research and Theory*, 22(1), 1–29.
Fleischmann, A. (2000). Regionalism and city: County consolidation in small metro areas. *State and Local Government Review*, 32(3), 213–226.
Florida, R. (2014). *The rise of the creative class revisited: Revised and expanded*. New York, NY: Basic Books.
Frederickson, H. G. (2005). Whatever happened to public administration? Governance, governance everywhere. In E. Ferlie, L. Lynn, & C. Pollitt (Eds.), *Oxford handbook of public management* (pp. 81–304). Oxford, UK: Oxford University Press.
Frieling, M. A., Lindenberg, S. M., & Stokman, F. N. (2014). Collaborative communities through coproduction: Two case studies. *The American Review of Public Administration*, 44(1), 35–58.
Friend, J. K., Power, J. M., & Yewlett, C. J. L. (1974). *Public planning: The intercorporate dimension*. London: Travistock Publications.
Hill, C., & Lynn, L. (2003). Producing human services: Why do agencies collaborate? *Public Management Review*, 5(1), 63–81.
Huxham, C. (1996). *Creating collaborative advantage*. Thousand Oaks, CA: Sage.
Huxham, C. (2000). The challenge of collaborative governance. *Public Management*, 2(3), 337–358.

Huxham, C., & Vangen, S. (2000). Leadership in the shaping and implementation of collaboration agendas: How things happen in a (not quite) joined-up world. *Academy of Management Journal*, 43(6), 1159–1175.

Im, E., Jeon, S. H., & Kim, J. (2017). Which local self-governments seek more collaboration? Evidence from interlocal collaboration for economic development in South Korea. *Lex Localis: Journal of Local Self-Government*, 15(2), 175–196.

Innes, J. E., & Booher, D. E. (1999). Consensus building and complex adaptive systems: A framework for evaluating collaborative planning. *Journal of the American Planning Association*, 65, 412–423.

Joshi, A., & Moore, M. (2004). Institutionalised co-production: Unorthodox public service delivery in challenging environments. *Journal of Development Studies*, 40(4), 31–49.

Kenis, P., & Provan, K. G. (2009). Towards an exogenous theory of public network performance. *Public Administration*, 87(3), 440–456.

Kickert, W. J. M., Klijn, E. H., & Koppenjan, J. F. M. (1997). *Managing complex networks, strategies for the public sector*. London: Sage.

Klijn, E. H., Steijn, A. J., & Edelenbos, J. (2010). The impact of network management strategies on the outcomes in governance networks. *Public Administration*, 88(4), 1063–1082.

Kooiman, J. (1993). *Modern governance: New government: Society interactions*. London: Sage.

Lee, I. W., Feiock, R. C., & Lee, Y. (2012). Competitors and cooperators: A micro-level analysis of regional economic development collaboration networks. *Public Administration Review*, 72(2), 253–262.

Mandell, M. P., & Keast, R. (2008). Evaluating the effectiveness of interorganizational relations through networks. *Public Management Review*, 10(6), 715–731.

McGuire, M., & Agranoff, R. (2007). Answering the big questions, asking the bigger questions: Expanding the public network management empirical research agenda. Paper presented at the 9th Public Management Research Conference, Tucson, October 25–27.

Meijer, A. J. (2014). From hero-innovators to distributed heroism: An in-depth analysis of the role of individuals in public sector innovation. *Public Management Review*, 16(2), 199–216.

Milward, H. B., & Provan, K. G. (2006). *A manager's guide to choosing and using collaborative networks*. Washington, DC: IBM Center for the Business of Government.

O'Toole, L. J. (1997). Treating networks seriously: Practical and research-based agendas in public administration. *Public Administration Review*, 57(1), 45–52.

OECD. (2011). *Together for better public services: Partnering with citizens and civil society*. Paris: OECD.

Ostrom, E., Parks, R. B., Whitaker, G. P., & Percy, S. L. (1978). The public service production process: A framework for analyzing police services. *Policy Studies Journal*, 7(s1), 381–389.

Parks, R. B., Baker, P. C., Kiser, L., Oakerson, R., & Ostrom, E. (1981). Consumers as co-producers of public services: Some economic and institutional considerations. *Policy Studies Journal*, 9(7), 1001–1011.

Pestoff, V. (2006). Citizens as co-producers of welfare services: Preschool services in eight European countries. *Public Management Review*, 8(4), 503–520.

Pfeffer, J. S., & Salancik, G. R. (1978). *The external control of organizations: A resource dependence perspective*. New York: Harper & Row.

Provan, K. G., & Milward, H. B. (1995). A preliminary theory of network effectiveness: A comparative study of four community mental health systems. *Administrative Science Quarterly*, 40(1), 1–33.
Sørensen, E., & Torfing, J. (2011). Enhancing collaborative innovation in the public sector. *Administration & Society*, 43(8), 842–868.
Weber, E. P., & Khademian, A. M. (2008). Wicked problems, knowledge challenges, and collaborative capacity builders in network settings. *Public Administration Review*, 68(2), 334–349.
Wise, E., & Høgenhaven, C. (2008, June). *User-driven innovation-context and cases in the Nordic Region. (Innovation Policy)*. Lund: Nordic Innovation Centre.

1 From competition to collaboration

Using cultural attractions to transform economic development strategies in the Detroit metropolitan region

Thomas Greitens and Nancy Quarles

Introduction

Competition over economic development dominates the practice of local governance in the United States. While such competition can be positive for localities that are successful in attracting economic development, negatives exist for those localities that either lose economic development to other areas or cannot attract new opportunities. Such negatives often include long-term economic decline, population loss, and degradation of governance capacity. To help offset such negatives, collaborative governance has emerged as a viable framework for effective local governance. However, the challenge for many local governments is how to engage in such collaborations given losses in economic development and corresponding declines in governance capacity and public service delivery.

Like many major urban areas, the city of Detroit has experienced extremes in terms of economic development. Until the latter half of the 20th century, the city enjoyed significant increases in economic development that continually transformed the city: from a small outpost for fur trading in the 1700s, to a military center by the early 1800s, to an industrial area known for building railroad freight cars and ships in the 1850s, to a major international center for automobile manufacturing in the 1900s (Hyde, 2001). This evolution helped the city of Detroit, and its surrounding suburbs, to become one of the largest industrial manufacturing areas in the world by the 1940s. Reflecting this might, the city of Detroit was the first American city to submit an application to house the newly formed United Nations (Mires, 2013). While that application was ultimately not successful, by the end of the 1940s the city was arguably at the zenith of its economic power with a population of close to two million residents and a resilience that allowed it to weather the complexity of transforming its industrial base from military production focused on the war effort back to automotive production (Sugrue, 1996).

However, weaknesses to the city's socioeconomic resilience were already starting to manifest. In 1943, the city experienced a significant race riot that reflected long-standing racial tensions within the city. Federal troops had to eventually be called to end the three-day riot that ultimately killed

34 individuals, injured 433 individuals, destroyed approximately $2 million in property, and wasted one million industrial production hours that could have been devoted to the war effort (Capeci & Wilkerson, 1990). The 1943 riot exposed the most significant weakness in the city during this time: a population divided by race, class, and culture.

Weaknesses within the city's economic base also manifested from the 1950s to the 1960s. While this decade is generally seen as the golden age of Detroit and the surrounding automobile industry, a closer inspection of history reveals a more complex reality. From 1949 to 1960, the United States experienced four significant economic recessions (specifically in 1949, 1953, 1958, and 1960). When considered in relation to the national economy, these recessions are often remembered as relatively minor events (Friedman & Schwartz, 1963). However, these recessions caused significant challenges for Detroit's automobile industry as their quick and unexpected nature made predicting the demand for automobiles nearly impossible given traditional modes of production. Consequently, as early as the 1950s, the city's industrial base of automobile manufacturing started to transform by implementing more agile production techniques and relocating factories outside of the city and the state of Michigan in order to maximize cost savings (Sugrue, 1996). As a result, between 1950 and 1960 the total number of blue-collar jobs within the city began to decline (Farley, Danziger, & Holzer, 2000). These trends, along with federal funding for the construction of new interstate highways and the social phenomena of "white flight," accelerated suburbanization around the nation and especially in the city of Detroit (Jackson, 1987; Thompson & Mahu, 2017). By the late 1960s, factors such as a lack of economic opportunity, discriminatory housing policies, and negative relationships between police and minority populations, especially the Black population, helped influence Detroit's race riot of 1967 (Herman, 2005). This riot, among the most destructive riots in the history of American urban areas, lasted five days, killed 43 individuals, injured 189 individuals, and caused over $75 million in property damage (Fine, 1989).

The impact of the 1967 riot on migration and economic development was significant. It accelerated Detroit's existing trends of outward migration and deindustrialization during the 1970s and beyond (Farley et al., 2000). Perhaps more than any event of its time, the 1967 riot fundamentally changed people's perception of the city of Detroit. The city was now the poster-child of urban decay and failure, whereas previously it was viewed as a hub of automobile and manufacturing innovation. Throughout the 1970s and 1980s, the city tried to reinvent itself and small successes often occurred. For example, in 1977 the Renaissance Center in the city of Detroit opened and hosted the 1980 Republican National Convention. But small successes could not stop the major long-term trends of decline. By the 2010s, the city's population had declined to approximately 700,000 residents and the number of manufacturing jobs in the city was barely over 25,000 (in 1947 the city had over 330,000 such jobs) (Thompson & Mahu, 2017). In addition, by the 2010s, the city had over 80,000 abandoned residential properties (Detroit Future City, 2012). The effects of such long-term economic decline coalesced in 2013 when the governor of Michigan placed the city under the control of a state appointed emergency financial manager, essentially ending local control of the city (Thomson, 2017). Quickly thereafter, the city entered municipal bankruptcy.

In many ways, entering municipal bankruptcy marked a turning-point for the city. In the municipal bankruptcy process, the city was eventually able to remove its state appointed emergency financial manager, reduce its long-term financial liabilities, and secure additional revenues for economic redevelopment and improved service delivery from the state of Michigan as well as nonprofit organizations (Jacoby, 2016). Further, the city experienced an increase in the number of economic development projects, especially in its downtown center, after exiting the bankruptcy process (Bomey, 2016). While these developments were positive, the city still faced significant challenges especially in terms of governance capacity, particularly in the formation and implementation of collaborative economic development strategies.

Collaborative economic development in Detroit

Collaborative efforts now define the current reality of local governments across the United States, especially those local governments struggling with fiscal stress, declining governance capacity, or significant policy challenges (Emerson & Nabatchi, 2015). At a foundational level, such efforts can be included in two distinct, but related categories: collaborative governance regimes and regionalism initiatives. Collaborative governance regimes involve a diverse set of governmental and nongovernmental actors engaging in continued collaborations to help implement some type of public serving endeavor or to help solve a complex policy problem (Agranoff, 2007; Agranoff & McGuire, 2003; Emerson, Nabatchi, & Balogh, 2012). Related to such efforts are regionalism initiatives in which local governments formally share services through interlocal agreements, share revenues as part of a fiscal arrangement, or even consolidate the structure of multiple governments into one single government to more effectively implement the operations of government (Chen & Thurmaier, 2009; Miller, 2002). Both collaborative governance regimes and regionalism initiatives involve a network of governmental organizations working outside their traditional boundaries. However, regionalism initiatives are generally viewed as being constrained to governments and their specific service deliveries while collaborative governance regimes involve a more diverse set of governance actors, including governments, nonprofit organizations, and private sector entities in the delivery of services.

Within either category, collaborative success depends on trust with more complex collaborations often building upon some type of existing relationship. These existing relationships help build the capacity for collaboration and often include basic agreements that allow knowledge sharing, repeated communications, and the eventual inculcation of shared values between different actors in a collaboration (Frederickson, 1999; Weber & Khademian, 2008a; Weber & Khademian, 2008b). In this way, preexisting cultural, political, organizational, and historical variables within a region can help build the ultimate social bonds that can make any type of collaborative endeavor successful (Andrew, 2009; Carr, LeRoux, & Shrestha, 2009; Feiock, Tao, & Johnson, 2004; LeRoux, Brandenburger, & Pandey, 2010; Thurmaier & Wood, 2002).

However, trust may be more difficult to achieve in regionalism initiatives rather than collaborative governance regimes. Achieving trust between local governments can be challenging as the history of local government emphasized the value of self-governance rather than collaborative approaches. Until relatively recently, most local governments in the United States did not possess a rich history of regional collaboration with other local governments. Interlocal agreements existed, but were not really widespread (Norris, 2001). Additionally, regional governments also existed, but were typically limited to a few cases of urban governments collaborating to implement complex policy projects (Teaford, 1979). Only with recent increases in the complexity of policy problems, mandates from national and state governments, and retrenchment in the budgets of many local governments has regional collaboration been embraced by more and more local governments (Miller & Cox, 2014). And even with those more recent trends, perceptions of competition rather than collaboration often dominate the theoretical justification for different types of local governments (Tiebout, 1956) and local perceptions of economic development (Johnson & Neiman, 2004).

For example, the "Tiebout Hypothesis of Local Government" shows the benefit of local governments competing with one another for residents. Viewed through the prism of public choice economics and utility maximization, the Tiebout Model theorizes that optimal service provisions from local governments will more likely occur from competition between local governments. With a marketplace of local governments providing services, residents can migrate to the jurisdiction that maximizes their perceptions of utility (Tiebout, 1956). Additionally, such a marketplace makes governmental services more efficient and effective as the pressure of competition forces all local governments to offer public services that are both low in price and high in quality in order to attract the most residents (Ostrom, Tiebout, & Warren, 1961).

Like much of the United States in the latter half of the 20th century, such ideas of competition, rather than collaboration, were dominant in the Detroit metropolitan area. Driven by suburbanization and social factors like "white flight," much of the white population of Detroit fled the city to the surrounding suburbs (Darden, Hill, Thomas, & Thomas, 1987). Essentially, the Detroit metropolitan area became divided by race, class, and income. This in turn, seemingly made trust-building between network actors in Detroit and the suburban governments more difficult. Such divisions had definite impacts on economic development in the region with collaborative networks weaker for policies like economic development (Leroux & Carr, 2010).

For example, in the 1970s the suburb of Pontiac, Michigan was able to lure sports teams such as the Detroit Lions in football and the Detroit Pistons in basketball away from the city of Detroit by building the publicly funded Pontiac Silverdome. Located approximately 30 miles from the city of Detroit, the Pontiac Silverdome also hosted a variety of cultural attractions such as music concerts, entertainment festivals, and even religious events such as a major Catholic Mass for 100,000 people held by Pope John Paul II in 1987 (Broda, 2017). However, since many local governments viewed (and continue to view) sports teams as a type of economic development opportunity, competition for these sports assets increased. By the late 1980s the neighboring suburb of Auburn Hills, Michigan attracted the Detroit Pistons from the Silverdome with a different, privately funded arena in Auburn Hills (i.e., the Palace of Auburn Hills) and by the early 2000s the city of Detroit was able to induce the Lions back to Detroit with another publicly funded stadium (i.e., Ford Field). While the actual economic impact of sports teams on local economies remains in doubt (Aaron, 2008; Groothuis, Johnson, & Whitehead, 2004), they showcase the local competition for economic development that pervaded the Detroit metropolitan region.

The lack of collaborative opportunities regarding economic development between local governments in the Detroit metropolitan region had significant implications for Detroit. With less opportunities for any type of collaboration, trust could not form, and more complex arrangements for economic development collaboration could not be made. Such arrangements are important, as positive interactions between a mother city and a suburb often lead to better economic development outcomes (Lewis, 2004). Arguably, without such coordination, the Detroit area fell further and further behind in terms of economic development from the 1960s onward.

By the 2010s, concerns about the city's fiscal state continued to build (Citizens Research Council of Michigan, 2010). Consequently, this uncertainty helped to generate new collaborative governance regimes in the Detroit metropolitan region, especially in economic development. These regimes started to form before the city of Detroit entered bankruptcy in 2013 and eventually helped the city regain some momentum regarding economic development by the end of 2017 (Detroit Future City, 2017). The circumstances surrounding these new collaborative governance regimes can best be observed by examining the Detroit Institute of Arts (DIA): a significant cultural attraction located within the city of Detroit that had to remain viable for continued economic development in the 21st century.

Cultural attractions play a significant role in economic development, especially in the 21st century. In order to attract populations of creative professionals, communities have to provide cultural attractions as part of their economic development strategy (Florida, 2014). However, providing access to these types of cultural attractions was always challenging in the city of Detroit given the metropolitan area's lack of a regional mass transit network (such as rail) and the rather unique funding and ownership model used on this cultural attraction.

Detroit Institute of Arts (DIA)

Formed in 1883 as the Detroit Museum of Arts, the Detroit Institute of Arts (DIA) is known for several paintings by significant artists such as Diego Rivera, Vincent van Gogh, Paul Gauguin, Pablo Picasso, Paul Cezanne, and Giovanni Bellini. However, its history has been punctuated by extremes in funding. In 1919 the museum was transformed from a nonprofit organization to an actual agency within the city of Detroit; by the 1970s cuts in funding from the city led the state of Michigan to become its guarantor of financing; and in 1998 the operation of the museum was subcontracted from the city of Detroit to a nonprofit organization (the Detroit Institute of Arts Founders Society) (Abt, 2001). Throughout all of these transitions, the DIA depended on significant support from private corporations, nonprofit organizations, individual donors, the state of Michigan, and the city of Detroit. Thus, in many ways an intersectoral collaborative governance regime already existed to help support the DIA. However, that regime was especially dependent on the actions of the city of Detroit and, to a lesser extent, on the state of Michigan (Abt, 2001). Typically absent from the regime were the other governmental actors in the Detroit metropolitan region. For instance, by the 1970s a majority of the DIA's visitors came from the rapidly expanding suburban areas outside of the city of Detroit in Wayne, Macomb, and Oakland counties; yet, those areas contributed no direct funding to the DIA other than ticket purchases (Abt, 2001).

Then, in 2010 the state of Michigan passed the "Art Institute Authorities Act" which enabled county governments to form a new type of governance structure that could collect local property tax revenues and transfer them to a provider of art services, namely an art museum (Art Institute Authorities Act, 2010). This act gave county governments official permission from the state government to form regional collaborations to help fund museums and also provided a template of governance by specifying the powers and structure of that regional governance entity. Facing another round of significant budget cuts, voters in Wayne, Macomb, and Oakland counties approved a ten-year increase in property taxes earmarked for the DIA in 2012 that was estimated to raise over $250 million in revenues for the DIA (Kennedy, 2013). In exchange, residents of the counties would receive free admission to the DIA and also receive additional services for children and the elderly (Cohen, 2012).

To implement this funding arrangement, Art Institute Authorities were formed in Wayne, Macomb, and Oakland counties. Thus, new governance actors entered the collaborative governance regime surrounding the DIA.

These new actors had direct access to the DIA since they supplied funding to the DIA, required the DIA to perform additional services to their residents, and also had five board members appointed by the county government to the authority to help hold the DIA accountable to specific interlocal agreements with each authority (Detroit Institute of Arts, 2012a, 2012b, 2012c). Specifically, as part of the revenue sharing agreement, each county art institute authority required the DIA to offer: 1) free admission to the residents of the county; 2) student curriculum development that required the DIA to work with school districts within the county so that students were actively engaged with the museum to help improve critical thinking skills; 3) professional development for teachers in the county to learn how to use the museum to engage students; 4) programs for specific tours for senior residents within the county; and 5) the formation of community partnerships that mandated the DIA bring their services to underserved communities within the county (Detroit Institute of Arts, 2012a, 2012b, 2012c).

Expenses for such arrangements were noteworthy. For instance, as shown in Table 1.1, the initial set-asides for each county's revenues for each of these mandates were often over $100,000. By 2016, financial reports detailing the expenses of these mandates revealed that the initial set-aside amounts had often been exceeded by the DIA (Plante-Moran, 2017a, 2017b, 2017c). Thus, the DIA gave back more to each county in terms of the mandates than required by the initial agreement. Nonetheless, the formation of such regional revenue sharing was noteworthy as regional collaborations regarding the transferring of revenues are often some of the most politically contentious regionalism endeavors possible (Miller, 2002). That such collaborative arrangements were possible in the case of the DIA show how uncertainty in the external environment, and especially funding uncertainty, can drive collaborative governance regimes to form tangible agreements that would most likely be impossible in ordinary, stable times.

As the city of Detroit entered municipal bankruptcy in 2013, uncertainty over the future of the DIA increased. As part of an effort to determine the value of the city's assets, the city's state appointed emergency financial manager, Kevyn Orr, asked Christie's auction house to appraise the DIA's collection, which technically was owned by the city of Detroit (Ohlheiser, 2013). This caused immediate concern that the assets of the DIA could be liquidated

Table 1.1 Initial Mandated DIA Investments for Each County

	Wayne County	*Oakland County*	*Macomb County*
Student Trips	$150,000	$150,000	$75,000
Senior Programs	$100,000	$100,000	$50,000
Community Collaborations	$300,000	$300,000	$75,000

Source: Detroit Institute of Arts (2012a, 2012b, 2012c).

during bankruptcy. Such liquidation would include the auctioning of actual paintings, sculptures, and other exhibits that comprised the entirety of the DIA's collection. Worth over $2 billion, this act of liquidation was attractive for financial reasons as it would potentially allow the city to pay back some of its debt, especially to pension systems. However, it was also supported by influential conservative commentators who suggested that the DIA's collection should be sold to pay off debts (Fund, 2013) or should be sold to reflect the realities of the nation in the 2010s; namely, that the collection would be more utilized by relocation to a more successful area like Los Angeles (Postrel, 2013). Such potential sales also activated the art institute authorities in Wayne, Macomb, and Oakland counties, with the Oakland county government even making a public announcement that such a sale would invalidate any revenue sharing agreement between the county's art authority and the DIA (Oakland County Board of Commissioners, 2013). Such uncertainty tested the collaborative governance regime surrounding the DIA.

The regime responded by rejecting any potential liquidation of the DIA's collection. This response is evident from a number of actors within the DIA's collaborative governance regime. First, as noted previously, the county governments publicly opposed such a liquidation. Additionally, the Michigan legislature even debated Senate Bill 401 that would amend the Art Institute Authorities Act to mandate that art institutes within the state had to follow the ethical code of the American Alliance of Museums, which only allowed the selling of art collections to advance the mission of the museum (Welch, 2013). And while that bill never passed the full legislature, dying in committee, the state of Michigan was overall against the idea of selling the DIA's collection. By 2014, state policymakers agreed to be part of the "grand bargain" that would save the DIA and prevent a liquidation of the collection while also preventing cuts to the city's pension obligations.

The "grand bargain" was officially included as part of the city's bankruptcy plan. For the DIA, the plan mandated that $816 million be raised to formally purchase the DIA's collection from the city of Detroit so that city pension obligations, a significant driver of the city's debt level, would not be significantly reduced (*In re City of Detroit, Michigan*, 2014). As part of this solution, the DIA agreed to raise $100 million to help purchase the museum's collection from the city and transfer formal ownership to a nonprofit organization running the DIA. Raising such funding depended on a variety of corporate and nonprofit actors contributing to the DIA. These partners that made significant funding contributions included General Motors, Ford, Chrysler, Penske Corporation, DTE Energy, Quicken Loans and Rock Ventures, Blue Cross Blue Shield of Michigan, Meijer, Toyota, Comerica Bank, JP Morgan Chase Foundation, Andrew W. Mellon Foundation, and the J. Paul Getty Trust of Los Angeles (Stryker, 2015). Other funding originated from additional contributions from national and local foundations such as the Kresge Foundation, which pledged $100 million for the "Grand Bargain" as well as the state of Michigan, which pledged $195 million immediately (quantified in the city's bankruptcy plan as equivalent to $350 million over 20 years) (*In re City of Detroit, Michigan*, 2014). By the end of 2015, the DIA had raised all of its required funding and had even started to fundraise an endowment that would eventually pay for the loss of regional revenue sharing funds from Oakland, Macomb, and Wayne counties once the property tax millage passed in 2012 expired in 2022 (Stryker, 2015).

Analysis

In collaborative governance regimes, four significant drivers influence the propensity for collaboration: uncertainty, interdependence, consequential incentives, and leadership initiative (Emerson & Nabatchi, 2015). These drivers played significant roles in the formation and sustained relevance of the DIA's collaborative governance regime. Indeed, the absence of many of these drivers before the 2010s helps to explain why economic development policies within the Detroit metropolitan region broadly construed were more individualistic and competitive rather than collaborative in nature, and why policies specifically devoted to the DIA were never fully realized.

For uncertainty, the nature of Detroit's economic crisis coupled with the prospect of the liquidation of the DIA's art collection formed a "wicked" type of problem that could only be addressed via collaboration. "Wicked problems" were initially described by Rittel and Webber (1973) as a way to recognize that some policy problems could not be solved by a rational analysis of data. Instead, some problems were so complex they required newer forms of collaboration and engagement whereby different sets of actors worked together in new ways to help solve the complex policy problem. Since it was so systemic and long-lasting, Detroit's decades-long economic decline could be viewed as a "wicked problem" that eventually forced the city, state of Michigan, surrounding suburban counties, and various nonprofit and private sector organizations to work together to help save a significant cultural attraction in the city, the DIA, that could help the city's future economic development. For by the 2000s, the city of Detroit, its surrounding suburban communities, and even the state of Michigan finally started to view themselves as being connected rather than separate. This may have been best exemplified during the immediate aftereffects of Detroit's municipal bankruptcy when many fiscally healthy suburban cities around Detroit discovered that they had to now pay more borrowing costs for bond issuances solely due to their location within the same state as Detroit (Walsh, 2013). Thus, finally after years of formal and informal prejudices that separated the city of Detroit from its suburban neighbors and state government, the various governance actors started to view themselves as linked and interdependent due to a financial nadir.

Additionally, by the 2010s, consequential incentives for collaboration started to be offered, often by the state government. As discussed earlier, the state of Michigan passed the Art Institute Authorities Act of 2010 that formally endorsed regional governance approaches for museums. Additionally, in 2011 the state passed the Economic Vitality Incentives Program (EVIP), which made additional funding from the state available to those local governments engaging in collaborative governance (as well as a variety of other ideals related to reducing pension and benefits costs and improving transparency) (Citizens Research Council of Michigan, 2012). And during the bankruptcy of Detroit, the state contributed significant funding to help avoid a liquidation of the DIA's art collection. Thus, the state government played a significant leadership role in helping form and sustain the collaboration necessary for the survival of the DIA.

But perhaps what made the most significant impact to the collaborative governance regime of the DIA was that the very nature of economic development started to change in the 2000s. Whereas residents used to flee urban areas, by the 2000s they started to flock to them, often attracted to the cultural attractions that help define urban life (Florida, 2014). The external environment for economic development changed and started to favor the large "mother city" that defines a metropolitan area. Consequently, the actors within the DIA's collaborative governance regime now had to respond to this fact and help protect and enhance the cultural attractions like the DIA that defined the Detroit metropolitan region. However, the price paid by the city of Detroit for such collaborations has been quite high. The city no longer has as much power over its cultural attractions like the DIA. For instance, in 2013 the city also lost control over another of its cultural attractions, Belle Isle Park, when the state appointed emergency financial manager signed a 30-year lease to allow the state of Michigan to operate the park (Pinho, 2013). For the city of Detroit at least, the solutions of collaborative governance often resulted in a consequential loss off control over its cultural attractions necessary for future economic development.

Conclusion

Cultural, political, historical, and financial factors within a region influence collaborative decisions in governments. With regional problems such as economic crises, environmental problems, and health concerns now dominating the agendas of many governments, traditional zero-sum policies that defined governance in the 20th century can no longer yield the needed policy solutions for 21st-century governance, especially regarding economic development. To solve these problems, governments have to increasingly emphasize collaborations with private vendors, nonprofit organizations, and other governments. When formalized by statute, this type of collaborative spirit is not without controversy. Many policymakers and public managers in government may view collaborations, especially those that include structural changes to government, as lost governmental power. In many ways, this happened to Detroit with the case of the DIA. But regardless of view, implementing any type of formal or informal coordinated response often depends on supportive influences that allow collaborations to occur. These can include sharing similar social and fiscal realities across governments and the election of political leaders willing to build collaborative partnerships with the private and nonprofit sectors as well as with other governments. But note that before anything can be implemented, collaborative arrangements must first be formed.

The formation of collaborative arrangements and networked governance occurs due to the existence of shared objectives between public and private entities that could not be achieved without some type of collaboration. In this way, the drivers of collaboration are often based in theories of resource dependency and contingency theory. Adaptation by groups and individuals in their survival and growth needs push stakeholders to collaborate. Additionally, crises, whether economic or environmental, can establish a network and help it adapt to new challenges as time goes forward.

These external challenges were especially prevalent in governments such as Detroit during the 2000s and 2010s as budget cuts, rising inequalities, changing demographics, and a changing natural environment made public policy problems vastly more complex and more costly to solve. As a result, collaborations during this time arguably became necessary to even attempt to solve public policy problems. However, as the rise of collaboration in government increased, the capacity of many governments to engage in certain types of collaborations declined. For example, from the late 1990s to the late 2000s, local governments in the United States experienced severe degradations in their ability to engage in effective contract management (Joaquin & Greitens, 2012). During this time, government became increasingly hollow with many traditional governmental functions lost due to retrenchment (Milward & Provan, 2000; Rubin, 2003). Decisions based in politics, rather than administration, also began to hold more weight during this time as interest groups were able to influence contracting decisions (Kelleher & Yackee, 2008; Witko, 2011). The resulting effect was that local governments lost much of their capacity to manage collaborative relationships, especially with private vendors, at the very time that effective management of collaborative relationships was needed.

Consequently, if governments are increasing their use of collaboration at the same time they are losing the capacity to manage those relationships, then management and policy failures can occur. But perhaps even more importantly, these failures may lead to new wicked problems or exacerbate existing ones. This brings up an interesting question that has never been fully addressed by the collaborative governance, networked governance, and even privatization literatures: namely, can hollowed-out governments effectively participate in collaborative governance regimes? Or, like the case of Detroit and the DIA, will their powers just be continually ceded to other units of government? Ultimately, the answer to that question will reveal whether collaborative governance regimes in Detroit and around the nation survive through the 21st century.

References

Aaron, K. (2008). A new stadium, a new city: The Dallas Cowboys' quest for a new playing field. In D. Watson, & J. Morris (Eds.), *Building the local economy: Cases in economic development* (pp. 176–189). Athens, GA: University of Georgia, Carl Vinson Institute of Government.

Abt, J. (2001). *A museum on the verge: A socioeconomic history of the Detroit Institute of Arts, 1882–2000*. Detroit, MI: Wayne State University Press.

Agranoff, R. (2007). *Managing within networks: Adding value to public organizations*. Washington, DC: Georgetown University Press.

Agranoff, R., & McGuire, M. (2003). *Collaborative public management: New strategies for local governments*. Washington, DC: Georgetown University Press.

Andrew, S. A. (2009). Regional integration through contracting networks: An empirical analysis of institutional collection action framework. *Urban Affairs Review*, 44, 378–402.

Art Institute Authorities Act, Mich. Comp. Laws §§123.1201–123.1229 (2010).

Bomey, N. (2016). *Detroit resurrected: To bankruptcy and back*. New York, NY: W. W. Norton & Company.

Broda, N. (2017, September 15). 30th anniversary of Pope's visit arrives as Silverdome demo nears. *Oakland Press*. Retrieved from www.theoaklandpress.com

Capeci Jr., D. J., & Wilkerson, M. (1990). The Detroit rioters of 1943: A reinterpretation. *Michigan Historical Review*, 16, 49–72.

Carr, J. B., LeRoux, K., & Shrestha, M. (2009). Institutional ties, transaction costs, and external service production. *Urban Affairs Review*, 44, 403–427.

Chen, Y., & Thurmaier, K. (2009). Interlocal agreements as collaborations: An empirical investigation of impetuses, norms, and successes. *American Review of Public Administration*, 39, 536–552.

Citizens Research Council of Michigan. (2010). *The fiscal condition of the city of Detroit* (Report No. 361). Livonia, MI: Citizens Research Council of Michigan.

Citizens Research Council of Michigan. (2012). *Using state shared revenues to incentivize local government behavior*. (State Budget Notes 2012–3). Livonia, MI: Citizens Research Council of Michigan.

Cohen, P. (2012, August 8). Suburban taxpayers vote to support Detroit museum. *New York Times*. Retrieved from www.nytimes.com

Darden, J. T., Hill, R. C., Thomas, J., & Thomas, R. (1987). *Detroit: Race and uneven development*. Philadelphia, PA: Temple University Press.

Detroit Future City. (2012). *Detroit strategic framework plan*. Detroit, MI: Detroit Works Project.

Detroit Future City. (2017). *139 square miles*. Detroit, MI: Inland Press.

Detroit Institute of Arts. (2012a). *Art institute service agreement between the Macomb County Art Institute Authority and the Detroit Institute of Arts, Inc.* Detroit, MI: Detroit Institute of Arts.

Detroit Institute of Arts. (2012b). *Art institute service agreement between the Oakland County Art Institute Authority and the Detroit Institute of Arts, Inc.* Detroit, MI: Detroit Institute of Arts.

Detroit Institute of Arts. (2012c). *Art institute service agreement between the Wayne County Art Institute Authority and the Detroit Institute of Arts, Inc.* Detroit, MI: Detroit Institute of Arts.

Emerson, K., & Nabatchi, T. (2015). *Collaborative governance regimes*. Washington, DC: Georgetown University Press.

Emerson, K., Nabatchi, T., & Balogh, S. (2012). An integrative framework for collaborative governance. *Journal of Public Administration Research & Theory*, 22, 1–29.

Farley, R., Danziger, S., & Holzer, H. J. (2000). *Detroit divided*. New York, NY: Russell Sage Foundation.

Feiock, R. C., Tao, J., & Johnson, L. (2004). Institutional collective action: Social capital and the formation of regional partnerships. In R. Feiock (Ed.), *Metropolitan governance: Conflict, competition, and cooperation* (pp. 147–158). Washington, DC: Georgetown University Press.

Fine, S. (1989). *Violence in the model city: The Cavanagh administration, race relations, and the Detroit riot of 1967*. Ann Arbor, MI: University of Michigan Press.

Florida, R. (2014). *The rise of the creative class revisited: Revised and expanded*. New York, NY: Basic Books.

Frederickson, H. G. (1999). The repositioning of American public administration. *PS: Political Science & Politics*, 32, 701–711.

Friedman, M., & Schwartz, A. J. (1963). *A monetary history of the United States, 1857–1960*. Princeton, NJ: Princeton University Press.

Fund, J. (2013, July 25). Detroit's precious art. *National Review*. Retrieved from www.nationalreview.com

Groothuis, P. A., Johnson, B. K., & Whitehead, J. C. (2004). Public funding of professional sports stadiums: Public choice or civic pride? *Eastern Economic Journal*, 30, 515–526.

Herman, M. A. (2005). *Fighting in the streets: Ethnic succession and urban unrest in twentieth century America*. New York, NY: Peter Lang Publishing.

Hyde, C. K. (2001). Detroit the dynamic: The industrial history of Detroit from cigars to cars. *Michigan Historical Review*, 27, 57–73.

In re City of Detroit, Michigan (2014, October 22). Case No. 13-53846, Eighth amended plan for the adjustment of debts of the city of Detroit. Detroit, MI: United States Bankruptcy Court, Eastern District of Michigan.

Jackson, K. T. (1987). *Crabgrass frontier: The suburbanization of the United States*. New York, NY: Oxford University Press.

Jacoby, M. B. (2016). Federalism form and function in the Detroit bankruptcy. *Yale Journal on Regulation*, 33, 55–108.

Joaquin, M. E., & Greitens, T. J. (2012). Contract management capacity breakdown? An analysis of local governments from 1997 to 2007. *Public Administration Review*, 72, 807–816.

Johnson, M., & Neiman, M. (2004). Courting business: Competition for economic development among cities. In R. Feiock (Ed.), *Metropolitan governance: Conflict, competition, and cooperation* (pp. 124–146). Washington, DC: Georgetown University Press.

Kelleher, C. A., & Yackee, S. W. (2008). A political consequence of contracting: Organized interests and state agency decision making. *Journal of Public Administration Research and Theory*, 19, 579–602.

Kennedy, R. (2013, August 20). Detroit Institute of Arts could lose regional tax funds. *New York Times*. Retrieved from www.nytimes.com

Leroux, K., Brandenburger, P. W., & Pandey, S. K. (2010). Interlocal service cooperation in U.S. cities: A social network explanation. *Public Administration Review*, 70, 268–278.

Leroux, K., & Carr, J. B. (2010). Prospects for centralizing services in an urban county: Evidence from eight self-organized networks of local public services. *Journal of Urban Affairs*, 32, 449–470.

Lewis, P. G. (2004). An old debate confronts new realities: Large suburbs and economic development in the metropolis. In R. Feiock (Ed.), *Metropolitan governance: Conflict, competition, and cooperation* (pp. 95–123). Washington, DC: Georgetown University Press.

Miller, D. (2002). *The regional governing of metropolitan America*. Boulder, CO: Westview Press.

Miller D. Y., & Cox, R. W. (2014). *Governing the metropolitan region: America's new frontier*. Armonk, NY: M.E. Sharpe.

Milward, H. B., & Provan, K. G. (2000). Governing the hollow state. *Journal of Public Administration Research and Theory*, 10, 359–379.

Mires, C. (2013, April 2). Detroit's quixotic bid to host the United Nations. *Foreign Policy*. Retrieved from www.foreignpolicy.com

Norris, D. F. (2001). Prospects for regional governance under the new regionalism: Economic imperatives versus political impediments. *Journal of Urban Affairs*, 23, 557–571.

Oakland County Board of Commissioners. (2013). *Oakland County Board of Commissioners unanimously voted to support maintenance of the Detroit Institute of Arts collection; Board will defund millions if art is sold in Detroit bankruptcy*. News Release from the Oakland County Board of Commissioners. Pontiac, MI: Oakland County Board of Commissioners.

Ohlheiser, A. (2013, August 5). Detroit's emergency manager could sell the city's art collection. *The Atlantic*. Retrieved from www.theatlantic.com

Ostrom, V., Tiebout, C. M., & Warren, R. (1961). The organization of government in metropolitan areas: A theoretical inquiry. *American Political Science Review*, 55, 831–842.

Pinho, K. (2013, October 1). Under 30-year state lease, Belle Isle to get up to $20 million in upgrades by 2017. *Crain's Detroit Business*. Retrieved from www.crainsdetroit.com

Plante-Moran, PLLC. (2017a). *Independent accountant's report on applying agreed-upon procedures (Macomb County Art Institute Authority)*. Detroit, MI: Detroit Institute of Arts.

Plante-Moran, PLLC. (2017b). *Independent accountant's report on applying agreed-upon procedures (Oakland County Art Institute Authority)*. Detroit, MI: Detroit Institute of Arts.

Plante-Moran, PLLC. (2017c). *Independent accountant's report on applying agreed-upon procedures (Wayne County Art Institute Authority)*. Detroit, MI: Detroit Institute of Arts.

Postrel, V. (2013, June 6). Detroit's Van Gogh would be better off In L. A. *Bloomberg*. Retrieved from www.bloomberg.com

Rittel, H. W., & Webber, M. M. (1973). Dilemmas in a general theory of planning. *Policy Sciences*, 4, 155–169.

Rubin, I. S. (2003). *Balancing the federal budget: Trimming the herds or eating the seed corn?* New York, NY: Chatham House.

Stryker, M. (2015, January 5). DIA hits its grand bargain goal. *Detroit Free Press*. Retrieved from www.freep.com

Sugrue, T. J. (1996). *The origins of the urban crisis: Race and inequality in postwar Detroit*. Princeton, NJ: Princeton University Press.

Teaford, J. C. (1979). *City and suburb: The political fragmentation of metropolitan America, 1850–1970*. Baltimore, MD: Johns Hopkins University Press.

Thompson, L., & Mahu, R. J. (2017). Local governments in Michigan I: Urban governments and Detroit. In J. Klemanski, & D. Dulio (Eds.), *Michigan government, politics, and policy* (pp. 78–99). Ann Arbor, MI: University of Michigan Press.

Thomson, D. (2017). Federalism and intergovernmental relations in Michigan. In J. Klemanski, & D. Dulio (Eds.), *Michigan government, politics, and policy* (pp. 52–77). Ann Arbor, MI: University of Michigan Press.

Thurmaier, K., & Wood, C. (2002). Interlocal agreements as overlapping social networks: Picket-fence regionalism in metropolitan Kansas City. *Public Administration Review*, 62, 585–598.

Tiebout, C. M. (1956). A pure theory of local expenditures. *Journal of Political Economy*, 64, 416–442.

Walsh, M. W. (2013, August 8). Woes of Detroit hurt borrowing by its neighbors. *New York Times*. Retrieved from www.nytimes.com

Weber, E., & Khademian, A. (2008a). Wicked problems, knowledge challenges, and collaborative capacity builders in network settings. *Public Administration Review*, 68, 334–349.

Weber, E., & Khademian, A. (2008b). Managing collaborative processes: Common practices, uncommon circumstances. *Administration & Society*, 40, 431–464.

Welch, S. (2013, May 30). Senate bill seeks to protect DIA artwork. *Crain's Detroit Business*. Retrieved from www.crainsdetroit.com

Witko, C. (2011). Campaign contributions, access, and government contracting. *Journal of Public Administration Research and Theory*, 21, 761–778.

2 Windsor

An international border city in Detroit's shadow

Robert Heuton

Introduction

The historical growth and economic trajectory of the City of Windsor mirrors that of the City of Detroit. These two neighbors are separated by a river and international boundary; however, they have much in common regarding early settlement by the French, expansion of industry and railroads into the interior of North America, and economic progress centered on automotive manufacturing. Regional cooperation pervades because of two international border crossings; the Ambassador Bridge and Detroit-Windsor Tunnel. These two facilities are the busiest border crossings for trade and commerce in the world. Nonetheless, Windsor's regional interests lie with its Canadian neighbors within the Windsor-Essex County region as they struggle to find their place within the larger shadow of Detroit. Economic decline has forced city planners to craft a vision for Windsor focused on attracting professionals and families by capitalizing on opportunities for tourism and greater economic prosperity. Windsor wishes to promote cooperative regional partnerships with the County of Essex and its constituent municipalities in southwestern Ontario along with Detroit and southeastern Michigan to achieve economic, social, and environmental improvements. These visions are a blueprint for the future; however, they lack scale and are instead implemented in a piecemeal fashion by local political and business actors within the Windsor community.

In this chapter, we address the challenges of collaborative governance within the Windsor-Essex Region. Emerson, Nabatchi, and Balogh (2011) discuss the drivers for building collective relationships within a complex geopolitical environment. A collaborative governance regime requires principled engagement, shared motivation, and the capacity for joint action. We ask the following questions to ascertain the extent that collaborative governance is functional in the Windsor-Essex Region:

1. To what extent has principled engagement been facilitated between local actors and citizens for development of a comprehensive planning strategy for the Windsor-Essex Region?

2. To what extent has the Windsor-Essex Region been able to facilitate a shared motivation and mutual understanding for collaborative governance as an economic development strategy?
3. What is the capacity of the Windsor-Essex Region to foster joint action to promote regional governance strategies?

Historical context

Several local historians have documented the historic relationship between Detroit and Windsor. Morrison (1954), Price and Kulisek (1992), Roberts (2006), Price (2010), Cangany (2014), and Brode (2014, 2017) are students of this rich history. Windsor's formative development as a metropolitan region was influenced by the arrival of the railroad in 1854. Windsor was the western terminus of the Great Western Railroad. Until Ford Motor Company, set up operations in 1904, the railroad was the hub of Windsor's commercial activity along the city's waterfront. The transshipment of rail freight cars via ferry across the Detroit River was a fixture on the waterfront until the 1980s. Remnants of the glorious age of rail remain intact along the river's edge.

By the 1890s, the Detroit-Windsor region emerged as an economic force within the North American economy. One of the consequences of the National Policy, adopted by Canadian Prime Minister John A. MacDonald and his Conservatives, was the location of branch plants across from Detroit. Implemented in 1879, the National Policy raised tariffs on manufactured goods and lowered the tariffs on raw materials. This gave incentives to industries in Detroit to move across the river to set up Canadian subsidiaries, including the Ford Motor Company, Park Davis Company, and Hiram Walker Distillery along with other ancillary manufacturing operations.

Workers would cross the Detroit River daily to labor in the new factories. Historian, Patrick Brode (2014, p. 141), writes that the existence of an international border was only a slight inconvenience. In the ensuing decades, cross-border movement was quite significant. On July 7, 1929, Morrison (1954, p. 272) reports that 20,000 cars and 100,000 people traversed the Detroit River on their daily commute back and forth to work in the local factories. This early 20th-century industrialization allowed Windsor to become the "motoropolis," coined by David Roberts (2006), as this international community emerged as one of Canada's major industrial complexes.

An article in the *Detroit News* in 1908 described the Detroit River as "the Greatest Commercial Artery on Earth." The *Detroit News* reported that 67,292,504 tons passed through the Port of Detroit, more than London and New York (Cangany, 2014, p. 202). With the United States Congress passing the 18th constitutional amendment in 1919, rum running became the commodity traded along the Detroit River. The narrow waterway and the numerous islands in the straights made the Detroit River a smugglers' paradise. Several distilleries along the Windsor shore took hold because of the new business opportunity.

Nevertheless, the Hiram Walker distillery has been a fixture on the Detroit River since 1857. Hiram Walker selected the Canadian side of the river for his operations because of early prohibitionists on the Michigan side of the river. Although Hiram Walker never overtly participated in the smuggling of whiskey between Windsor and Detroit, during the height of Prohibition in the 1920s, it nevertheless profited from prohibition. From these roots, Canadian Club whiskey has become world famous and is still produced today under the Wiser's label. One other important point about Hiram Walker, he built a planned factory town around his distillery known as the Town of Walkerville, which included workers' homes, schools, and churches. *This Old House Magazine* rated Walkerville as one of the top old house communities in Canada in February 2012.

By 1930, industry and more specifically, the automotive sector was the driving force for the economic vitality of the Detroit-Windsor region. Although the Great Depression slowed production, Detroit symbolized the modern industrial city and the power of American capitalism. Henry Ford, the father of mass production, founded the Ford Motor Company in 1903. Later, in 1908, Henry Ford introduced the Model T and the assembly-line which revolutionized automotive production. Ford Motor Company led automotive production in the region; however, 125 other automotive companies were at work in the region, including Chrysler, General Motors, and Packard. Shipping via the Detroit River gave industries in both Detroit and Windsor access to raw materials, such as iron ore, from the Mesabi Range in Minnesota. At the time of World War II, the Detroit-Windsor region was known as the "Arsenal of Democracy" (Baime, 2014).

The motor cities, Detroit and Windsor, live by the automobile and die by the automobile. The Detroit region was at its industrial peak in the post-World War II era. However, deindustrialization of the central city and the movement of manufacturing to suburban and Sunbelt locales led to the decline of the auto sector centered in southeast Michigan. Many of the large factory buildings of the glory years of the automotive industry now remain vacant.

The riot in Detroit in 1967 gave the city a black eye and a negative image and the city for decades later continued to hemorrhage both population and investment. Furthermore, the rise of international competition from both Japanese and German auto companies has further weakened the once mighty metropolis of the Midwest. Chrysler filed for bankruptcy in 1979 and again in 2008. Even General Motors filed for bankruptcy in 2008 during the Great Recession. The population of Detroit stands at 673,100 people and unemployment during the Great Recession ballooned to almost 30% of the workforce, although it has now fallen to 8.7% (Detroit News, 2018). Detroit is no longer a boomtown and can be more appropriately labeled as the "preeminent urban basket case," as reported by the *Washington Post* in 1997. Yet, a lot has changed since bankruptcy and the downtown area of Detroit is on the rebound.

Although Windsor has not experienced the same social unrest as observed in Detroit, the community relies on its survival based upon the automotive sector. The world-famous Mini-Van is built by Chrysler in Windsor; however, General Motors has closed shop in the city leaving vacant brownfield space. Ford Motor Company still produces engines at its old Ford City site as the manufacturer has since 1904. Nonetheless, unemployment in Windsor has remained high, at over 10% of the workforce, the highest rate in Canada. Currently, the automotive sector has regained some economic clout as the Chrysler Assembly plant is running a third shift to assemble the new Pacifica SUV and the ancillary tool and mold sector has seen jobs return from offshore assembly because of offshore quality problems.

Windsor's economy has transformed somewhat from a manufacturing-based economy to a consumer-based economy driven by entertainment and lively urban scenes as exemplified by the growth of the casino gaming. Caesars Windsor, opened in 1998, is one of four casinos in the Detroit-Windsor area. Motor City (1999), Greektown (2000), and MGM (2007) casinos opened respectively to add competition for the Windsor casino. The competition for entertainment dollars has seen layoffs at the Caesars Windsor.

This brief economic history of the Detroit-Windsor region highlights the challenges for two neighbors on the banks of the Detroit River. The key concern is how to reinvigorate the meaning of place when civic leaders make claims that their city is making a comeback and there is hope for the future (Archer & Watkins, 2017; Michael Duggan, 2017; Windsor Star, 2018).

Figure 2.1 Windsor: An International Border City in Detroit's Shadow

Source: Author.

Regional planning and cooperation in the Windsor-Essex region

Windsor was not the point of original settlement on the south shore of the Detroit River. The Town of Sandwich, located two miles west of downtown Windsor, was created as a planned community to be the capital of the Western District. However, Windsor became the focal point of economic activity being the site for the main river crossing to Detroit in the 1830s. Other rival communities also developed along the south shore of the Detroit River. As noted earlier, Hiram Walker moved his whiskey distillery to Canada in 1857 and created a planned community known as the Town of Walkerville. A little further east, Ford City came into being when Ford Motor Company purchased the Walkerville Wagon Works and started producing automobiles in 1904. These four separate communities were known as the Border Cities.

In the early days of the 20th century, the Border Cities grew as industrial growth, centered on automotive production, took hold in the Detroit-Windsor Region. The Border Cities were in stiff competition to be part of the new wave of economic opportunity. Nonetheless, civic leaders began to realize the need to improve basic services, such as water, sewers, and road infrastructure. The first step toward the crafting of metropolitan solutions was the establishment of the Essex Border Utilities Commission by the Ontario legislature in 1917. All communities in the region were included in the new regional authority, which had responsibilities for area-wide public health, water supply, sewer systems, a metropolitan hospital, and regional planning. This governing body came to be because of negative reports from the International Joint Commission regarding water quality in the Detroit River.

The next steps to amalgamate the Border Cities was through the initiation of a master plan for the region. Thomas Adams was commissioned to develop a growth plan for the City of Windsor, which supported a more integrated approach to regional planning for the Border Cities. As well, the Border Cities Utilities Commission sought amalgamation through a plebiscite held in 1925, which failed to gain approval of Sandwich and Walkerville residents. Furthermore, the Ontario Bureau of Municipal Affairs was directed by the Attorney General for the province of Ontario to undertake a financial analysis of the Border Cities in 1928. The provincial study confirmed that Border Cities should be amalgamated. Price and Kulisek (1992) are the scholars that have researched this case in depth.

The issue of amalgamation came to a boiling point with the onslaught of the Great Depression and the widespread default on municipal debenture debt. A huge amount of borrowing took place in the 1920s to finance new capital infrastructure that could only be paid through continued prosperity and rising property taxes, none of which were sustainable. This dire fiscal situation led to support for amalgamation of the Border Cities with the exception of Walkerville, which was still able to service its debt load. The Mitchell Hepburn Liberal government at Queen's Park (Ontario legislature) recognized the need for fast action and appointed a royal commission with former Windsor Mayor David Croll as the chairman to report on the fiscal crisis facing the Border Cities. The result was the amalgamation of the Border Cities – Windsor, Sandwich, Walkerville, and Sandwich East (formerly Ford City) in 1935.

Urban sprawl has been one of the greatest economic challenges to the supremacy of the City of Windsor within the Windsor-Essex County region. Since World War II, there has been a steady movement of population and economic activity to the fringes of the city spilling over into the neighboring suburban communities. At the end of World War II, 85% of the metropolitan population lived in Windsor. By 1956, the suburban shift in growth saw only 65% of the metropolitan population residing in the city (Price & Kulisek 1992, p. 36). The outward movement of population and economic growth was spurred on by new subdivisions, retail expansion, and modern industrial facilities. The City of Windsor was neglected and a hodgepodge of disjointed growth as the result of being the four separate Border Cities for long.

The need to get a handle on urban expansion led to calls for annexation of the new suburban communities. It was recognized that better planning of roads, public transportation, and water and sewer infrastructure was required. Regional planning was not happening in any coordinated fashion. An annexation battle lasted for five years from 1961 and 1965 between the City of Windsor and its neighboring suburbs. The Ontario Municipal Board ruled on the proposal in 1966, calling for the Township of Sandwich East, the industrial and built-up portions of Sandwich West Township, the Town of Riverside, the Town of Ojibway, and a portion of Sandwich South Township to become part of the City of Windsor. Currently, it has been over 50 years since this significant annexation of surrounding suburban growth, yet the Windsor metropolitan region is still reeling from poor road infrastructure, inadequate public transportation infrastructure, and water and sewage systems that regularly backup during heavy rain conditions.

Although there have been various annexations by the City of Windsor to consume sprawling suburbs within its jurisdiction, there has never been a full review of the city-county system of local government adopted in the 1840s. To rationalize service delivery and eliminate political duplication in the Windsor-Essex Region, the provincial government commissioned the *Essex County Local Government Restructuring Study*, which delivered a report on June 30, 1976 (Windsor Star, 1976). University of Toronto professor, Peter Silcox, recommended several changes, including: a new two-tier governance structure that would include the City of Windsor along with the neighboring suburban and rural communities of Essex County, reducing the role of local councils within the new regional form of government; a reduction in the number of lower tier municipalities from 22 to eight; abolition of special boards and commissions, such as planning boards, utilities commissions, the region conservation authority, and the metro health unit by placing these functions with the upper-tier county government; a reduced role of the Ontario Provincial Police in the region by the creation of new local police forces; promotion of industry and tourism by the county council; and the transfer of income redistribution programs for the Windsor-Essex County region to the new upper-tier county government.

The restructuring plan was placed on the shelf to collect dust for many years; however, over time several of the recommendations from the Essex County Local Government Restructuring Study have been implemented indirectly. The election of Mike Harris as Premier of Ontario in 1995 marked a change in provincial-local relations across the province. His Common-Sense Revolution advocated measures to cut taxes and reduce duplication in the delivery of municipal services. The government adopted Bill 26, the *Savings and Restructuring Act* and Bill 25, *Fewer Municipal Politicians Act*, which led to the number of municipalities across the province being reduced from 850 to 444 in the period between 1995 and 2000. The impact of these legislative changes culminated on January 1, 1999, when the number of municipalities in Essex County was reduced to eight, as recommended by the *Local Government Restructuring Study*, 1976.

Since that time, the Windsor-Essex Region has evolved even further. On January 1, 2003, the City of Windsor annexed a parcel of land from the Town of Tecumseh, including the airport. The City of Windsor paid the Town of Tecumseh and Essex County $3.7 million to compensate for the 5,800 acres of land annexed (Windsor Star, 2002). Furthermore, cooperative service delivery approaches have now transpired between the City of Windsor and the County of Essex. Court services, income redistribution programs, and regional economic development strategies are a few examples whereby regional cooperation prevails as was recommended in the *Local Government Restructuring Study* in 1976. Several key questions remain. Would a regional approach to police and fire protection better serve the residents of the Windsor-Essex Region? Are there possibilities to improve public transit across the region? Would a regional planning approach reduce urban sprawl and lead to rationalized service provision through an urban growth boundary? Would a tax-based share mechanism create opportunities to reduce competition for commercial development between Windsor and the surrounding suburban communities? These are all important queries to build a cooperative regional character.

The Detroit-Windsor region opportunities and challenges

There have been big ideas presented to consider Detroit-Windsor as a singular metropolitan region. A conference was held at the University of Windsor in 1966 to present the key themes surrounding concept of the "Great Lakes Megalopolis." Greek planner, Constantin Doxiadis, was commissioned by the Detroit Edison Company to analyze growth and development taking place in the Detroit urban region. The discussions explored ways whereby regional thinking could be carried out effectively in a fragmented political mosaic (Wade, 1969, p. viii). As well, discussion ensued about the environmental concerns and possibilities for the region. The importance of the international crossings for trade and commerce presented challenges in protecting the surrounding region from environmental degradation as manufacturing production continued to thrive in the region. Conversations focused on the following: how to develop and maintain centers of industry, commerce, and culture; provisions for quality housing and viable neighborhoods; efficient transportation networks; efficient regional systems for utilities, fuel, telecommunication, water, and waste treatment; and appropriate financing for public and public investments (Wade, 1969, p. xvii).

In the mid-1960s, another more formal regional thought process evolved across Ontario that had implications for the Detroit-Windsor region. In 1965, the Canadian federal government and the province of Ontario sponsored a conference discussing areas of economic stress in Canada at Queen's University in Kingston, Ontario with more follow-up at the International Conference on Regional Development and Economic Change. In the following year, the Ontario government released a white paper titled *Design for Development* outlining the objectives and administrative mechanisms to create a program for planning regional development across the province. The proposal was to divide Ontario into ten economic regions to effectively plan for potential development, both social and economic; the conservation of the natural environment; and to improve the coordination of provincial service delivery and improve provincial-local relations. Windsor was included in the St. Clair region as defined by the planning initiative (Ontario Government, 1972). Most important, the report recognized the need for international cooperation to improve the economic vitality for the province of Ontario but also the fact that Windsor was a key gateway to this economic opportunity.

From the above notations, it is important to understand these were the early initiatives considering the need for "regional thinking" in terms of growth and economic development opportunities for the Detroit-Windsor region. Although no specific regional economic development strategy was implemented, the discussions recognized the importance of the connectivity between Detroit and Windsor via the Ambassador Bridge and Detroit-Windsor Tunnel. Today, an estimated $500 million of trade crosses the border between Detroit and Windsor, making it the busiest border crossing in North America. The 2010 census shows that 28,814 trucks and 140,728 cars and other vehicles cross the border daily (CBC News, 2011).

Two major international agreements that have had impact on trade and economic development of the Detroit-Windsor region are the Auto Pact and subsequent Canada-U.S. Free Trade Agreement, and the North American Free Trade Agreement (NAFTA). From a Canadian perspective, the Auto Pact signed in 1965 saved the automotive industry in Canada. The Canadian market was too small to make car production cost effective. A policy debate ensued in Canada over protectionism or freer trade with the United States. The Detroit 3 automakers wanted an integrated market, so they could use a single plant to produce vehicles for both markets to achieve greater efficiency and economies of scale. The Canadian government relented when minimum guarantees for Canadian production were satisfied. Headwinds from foreign competition as well as automation have impacted automotive production in the Detroit-Windsor region, but Windsor's economy is quite dependent upon the production of the Mini-Van by Fiat Chrysler and engines by Ford Motor Company.

With continued global competition, particularly in the automotive sector, there was increased pressure to have a free trade zone between the United States and Canada. After the 1984 Canadian federal election, Canada entered negotiations to formulate the Canada-U.S. Free Trade Agreement in 1989. This agreement helped foster the two-tiered manufacturing system, allowing a formative automotive parts manufacturing network to take hold in the Detroit-Windsor region not only serving the Big 3 but also the offshore competition from Asian markets (Melanson, 2009).

The current trading environment falls under the parameters of the North American Free Trade Agreement (NAFTA) signed in 1994. NAFTA essentially is the largest free trade zone in the world; however, it hollowed the Auto Pact and allowed companies to outsource production to anywhere in Canada, the United States, and Mexico thus ending protections for Canadian content rules. Although manufacturing operations continue to operate productively within the Detroit-Windsor region, there is the ever-present pressure

Figure 2.2 FIAT Chrysler Canadian Headquarters

Source: Author.

to consider the bottom-line and saving labor costs by moving to Mexico. For example, General Motors no longer has a production footprint in Windsor as the trim plant and transmission plant have been closed and demolished as production has been outsourced or moved to Mexico and other developing countries. This economic reality has impacted the Detroit-Windsor region over the past several decades as blue-collar jobs have moved to Mexico, leaving abandoned industrial space and higher than average unemployment.

The current challenges for Windsor as an international border city

Although Windsor's waterfront has a wholesome natural look, Windsor itself feels like a tired post-industrial city. Traveling around the city streets, you experience aging road infrastructure and you see worn-out neighborhoods. Much of the commercial and retail space in the downtown core is vacant and dotted with small takeout food outlets or thrift stores. The same feel permeates the main arteries. Along University Avenue and Wyandotte Street, you see vacant store fronts. Pockets of regeneration exist in Old Walkerville and Pillette Village through the efforts of Business Improvement Associates with committed shop owners. Erie Street, with its Italian cultural base, and Ottawa Street with its long history of Jewish family businesses, such as Freed's, have sustained the mom-and-pop neighborhood aesthetic.

On a larger scale, several industrial sites remain vacant. General Motors closed its Trim Plant in 2008 after contracting out the site to Lear Corporation, leaving 2,400 employees out of work. As well, General Motors closed the Transmission Plant in 2010, resulting in another 1,400 job losses. Nonetheless,

Figure 2.3 Site of Former G.M. Transmission Plant

Source: Author.

Ford Motor Company still employs 1,400 workers who produce engines in Windsor. Windsor's largest manufacturing employer with 5,800 employees is the Fiat Chrysler Plant where the Mini-Van and Pacifica are produced. On a smaller scale, there are examples of office space vacancies. Green Shield Canada, a $1.5 billion health-care provider, relocated its office to a suburban industrial park, leaving vacant space in the downtown core.

The magnitude of retail sprawl is magnified by the nearly 76,000 square feet of vacant shops at the Dorwin Plaza (Windsor Star, 2017a). The Plaza opened in 1956 as a part of the move to create new strip malls and enclosed climate-controlled retail environments across North America in the mid-1950s. These retail configurations fit the "car-centric" environment that arose after World War II and through the Baby-Boom Era. While this type of retail space struggles for a new identity, the fully climate-controlled Devonshire Mall built in 1970 faces similar challenges. Sears closed 200,000 square feet of retail space at this 1,000,000-square foot site. All older retail districts in Windsor now must compete with new Big Box Outlets located in the suburban fringe.

The challenge for Windsor going forward is the need to create viable employment in the post-industrial era. Windsor-Essex Economic Development Corporation (2017) reports the current population is estimated at 217,188 (210,891 in 2010). Overall population growth has been limited (CBC News, 2017a). New immigrants account for 22% of the city's population growth. A significant number of Syrian refugees have relocated to Windsor from their war-torn land. Several of these new arrivals have taken the opportunity to start new businesses. This urban enclave has taken hold in the near downtown area along Wyandotte Street east.

By contrast, 17% of Windsor's population is composed of the senior age group. Retirees have not only remained in the Windsor area after a long working career in an automotive factory, other folks are moving in from Toronto and other parts of Ontario where real estate prices have grown exponentially in the past decade. These folks have cashed in their assets and have moved to Windsor where real estate values are still affordable. These recent migrants have placed greater demands on the health-care system. The combined socioeconomic impacts of these recent events that have changed local demographics have not been considered by policy decision-makers in their long-term health infrastructure planning.

An ominous number is Windsor's 6.2% unemployment rate. This number is close to the national average in Canada; however, since the recession of 2009, Windsor has had the highest unemployment rate in the country. To this point, an estimated 14,600 manufacturing jobs have been lost since 2005. These job losses have brought economic hardship for many local families. Homelessness in the downtown area has stressed various social services agencies working in the community. An estimated 200 people sleep on the streets of Windsor nightly as shelters are stretched to capacity (Windsor Star, 2017b).

The renegotiation of NAFTA wrestles heavily on the mind of Windsor's political elites, corporate actors, and union brethren alike. Over 6,000 residents of Windsor commute to Detroit daily for employment opportunities in the health sector, engineering positions in the automotive sector, and other high-technology related employment opportunities. The potential impacts on cross-border trade restrictions could have a potential devastating impact on Windsor's economy. Table 2.1 displays employment by industry in Windsor. Note the heavy dependence on manufacturing and trade-related employment within the Windsor region.

Given Windsor's economic situation, the political elites continuously project a positive future for the city. The *20-Year Vision for Windsor* calls for a focus on jobs, building reputation, and promoting quality of life for all. Here are a few quotes from the Vision:

> "For century, Windsor has been a center of people who know how to build and make things. We need to build on that tradition and create a new diversified knowledge-driven economy."
>
> "To change our future, we need to change our attitude about our city, our partners and our prospects."
>
> "In Windsor, you can have the perfect mix of access to 'big city' amenities in Detroit while enjoying the 'small town feel' of Windsor."

This Vision for the City of Windsor fits into the economic development scheme to explain city building as presented by Terry Clark (2004) and his colleagues at the University of Chicago.

Table 2.1 Employment by Industry in Windsor

Categories	*2017*	%
Agriculture and Mining	4,640	2.5
Utilities	779	0.5
Construction	11,479	6.0
Manufacturing	31,582	18.0
Trade	26,210	15.0
Transportation & Warehousing	8,318	4.5
Finance, Insurance & Real Estate	8,629	4.5
Professional, Scientific & Technical	6,820	4.0
Business, Building & Other Services	9,552	5.0
Education Services	14,518	8.0
Health Care & Social Assistance	22,456	12.0
Information, Culture & Recreation	7,371	4.0
Accommodation & Food Services	13,227	7.0
Other Services	10,818	5.5
Public Administration	7,066	3.5
Total	**183,465**	**100.0**

Source: Windsor-Essex Economic Development Corporation, Monthly Monitor – December 2017.

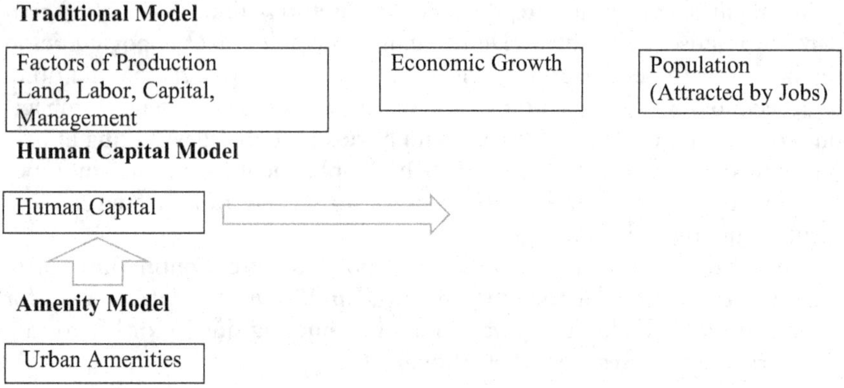

Figure 2.4 Three Models of Urban Development
Source: Clark (2004, p. 106).

The traditional model focused on factors of production, including land, labor, capital, and good management to generate economic growth as population would be attracted to the jobs. The human capital model is centered on building on the ideals of talent, technology, and tolerance as advocated by Richard Florida and his discussion on the creative class (Florida, 2003). Terry Clark builds additional thoughts on a successful city by suggesting it is important to package an urban scene. According to Clark and Silver (2016), a scene is more than a neighborhood, physical structures, and persons labeled by race, class, or gender. The ideal situation is to package all the amenities of a city to create a meaningful sense of identity.

To achieve these objectives, local resources need to cultivate a positive and diverse economic environment for business growth. There is need for community leaders and local government to partner to stimulate the economy. Promoting tourism and hospitality as the gateway to Canada is one aspect of a marketing strategy for the City of Windsor. Working with local education institutions to develop a skilled and adaptable workforce is another component of fostering new opportunities in the post-industrial economy. The City of Windsor has a responsibility to ensure public safety, invest in convenient city services, ensure access to comprehensive health care, encourage the development of quality neighborhoods, and maintain and improve physical infrastructure. City council can achieve these objectives by facilitating partnerships between the public, private, and not-for-profit sectors as well as engaging citizens openly and frequently to build collaborative, cooperative, and creative ways to lead Windsor in the next great era.

City Council has undertaken several initiatives that are unfortunately piecemeal and their impacts on the economic vitality going forward have been and will continue to be limited. For example, the Canderel Building, the site for the headquarters for Chrysler Canada, was developed in 1999 as a private-public partnership to keep the headquarter office complex in Windsor. The project cost the City of Windsor tens of millions of dollars. A good portion of its leasable space has remained vacant for two decades. The city finally renegotiated the operating arrangement with the new owner of the building, EuroPro (Windsor Star, 2017c). The new arrangement sees the city selling the parking garage and walking away from other financial obligations. The building has been underutilized since construction was completed. There is much urban decay in the surrounding retail district as shops and restaurants have closed in the past decade.

Positive signs of life in the downtown core have seen St. Clair College and the University of Windsor create new educational opportunities. In 2010, St. Clair College refurbished the vacant space previously home to the Salvation Army and built a state-of-the-art Media Plex. St. Clair College received $5 million of Federal funding from the Community Adjustment Fund along with the site being donated by the City of Windsor. The facility offers teaching space for journalism students to learn new methods on a variety of media platforms from radio and television to print and online formats.

Furthermore, the University of Windsor in 2015 opened classroom space in the downtown. The School of Social Work and the Centre for Executive and Professional Education moved into the restored site of the former Windsor Star newspaper building. In the second phase, the university's footprint in the downtown core will see the School of Creative Arts move into the former Windsor Armories. All these moves will bring approximately 2,000 students and faculty into the downtown core. These investments will help drive economic revitalization both with new residential land uses along with expansion of restaurants and cafes.

In 2014, Adventure Bay, a new indoor water park, opened in the downtown area. The $78 million facility includes competitive swimming and diving space. This facility provides recreational opportunities for both students and young families; however, the attendance numbers at the pool facility have declined the past three years. CBC News (2017b) reports that in year one attendance stood at 184,000 participants annually but by year three attendance has dropped off to 105,000 participants. The swimming facility is struggling to meet budgeted revenue projections.

Seeking out synergies, a better recreation and entertainment strategy would have seen the Windsor Family Credit Union (WFCU) located adjacent to the downtown swimming pool complex. Built in 2007, home to the Windsor Spitfires Major Junior A hockey franchise, the arena would have created economies of scale and would have been a catalyst for revitalization of the downtown core of Windsor. Instead, the WFCU arena sits adjacent to the brownfield site left behind by the General Motor Trim Plant that closed in 2008 without a redevelopment strategy for the vacant space. Positive spin-off economic opportunities are not being maximized either downtown or surrounding the arena complex.

A regional planning effort for the Windsor-Essex County area calls for plans to construct a new mega-hospital. The projected $1 billion state-of-the-art facility is planned for a new site at the periphery of the city adjacent to Windsor Airport. This project is a public-private partnership between the province of Ontario, the City of Windsor, and the County of Essex with the project to be completed by Infrastructure Ontario as a Design-Build-Finance-Maintain model. Infrastructure Ontario will take the lead on handling the project, including the call for proposals and the construction of an acute-care facility that will replace two aging buildings located in the central city. The Metropolitan campus is to be torn down and the land sold for other uses. The Hotel-Dieu campus will be redeployed for outpatient mental-health and chronic-disease management. An acute-care clinic is proposed for the former Grace campus. An issue of public concern is that the new medical facility, to be located at the edge of the city, will have minimal economic spin-off in downtown Windsor.

A continuing festering problem for the City of Windsor is the future of the Ambassador Bridge and the proposed construction of the Gordie Howe Bridge. These two projects have created urban blight and have left the west side of the city as a zone of transition. Matty Moroun, owner of the Ambassador Bridge, wishes to twin the existing facility. In the process, he has purchased several buildings and has boarded them up. The Canadian federal government has recently given approval for the twinning of the Ambassador Bridge. This approval is in addition to the government's commitment to build the Gordie Howe Bridge. It remains unclear what the future holds for these international crossing projects. Nevertheless, it is important for planners and developers to be prepared for the economic opportunities. Cross-border movement could generate many possibilities for the local regional economy of Windsor and Essex County.

All these mega-projects, in sum, are an amenity driven approach to economic development as depicted by Terry Clark's model. Each project is the foundation for a community focused on building and making things in the new diversified knowledge-driven economy, but each project is a standalone effort. What is required to build a successful community is a "wrap around" approach. There is a requirement to bring all interested local actors – political leaders, industrial leaders, institutional leaders, and community leaders into a collaborative working framework in order to facilitate effective local decision-making. All hands must work together in conjunction to generate regional growth strategies to rebuild Windsor and neighboring Essex County as a vibrant economic engine for the 21st century.

Collaborative governance analysis in the Windsor-Essex region

This chapter highlights the efforts to initiate regional collaborative governance with the Windsor-Essex Region through the lens of Emerson et al.

(2011). To conclude, an assessment of the key questions associated with addressing an effective regional collaborative model must be evaluated.

1 To what extent has principled engagement been facilitated between local actors and citizens for development of a comprehensive planning strategy for the Windsor-Essex Region?

As we note, the City of Windsor has undertaken a comprehensive strategic planning exercise. The *20-Year Vision for Windsor* calls for a focus on jobs, building reputation, and promoting quality of life for all (City of Windsor, 2014). It provides a benchmark for the future; however, the strategic effort needs to establish measurable results through the efforts of building upon both public and private partnerships. An example of this collaborative approach is the proposed construction of a $1 billion acute-care hospital. Both the City of Windsor and the County of Essex are contributing to the project. The measurable result will be completion of the new hospital facility.

Yet, in other instances, regional collaboration seems to wane. There has never been a comprehensive review of the political governance structure of the Windsor-Essex Region since the Silcox Report published in 1976. To engage local actors in collaboration, comprehensive regional partnerships between the City of Windsor and County of Essex along with constituent municipalities in southwestern Ontario need to be fostered. Also, the City of Detroit and the communities of southeastern Michigan should be part of a broader economic, social, and environmental regional strategy. A scaled set of visions must be established as a blueprint for the future.

2 To what extent has the Windsor-Essex Region been able to facilitate a shared motivation and mutual understanding for collaborative governance as an economic development strategy?

There has not been a "big vision" for the Windsor-Essex Region since the Great Lakes Megalopolis idea promoted by Constantin Doxiadis (1966). As discussed, the City Windsor and the Essex County Region should work more closely with the City of Detroit and the communities of southeastern Michigan to foster cooperative ventures. With the ongoing NAFTA negotiations between Canada and the United States, it is imperative that the two international communities collaborate to protect the vital automotive supply chain that the region is dependent upon for economic prosperity.

A good example of collaboration was the Detroit-Windsor Amazon Headquarters Two proposal. The City of Windsor partnered with Dan Gilbert's office, the Mayor of Detroit, and economic development officials on both sides of the Detroit River. Although the Detroit-Windsor presentation did not make the final cut, much valuable information was gleamed from the outcome. One of the most important pieces shared by representatives from

Amazon is that the quality of elementary education, the "brain drain" of tech-savvy post-secondary graduates, and Detroit's difficulty in attracting and retaining talent (Detroit Free Press, 2018; Windsor Star, 2018). These points are keynotes in the City of Windsor's civic vision discussed earlier in the chapter.

The twinning of the Ambassador Bridge and the construction of the Gordie Howe Bridge lend themselves to new possibilities for regional collaboration. There has been limited discussion by political leaders and the business community of the potential spin-off business opportunities in the Windsor-Essex Region for warehousing and just-in-time ventures that will be able to easily access the expanded border facilities. With the inevitable expansion of online retailing and commercial purchasing, the Detroit-Windsor Region has available vacant industrial space and the infrastructure to support economic opportunities that wish to connect to the heartland of North America. The region is the perfect strategic location to maximize new potential.

3 What is the capacity of the Windsor-Essex Region to foster joint action to promote regional governance strategies?

There is a need to build on the strengths and opportunities for the Windsor-Essex Region. Certainly, the automotive and the manufacturing sector is the economic engine for the region. Nonetheless, high-tech employment in the pharmaceutical and medical fields should be expanded. The potential of a new regional medical facility with specialized patient care presents this possibility. Working with the University of Windsor and St. Clair College, the intellectual capacity exists for public and private partnerships to collaborate in new research opportunities. For example, computer aided research and design in such specializations as robotics should be explored. In another collaborative business venture, Essex County has the climate and soil conditions to strengthen agri-business opportunities in the Greenhouse sector and wine industry situated in southern Essex County.

The infrastructure is in place. Collaborative partnerships with new innovative ideas in terms of specialized training and job opportunities must be capitalized upon. Results-based leadership is required at a regional level. Piecemeal projects have not achieved the desired economic impacts for the Windsor-Essex Region. The Windsor-Essex Region must build stronger economic partnerships. Planning and economic development officials along with venture capitalists and various business partnerships should join in the discussions with such organizations as Automation Alley based in southeastern Michigan. Automation Alley is a partnership of political and corporate elites that have come together to promote technology and manufacturing business associations that connect industry, academia, and government to drive Southeast Michigan's economy and accelerate innovation. Automation Alley focuses its efforts on entrepreneurship, talent development, and international business by providing resources, funding, and actionable intelligence to help members grow and prosper in the digital age. Such broader collaborative partnerships would facilitate new business ventures, which might help mitigate the social and economic challenges the City of Windsor is experiencing in the downtown core by providing viable job opportunities, reducing unemployment. Joining into a broader regional collaboration would be a win-win opportunity for all involved in promoting Windsor as an international border city in Detroit's shadow.

Bibliography

Archer, D. W., & Watkins, E. A. (2017). *Let the Future Begin*. Detroit: Atkins and Greenspan Writing.

Baime, A. J. (2014). *The Arsenal of Democracy: FDR, Detroit and an epic quest to arm an America at war*. New York: Houghton Mifflin Harcourt.

Brode, P. (2014). *The river and the land: A history of Windsor to 1900*. Windsor: Biblioasis.

Brode, P. (2017). *Border cities powerhouse: The rise of Windsor 1901 to 1945*. Windsor: Biblioasis.

Cangany, C. (2014). *Frontier seaport: Detroit's transformation into an Atlantic Entrepôt*. Chicago: University of Chicago Press.

CBC News. (2011). *The Canada U. S. border by numbers*. Canadian Broadcasting Corporation, online May 18, 2017.

CBC News. (2017a). *Census data shows Windsor's population has grown by 3 per cent*. Canadian Broadcasting Corporation, online May 18, 2017.

CBC News. (2017b). *Adventure changes rules and prices to combat sagging attendance*. Canadian Broadcasting Corporation, online May 18, 2017.

City of Windsor. (2014). *20-Year strategic vision*. Corporation of the City of Windsor, online October 20, 2017. Retrieved from www.citywindsor.ca

Clark, T., & Silver, D. (2016). *Scenescapes: How qualities of place shape social life*. Chicago: University of Chicago Press.

Clark, T. (2004). Urban amenities: Lakes, opera, and juice bars: Do they drive development. In Terry Nicholas Clark (Ed.), *The city as an entertainment machine* (pp. 103–140). San Diego, CA: Elsevier Inc.

Detroit Free Press. (2018, January 18). *Amazon to Detroit: You didn't have enough talent for HQ2* online January 21, 2018.

Detroit News. (2018, May 24). *Detroit's population loss slows, but rebound elusive* online August 20, 2018.

Duggan, M. (Mayor). (2017). State of the City Address. *Detroit Free Press* on-line February 21, 2017. Retrieved from www.freep.com

Emerson, K., Nabatchi, T., & Balogh, S. (2011). An integrative framework for collaborative governance. *Journal of Public Administration Research and Theory*, 22, 1–29.

Essex County Local Government Restructuring Study. (1976). *Final report: Peter Silcox, commissioner; John A. Jackson, research director*. Corporation of the County of Essex.

Florida, R. (2003). Cities and the creative class. *City and Community*, 2(1), 3–17.

Melanson, S. (2009). *Learning from the past: Volume 1: The automotive industry and economic development in Ontario; a historical perspective (1904 to the present)*. Toronto: Martin Prosperity Institute, University of Toronto.

Morrison, N. F. (1954). *Garden gateway to Canada*. Toronto: Ryerson Press.

Ontario Government. (1972). *Design for development: Prospects for the St. Clair region*. Toronto: Ministry of Treasury, Economics and Intergovernmental Affairs.

Price, T. (2010). *Heritage along the Detroit River*. Windsor: Essex County Historical Society.

Price, T., & Kulisek, L. (1992). *Windsor 1892–1992: A centennial celebration*. Windsor: Chamber Publications.

Roberts, D. (2006). *In the shadow of Detroit: Gordon M. McGregor, Ford of Canada, and motoropolis*. Detroit: Wayne State University Press.

This Old House (2012, February). *Best old house neighborhoods 2012: Canada*, This Old House Ventures, LLC, online October 1, 2017. Retrieved from www.thisoldhouse.com

Wade, M. (ed.). (1969). *The international megalopolis*. Toronto: University of Toronto Press.

Washington Post. (1997, February 19). *For first time in generation, hopes for rebirth are high in Detroit* online January 21, 2018.

Windsor Star. (1976, June 30). *Silcox drafts a new Essex County* online A1.

Windsor Star. (2002, October 12). *$3.7M land transfer OK'd; annexation by Windsor brings regional 'peace'* online A3.

Windsor Star. (2017a, July 31). *Mostly vacant Windsor plazas seen as an opportunity for 'sprawl repair'* online August 1, 2017.

Windsor Star. (2017b, October 13). *Homeless epidemic in the downtown is taxing residents and service groups* online October 15, 2017.

Windsor Star. (2017c). *City disentangles itself from costly Canderel Building Deal* online November 6, 2017.

Windsor Star. (2018, January 8). *Mayor Drew Dilkens reflects on 2017 accomplishments, hopes for 2018* online January 8, 2018.

Windsor Star. (2018, January 18). *Why did Detroit-Windsor fail in our bid for Amazon HQ2?* online January 21, 2018.

Windsor-Essex Economic Development Corporation. (2017). *Monthly Economic Monitor* online August 20, 2018.

3 Next steps for social impact bonds

Moving from an economic tool to a trust-based collaboration

Emma Powell

Introduction

The genesis of a social impact bond is present with Ansell and Gash's (2008) definition of collaborative government: "a governing arrangement where one or more public agencies directly engage non-state stakeholders in a collective decision-making process . . ." (p. 544); however, Emerson, Nabatchi, and Balogh's (2011) definition is better suited; calling attention to "multi-partner governance," which encompasses the variety of stakeholders that strive to make new partnerships a better option for wicked problems in our social sector. For the sake of this chapter, Emerson et al.'s definition of collaborative governance is extended into the realm of social impact bonds (SIB) as a tool for economic growth and program oversight:

> The processes and structures of public policy decision making and management that engage people constructively across the boundaries of public agencies, levels of government, and/or the public, private, and civic spheres in order to carry out a public purpose that could not otherwise be accomplished.
>
> (p. 2)

Social impact bond review sits nicely in the collaborative governance regime's (CGR) three primary dimensions (Emerson et al., 2011): *system context*, *drivers*, and *collaboration dynamics*. Additionally, Denita Cepiku (2017) addresses the collaborative mindset and the "collaboration continuum" of governance and oversight. The continuum starts with *cooperation*, a short-term relationship with limited information sharing; moves to *coordination*, a relationship of separate behaviors toward an agreed on action; finally, *collaboration*; a notably risky relationship that is based on mutual commitment to the overarching efforts and concerns being addressed (Mandell & Keast, 2008).

The SIB experiments make evident collaborative governance partners, which include public, private, and nonprofit stakeholders, to improve governance relationships, foster community development within and between all sectors of public life, as well as establish a trust-based collaboration across the sectors. Social impact bonds, within contemporary civil society, have a possible long-term impact but do not come without legitimate trepidations due to the innovative service/funding model.

This research uses social impact bonds to examine the relationship between community needs, public expectations, government restrictions and/or limitations, financial resources, and the nonprofit sector's ability to fill the gaps of market and government failure. These variables are the ultimate determiners of economic development within communities, regions, and the country. SIBs best demonstrate the interconnectedness of constituents and stakeholders and thus acknowledge the core of the collaborative governance framework from Emerson et al. (2011) and Emerson and Nabatchi (2015). This theory is used to specifically highlight the social impact bond opportunities and threats to engage and solicit funding/support for the oversight and implementation of social impact programs. The principal question reveals the unique construct of the SIB model and the need for continued understanding of the value of collaborative governance as it pertains to economic development efforts. *How do social impact bonds help demonstrate collaborative activity within and across sectors?*

Social impact bonds are a tool in the redesign of human services through a market approach. SIBs call to question the responsibility of financial/economic structures to social welfare (Schinckus, 2017). While the literature suggests that SIBs are not the "magic wand" to fix all massive problems, the SIB approach is a new model that is meant to develop a relationship with the for-profit sector and to gain buy-in from the stakeholders that have the wealth to help offset the large-scale costs that seem to match the large-scale problems being addressed.

Social impact bonds are understood as a contract between a private funder and the public sector (NCSL, 2016). At the core, SIBs are positioned to engage investors to fund programs meant to disrupt the cycle of distress for those most burdened. This market-driven approach to paying for social service areas of problem-solving is centered on trust between the service provider, government oversight, and the private funder. As a type of "Pay for Success" model, SIBs are funded through private capital and/or philanthropy to manage public projects in an effort to reduce government spending and increase the risk/reward calculation toward innovation (Hartley, 2014; Katz, Brisbois, Zerger, & Hwang, 2018; Schinckus, 2017). These investors assume the risk of under producing, innovative, and/or scaled-up program opportunities. However, if the programs are successful while using the funding of the private investor through the SIB model, then the government agrees to repay the investor with interest. As a market-based approach, SIBs are an illustration of traditional public, private, and nonprofit relationships extended to engage new dollars, oversight, outputs, and measures that assist the typical governance and service model.

Why they are touted?

The crucial distinction SIBs offer is that taxpayers do not pay for failed programs. The tax dollars are only used to repay the investor after program success has been determined. In theory, SIB's should shift the traditionally risk-averse service provider mentality to better consider innovation, risk/reward limitations, evaluation of service delivery, and outcomes. Local Initiatives Support Corporation's program manager, Anna Smukowski, told the SIB Review that "investors are interested in the model because it provides a forum for impacting investing which produces social and/or environmental returns, as well as a financial return" (as cited in Welch, 2017). This type of investing connects mission-focused organizations to the financial institutions and corporate social responsibility interest of banks and business. Smukowski continued, "Through measurement of program effectiveness, it ensures investments measurably improve the lives of the people served" (2017). Lastly, the design of social impact bonds requires evaluation to be the driver of investment repayment. Using a comprehensive evaluation plan, SIBs change the program review from anecdotal evidence of execution to quantitative long-term outcome measurement that indicates achievement.

Much research notes that social impact bonds are shifting the social policy environment in advanced economic countries. Moreover, social impact bonds can be seen as ". . . a useful new strategy for mobilizing private and public capital for social purposes in a period of great change in the global economy" (Jackson, 2013, p. 610). Enlisting the SIB model provides a tool for funding strategies that were previously frowned upon in the nonprofit sector. Ideally, this model allows for innovative program design and funding mechanisms to address such deeply rooted problems.

The nonprofit sector's role in social welfare is obvious to those who use and distribute services to the marginalized or disenfranchised constituents. However, through the lens of the SIB model, there is significant cause to evaluate the system as it contributes to economic development efforts of participating areas. The efforts associated with strengthening the well-being of the communities' social, political, and economic tenets are understood to be "economic development." In that, there is a legitimate case to be made that the initial private funding source (which alleviates the startup financial burden for the nonprofit service provider and lessens the tax pressures of the citizens), the nonprofit service providers (who employ those with the expertise and training to serve the program's mission, as a priority), and the government repayment for successful programs (to ensure that taxpayers are paying for proven and successful programs to contribute to the economic development and social welfare after program completion) are a trifecta of engage stakeholders in the area of economic growth. The social impact bond model is steeped in securing the support and resources of all three sectors for community advancement.

Why they are refuted?

The SIB model has been touted by politicians as a substitute for government funding on social services. SIB's are a fit in select circumstances, but not all. Many investors require target measures that are unrealistic and impossible to measure accurately (Jackson, 2013). SIB naysayers would argue that the use of SIBs encourages the government to remove themselves from the direct care and concern of the nation's most vulnerable. Ultimately, government should care about program development and implementation without private investment as a tool for economic relief. Moreover, in light of the required SIB evaluation standards, some have argued that a SIB transforms the citizens whom are receiving the services into commodities to count and measure to determine investment payout (Roy, McHugh, & Sinclair, 2018). Considering the evaluation requirement, the increased oversight and administrative burden offers a less flexible environment for service and may affect the care or program delivery, given the predetermined evaluation criterion. Often, indicators for success are selected at the front-end of the SIB agreement and therefore may not consider confounding variables that could demonstrate success or challenge the success rate, but ultimately has no bearing on the SIB program at all. For example, NYC Rikers Island, the juvenile recidivism case example (which is considered in more depth, later in the chapter) indicates that there were fewer men released and reconvicted, over the span of the SIB. Recidivism number/measurement is a prescribed indicator of program success. However, what is not considered is the policy change that minimized the police force and focus in certain neighborhoods. This could be a reason for decreased reconvictions versus the actual success of the SIB program, specifically. Lastly, outcomes are measured based on condition change and the time to assess is too far out to know if the SIB was successful within the contract terms.

Nonprofit partners are engaged to do the work of the SIB and are held accountable for the evaluation measures. These same partners are supporting program constituents in other ways, not measured by the SIB. These efforts, outside of the SIB evaluation measures, can exhaust resources (time and talents) and are often not a direct measure pre-established by the SIB agreement. Such efforts are needed for the organization to execute the mission but are not an indication of success for the contract and therefore may go unnoticed (Sanders, Teixeira, & Truder, 2013). SIBs are designed to create outcome change (generally a long-term measure) but are implemented to count outputs (typically a short-term measure). This dichotomy challenges the purpose and value of SIB as a change agent for the wicked problems they are constructed to combat.

Social impact bond overview

This chapter seeks to illustrate the use of social impact bonds as a tool for collaborative governance to support economic development efforts. A review of the social sector, the limitations of government resources, and private sector interest in wicked problem solutions calls attention to the need for unique strategies that affect social change. Emerson et al's. (2011) collaborative governance theoretical advancement will be evaluated through the lens of two of the United States' instrumental social impact bond experiments; New York City's 2012 *ABLE Project for Incarcerated Youth* and the 2016 *Strong Beginning's Project*. These two cases illustrate the SIB model over different time periods, geographies, funding amounts, funding sources, and scope of services. It is important to call attention to the early stages of SIB use. Considering that reports are typically not available to the public until all the details are finalized in the project, there are a limited amount of final reports available for review. Instead, the author conducted a thorough literature review and chose an exploratory case analysis of two SIBs through which the Emerson and Nabatchi's (2015) collaborative governance framework principles can be evaluated. In this research, both SIBs are examples of private and/or hybrid model funding used to support traditional government and social service programs while using a nonprofit organization to implement/manage the project and a third-party evaluator to measure success.

In addition to Michigan and New York, other states have taken to the SIB model since their first inception in the U.S. According to the Rockefeller Foundation, author Kippy Joseph (2013) compiled a brief highlight of states zeroing in on critical community needs. California is interested in SIBs that address issues of health care and housing, Texas is using SIBs for chronic disease management, specifically cardiovascular and lung disease, within low-income communities, and South Carolina is framing programs that address reducing infant mortality rates. Across the country, cities and states are continuing to investigate the benefits and challenges of the SIB model in an effort to address such wicked problems that drain resources and affect society at its core. Table 3.1 illustrates the domains for which the 108 contracted social impact bonds exist, globally (as reported in 2018) and Table 3.2 drills down to highlight the 20 U.S. contracted SIBs, to-date (Social Finance, 2018).

Table 3.1 Global SIB by Domain

Domain	*No.*
Workforce Development	36
Health	18
Housing/Homelessness	19
Child/Family Welfare	13
Criminal Justice	11
Education/Early Years	8
Environment	1
Adults with Complex Needs	1
Education	1

Source: Social Finance, Impact Bond Global Database, 2018.

Table 3.2 U.S. SIB by State

	Location	*Domain*	*Launch Date*	*Capital Raised*	*Max. Outcome Payment*
1	Ventura County, CA	Recidivism	Nov. 2017	$2.6 M	$2.85 M
2	Los Angeles, CA	Homelessness & Recidivism	Oct. 2017	$10 M	$11.5 M
3	Alameda County, CA	Juvenile Justice	Sept. 2017	$M-Unavailable	$M-Unavailable
4	Oklahoma	Female Incarceration	April 2017	$10 M	$2M
5	Massachusetts	Immigrant & Refugee Employment	March 2017	$12.4 M	$15 M
6	Salt Lake County, UT	Homelessness	Dec. 2016	$4.4 M	$5.5 M
7	Salt Lake County, UT	Recidivism	Dec. 2016	$4.6 M	$5.95 M
8	Connecticut	Family Stability	Sept. 2016	$11.2 M	$14.8 M
9	Washington, DC	Green Infrastructure	Sept. 2016	$25 M	$28.3 M
10	**Kent County, MI**	**Preterm Births *(Strong Beginnings)***	**August 2016**	**$8.5 M**	**$M-Unavailable**
11	Denver, CO	Homelessness	Feb. 2016	$8.7 M	$11.4 M
12	South Carolina	Early Childhood Development	Feb. 2016	$30 M	$7.5 M
13	Santa Clara County, CA	Homelessness	Sept. 2015	$6.9 M	$8 M
14	Ohio	Child Welfare & Family Homelessness	Jan. 2015	$4 M	$5 M
15	Massachusetts	Homelessness	Dec. 2014	$3.5 M	$6 M
16	Chicago, IL	Preschool Education	Oct. 2014	$16.9 M	$34.5 M
17	Massachusetts	Juvenile Recidivism	Jan. 2014	$22 M	$27 M
18	New York State	Recidivism & Employment	Dec. 2013	$13.5 M	$21.5 M
19	Salt Lake County, UT	Education & Early Years	Sept. 2013	$7 M	$M-Undisclosed
20	**New York City**	**Juvenile Recidivism (ABLE)**	**Jan. 2013**	**$9.6 M**	**$11.7 M**

Source: Social Finance, Impact Bond Global Database, 2018.

SIBs are a special type of social venture that bring together for-profit and nonprofit sectors through investment and are an example of the larger realm of new philanthropy that utilizes tools from the business sector in the human service and social welfare arenas. Foundations can function as philanthropic banks and serve as key actors as they bring along the requisite private investors (Salamon, 2013). "Social impact bonds are fast becoming part of the social policy landscape across the advanced economies" (Jackson, 2013, p. 614).

Social impact bonds are, at best, a tool that has worked in some cases and an option that could produce a scaled-up version of a successful program. From the extensive SIB literature review, it is clear that SIBs are not a one size fits all or a "silver bullet" to remedy all wicked problems. However, the literature does provide examples of best-case scenarios/environments for SIB success (Costa, 2014; Kohli, Besharov, & Costa, 2012).

SIBs are more likely to succeed if:

- Outcomes can be clearly defined, and historical data are available
- Outcomes are observable and measurable within three to eight years
- Preventive interventions exist that cost less to administer than remedial services
- Government agencies believe they will save money as a result of the outcome being achieved
- Social interventions are shown to be effective in achieving the outcome
- Some interventions with high levels of evidence already exist
- Political will for traditional direct funding can be difficult to sustain
- Few negative consequences exist if the external organization determines it cannot achieve the outcome and discontinues services

A working paper, from the Organization for Economic Cooperation and Development prepared by Galitopoulou and Noya (2016), further highlights that from the short time SIBs have been an option they are most "appropriate for policy areas in which there are target groups that can be easily identified, when there are measurable outcomes, and when investors are familiar with nonprofits, social enterprises and social policies" (p. 16). Wicked problems seeking large-scale solutions continue to be the best environment to consider a SIB as a tool for economic growth and system change.

How are SIBs, as an economic development tool, relevant to collaborative governance?

An approach similar to SIBs are traditional performance-based contracts and/or pay for success models. However, according to Third Sector Capital (2013), social impact bonds offer three distinct differences. First, the use of data is ongoing and adds heightened attention to outside evaluation. Third party evaluators are a norm for SIB management and oversight. Taking evaluation away from the success stories and instead quantifying measures to translate to all sectors for review. Second, there is flexibility to service providers. Instead of the traditional performance-based contract as a prescriptive approach, the SIB model allows for funding around measurable results. Third, there is an increased financial incentive compared to a performance-based contract. SIBs are only repaid with interest based on results. Moving beyond the typical service contract into a model of social impact bonds recognizes private finance dollars for public goods and services. Moreover, although SIBs are considered a subset of payments-by-results, pay-for-performance or results-based financing mechanisms, these models are different from a true social impact bond. According to the OECD (Galitopoulou & Noya, 2016), critical differences include:

1. SIBs involve private sector investors. This demonstrates a broader stakeholder analysis and reliance on effective cooperation and coordination between funding, implementation, and evaluation.
2. SIBs are outcome-centered rather than results or outputs oriented. The primary purpose is to see lasting/long-term change in condition of such wicked problems the program was designed to address instead of aggregate numbers of short-term outputs.
3. SIBs secure funding up-front (or in predetermined installments/payment schedules tied to specific measures or milestones) so that the organization can focus on service delivery efforts instead of the typically-present demand for fundraising initiatives.
4. SIBs transfer the financial and implementation risk from the service provider organization to the private sector investor. This risk transfer allows for public sector or nonprofit service stakeholders to participate in innovative programing without bearing the financial stress or tax dollar appropriation for untested programing.

Social impact bonds speak truth to the ideals of collaborative governance. The SIB is a tool for fiscal relief from the public sector as well as a stakeholder engagement mechanism that expands that of the normal players for service and community building programs. Instead SIBs call more for-profit entities to invest and care about the mission work that the public sector is already generating solutions to.

The use of a collaborative governance regime concept recognizes the patterns of behavior, norms, and structures used in a cross-boundary system for public decision-making (Emerson et al., 2011; Crosby & Bryson, 2005; Krasner, 1983). More specifically, Table 3.3 shines a light on the system approach to collaborative governance and the multiple stakeholders. The Collaborative Governance Regime (CGR) is illustrated as a logic model flow chart within the Emerson et al. (2011) text, highlighting the multifaceted approach to understanding and reviewing the integrative framework for collaborative governance (p. 7). Collaborative governance is steeped in the

Table 3.3 Rikers Island Social Impact Bond Payment Schedule

Reduction in Re-incarceration Rate	*City Payment*	*Return on Investment*	*Projected Long-term City Net Savings*
>20%	$11,712,000	22%	$20,500,000
>16%	$10,944,000	14%	$11,700,000
>13%	$10,368,000	8%	$7,200,000
>12.5%	$10,272,000	7%	$6,400,000
>12%	$10,176,000	6%	$5,600,000
>11%	$10,080,000	5%	$1,700,000
>10%	$9,600,000	0%	>$1,000,000

Source: Goldman Sachs, 2012.

recognition of stakeholders, varying lenses, problem-solving, and the ideals of cross-sector comprise and mutual understandings. Such collaboration management provides an environment for collaborative outputs and outcomes (Cepiku, 2017). A systems approach continues to call attention to the interconnected variables that create a collaborative governance environment.

Case review

The first social impact bond launched in September 2010. The Peterborough Prison, based in the United Kingdom, focuses on the re-offending rate of prisoners leaving the prison (Disley & Rubin, 2014). In July of 2017, independent evaluators concluded the program a success; whereby the target success measure of 7.5% reduction, as indicated by the Ministry of Justice, was met or exceeded. According to the evaluations, Peterborough social impact bond effectively reduced re-offending of short-sentenced offenders by 9% (compared to a national control group). Investors were repaid in full, with a 3% annualized return on the initial investment (Helbitz, 2017).

The 2012 New York City *ABLE Project for Incarcerated Youth* program was the United States' first social impact bond aimed at reducing juvenile recidivism. Prison projects appear to meet the needed SIB criterion; as a social problem, a human concern, and also a financial drain, incarceration is expensive for the taxpayer. Reducing reoffenders can have a tremendous savings on the criminal justice system and results are easily quantifiable (Murray, 2018).

The ABLE Project contract secured a $7.2 million investment from Goldman Sachs to reduce recidivism at Riker's Island prison in New York City. The Adolescent Behavioral Learning Experience (ABLE) focused on education, training, and counseling through the *Young Men's Initiative*. The project was an evidenced-based intervention, designed to develop responsibility and support decision-making skills of the young men involved in the program.

The private funding from Goldman Sachs was structured as a loan to the nonprofit organization, MDRC. MDRC managed the implementation of the ABLE program. At the onset, Bloomberg Philanthropies guaranteed up to $6 million if the ABLE program was unsuccessful. According to the August 2, 2012 City of New York Press Release, The Vera Institute of Justice is the independent evaluator to determine if the program met the specified target for success and thus repaying Goldman Sachs their initial investment plus interest. Success measures were determined to be: a 10% or more reduction of re-admission rates – measured by total jail days avoided. If the reduction rate exceeded 11%, Goldman Sachs would also receive a financial return that was consistent with typical community development lending (City of New York, 2012). Table 3.3 illustrates potential return on investment based on reduction of re-incarceration rates.

In the case of ABLE, and in contrast to the 2017 UK success of the Peterborough Prison project, the program fell short of the approved measures and Goldman Sachs lost $1.2 million of the initial $7 million investment (Misner, 2013).

In 2016 Michigan launched a pilot program expanding a current collaborative that focuses on infant mortality rates in Kent County, Michigan. In 2011 the W.K. Kellogg Foundation initiated support for *Strong Beginnings* program, managed by Spectrum Health. The program was conceptualized at the local hospital and has since proven successful in improving healthy birth outcomes for high-risk mothers. *Strong Beginnings* uses eight community partner agencies to conduct home visits, produce quality community programing/education events, and coordinated efforts for care from pregnancy through age two (Spectrum Health Newsroom, 2016). With the *Strong Beginnings* success, the state of Michigan chose to leverage the existing program model with the infusion of social impact bond financing to scale-up and serve an additional 1,700 families in Kent County, alone.

The *Strong Beginnings* program is Michigan's first SIB. Such a multi-stakeholder initiative highlights the economic advantages of aligning the program for the community good; there is a cost savings for the government, improved patient health, and ultimately a financial return for the investors (Crowley, 2014). Specifically, this SIB was funded by private and philanthropic partners to support the work of the eight partner agency collaboration efforts, all managed through the Spectrum Health coordination and oversight. The program was selected to be the first in Michigan after receiving an American Hospital Association NOVA Award, meant to congratulate collaborative efforts that improve community health, organized by a hospital (Beck, 2016). With proven success and awards under the belt of the collaborative, Michigan's governor selected *Strong Beginnings* as the first "pay-for-success" model in the state.

The *Strong Beginnings* program is a federally funded Healthy Start program, a recipient of the Health Resources and Services grant, as well as the recipient of Kellogg Foundation investment. The pay-for-success contract provides $1 million of the estimated $1.4 million operating budget for the program (Dewey, 2016). Over a five-year period, the Health Resources and Services Administration awarded the *Strong Beginnings* program $4.9 million to increase capacity to serve more African-American women, men, and children. During the same five-year period, the Kellogg Foundation approved $4.3 million to focus on and improve Latino families (Spectrum Health Newsroom, 2018). This $9 million investment expands the programs initial model to serve the populations most vulnerable in west Michigan. This hybrid funding and implementation model is yet another example of government, private sector, foundations, and nonprofit service providers becoming more creative in an effort to leverage resources for large-scale impact and success.

The economic impact is most obvious in the reports to-date. Not a single infant life lost from mothers enrolled in the program (over the last three years), 4,000 families have been served, and low-birth weight and infant mortality rates have been reduced by half in comparison to other African Americans in the community. Economic development is the improvement of the communities' social, political, and economic environment. Through the *Strong Beginnings* program, it is clear to see such advancements have strengthened the community in which the program serves.

Discussion

Collaborative governance is present in new models of funding and oversight throughout multiple facets of government, civic intermediaries, agencies, and nonprofits. New York City and the Michigan SIB agreements are used as examples to understand how social impact bonds support collaborative activity within and across sectors, using the integrative framework for collaborative governance. Collaborative governance regime, according to Emerson et al. (2011) introduces ten propositions. Six of them can be addressed specifically using the SIB model. Proposition 1, 2, 3, 5, 9, and 10 are specific and relevant to the SIB model review.

Proposition One considers the drivers of collaborative governance. What helps instigate these behaviors and supports the collaborative governance regime values? Social impact bonds, as a tool for economic growth, demonstrate those same drivers Emerson et al. recognizes for collaborative governance, in action. Leadership, incentives, and interdependence are all clearly critical to the design, implementation, and success of the SIB agreement. Through the Rikers Island case example, leadership for the financial contribution of the private sector investment as well as the nonprofit implementer and the government participation show forward thinking to design a new initiative for change. Incentives are obvious in that there is a financial gain for the investment partner and the possibility of key outcomes to change major social problems. These incentives are key "wins" for the stakeholders involved in a specific SIB. Lastly, the design of a SIB is

Table 3.4 Propositions as Presented by Emerson et al. (2011)

Proposition	*Description*
Proposition One	One or more of the drivers of leadership, consequential incentives, interdependence, or uncertainty are necessary for a CGR to begin. The more drivers present and recognized by participants, the more likely a CGR will be initiated.
Proposition Two	Principled engagement is generated and sustained by the interactive processes of discovery, definition, deliberation, and determination. The effectiveness of principled engagement is determined, in part, by the quality of these interactive processes.
Proposition Three	Repeated, quality interactions through principled engagement will help foster trust, mutual understanding, internal legitimacy, and shared commitment, thereby generating and sustaining shared motivation.
Proposition Four	Once generated, shared motivation will enhance and help sustain principled engagement and vice versa in a "virtuous cycle."
Proposition Five	Principled engagement and shared motivation will stimulate the development of institutional arrangements, leadership, knowledge, and resources, thereby generating and sustaining capacity for joint action.
Proposition Six	The necessary levels for the four elements of capacity for joint action are determined by the CGR's purpose, shared theory of action, and targeted outcomes.
Proposition Seven	The quality and extent of collaborative dynamics depends on the productive and self-reinforcing interactions among principled engagement, shared motivation, and the capacity for joint action.
Proposition Eight	Collaborative actions are more likely to be implemented if: 1) a shared theory of action is identified explicitly among the collaboration partners and 2) the collaborative dynamics function to generate the needed capacity for joint action.
Proposition Nine	The impacts resulting from collaborative action are likely to be closer to the targeted outcomes with fewer unintended negative consequences when they are specified and derived from a shared theory of action during collaborative dynamics.
Proposition Ten	CGRs will be more sustainable over time when they adapt to the nature and level of impacts resulting from their joint actions.

based in interdependence. Without the finance partner, the implementation organization/program, and the government approval/acceptance of the plan, the SIB would be just another donation or single attempt at program design by a local partner agency. Through the SIB, the interdependence becomes a valued tenet of the model.

Proposition Two focuses on the engagement and ultimately the interactive process of such engagement. Social impact bonds rely on the buy-in for the program and outcomes from each actor but also strive to maintain the engagement through evaluation. Using predetermined success measures is an illustration of Emerson et al's. proposition two; seeking to create an interactive process of development. Collaborative governance needs critical stakeholders to be engaged and concerned. In the Michigan *Strong Beginnings* program, the project design enlisted not only the oversight organization and the funders, but also included eight social service providers to have a holistic approach to care and education using as many stakeholders as possible at the onset. Through the process of outcome determination and success measures, each stakeholder is a key player in the interactive process of SIB determination and establishment. Using this engagement, *Proposition Three* can be met. While proposition two seeks to create engagement, proposition three suggests that collaborative governance can be crafted through repeat engagement opportunities to create and maintain shared commitment and common motivation for the continued SIB activity. Proposition three suggests that building shared understanding fosters trust in the partnership of collaborative governance actors. Building a shared commitment is understood through individual partner motivations. Each actor participates in the collaborative governance regime through the SIB tool because they are motivated through specific outcomes; financial, social change, risk/rewards, etc. Recognizing these separate, yet shared, motivators allows for the SIB to be used as a tool that generates trust and seeks to oversee programs that foster community development as well as financial output for the investor.

Proposition Five suggests that proposition two and three, working in tandem, will generate the institutional arrangements, leadership, knowledge, and resources necessary for capacity for joint action. In essence, enacting proposition two and three will support proposition five, which is a SIB in action.

Proposition Nine of the collaborative governance regime ideals is visible in a SIB's role in innovative solutions and shared understanding of success. Proposition nine put forward that once collaborative governance practices are implemented, there is a greater chance for success and fewer opportunities for unintended consequences. When all the stakeholders are a part of the dialogue and design, collaboration helps understand the scaling up process that SIBs can best be used for. Due to the heavy emphasis on outcome agreement and measurement, SIBs demonstrate a shared understanding for the actors to move the program(s) forward toward mutually agreed upon targets.

Lastly, *Proposition Ten* of collaborative governance regime ideals suggests that long-term sustainability is more viable when governance of the program can adapt to the nature of the impact. In the case of a SIB, after success is demonstrated, a vital component is the transition to government payout and administrator oversight. In that, government resumes control and financial responsibility once program success is confirmed. This model alleviates initial fiscal strain on government, nonprofit program implementer resources to scale-up the model, as well as taxpayer hesitation to support an unknown. The SIB model transitions the program back to government or nonprofit oversight and therefore supports proposition ten given that the initial hesitations have been answered and the community or system is able to adapt to the model that has been established to continue the proven successes of the initial SIB.

Conclusion

Wicked problems endure. Nonprofit organization's role in those problems continues to evolve. With tools like the social impact bond, nonprofit, for-profit, and government stakeholders become a trifecta voice in solution-based program design and implementation. From this review, the reader has a brief glimpse at the extent to which such massive and interconnected problems can span. Calling attention to the tools our public, private, and nonprofit sector may have to address these social complexities is prudent, given the constant plea for resources to attempt any probable remedy. Therefore, understanding the social impact bond as a possible tool for collaborative governance is one opportunity that continues to gain momentum.

At the onset of this chapter, the principal question was posed, *how do social impact bonds help demonstrate collaborative activity within and across sectors?* Emerson et al.'s Ten Propositions were reviewed, and consideration of the collaborative governance core areas were explored. Using a brief overview of two U.S.-based social impact bond contracts, six of the ten propositions are better revealed to demonstrate critical components of collaborative governance; system context, drivers, and collaboration dynamics.

The SIB tool has examples, worldwide. Given the infancy for the SIB concept, it is still difficult to determine a correct and consistent formula for success. However, after extensive review, a focus on collaborative governance allows principle engagement, shared understanding, and a transition of the program for long-term success. The propositions presented in Emerson et al's. CGR article (2011) provide a framework for this review from which SIBs can be determined to be a fit with the collaborative governance regime values and practices. Although SIBs can and have failed, this review posits that such a tool has, and might continue to be used as a demonstration of trust via a collaborative governance model. Ultimately suggesting that there is an opportunity for SIBs to morph from an economic tool with a market approach strategy that simply funds scaled-up projects to a comprehensive, trust-based collaboration approach for massive scale success.

References

Ansell, C., & Gash, A. (2008). Collaborative governance in theory and practice. *Journal of Public Administration Research and Theory*, 18(4), 543–571.

Beck, M. (2016, October). Program created to reduce infant deaths gives new moms a 'strong beginning'. *Mlive*. Retrieved from www.mlive.com/news/grand-rapids/index.ssf/2016/10/program_created_to_reduce_infa.html

Cepiku, D. (2017). Collaborative governance. In T. R. Klassen, D. Cepiku, & T. J. Lah (Eds.), *The Routledge handbook of global public policy and administration* (1st ed.).

City of New York. (2012, August 2). *Fact sheet: The NYC ABLE Project for Incarcerated Youth*: America's first social impact bond [Press release]. Retrieved from http://www.nyc.gov/html/om/pdf/2012/sib_fact_sheet.pdf

Costa, K., & Kohli, J. (2012, November). *Social impact bonds: New York City and Massachusetts to launch the first social impact bond programs in the United States*. Center for American Progress. Retrieved from https://www.americanprogress.org/issues/economy/news/2012/11/05/43834/new-york-city-and-massachusetts-to-launch-the-first-social-impact-bond-programs-in-the-united-states/

Costa, K. (2014, February). *Social impact bonds in the United States* [Fact sheet]. Center for American Progress. Retrieved from https://www.americanprogress.org/issues/economy/reports/2014/02/12/84003/fact-sheet-social-impact-bonds-in-the-united-states/

Crosby, B. C., & Bryson, J. M. (2005). *Leadership for the common good: Tackling public problems in a shared-power world*. San Francisco, CA: Jossey-Bass.

Crowley, D. M. (2014). The role of social impact bonds in pediatric health care. *Pediatrics*, 134(2), 331–333.

Dewey, C. (2016, October). Strong beginnings to pilot pay-for-success model. *Grand Rapids Business Journal*. Retrieved from www.grbj.com/articles/86316-strong-beginnings-to-pilot-pay-for-success-model

Disley, E., & Rubin, J. (2014). Phase 2 report from the payment by results social impact bond pilot at HMP Peterborough. *Ministry of Justice*. Retrieved from www.rand.org/pubs/research_reports/RR473.html

Emerson, K., & Nabatchi, T. (2015). *Collaborative governance regimes*. Washington, DC: Georgetown University Press.

Emerson, K., Nabatchi, T., & Balogh, S. (2011). An integrative framework for collaborative governance. *Journal of Public Administration Research and Theory*, 22, 1–29.

Galitopoulou, S., & Noya, A. (2016). Understanding social impact bonds. *Organization for Economic Cooperation and Development*. (Working Paper). Retrieved from www.oecd.org/cfe/leed/UnderstandingSIBsLux-WorkingPaper.pdf

Hartley, J. (2014, September 15). Social impact bonds are going mainstream. *Forbes*. Retrieved from www.forbes.com/sites/jonhartley/2014/09/15/social-impact-bonds-are-going-mainstream/#a278ed86306b

Helbitz, A. (2017, July 27). World's 1st social impact bond shown to cut reoffending and to make impact investors a return. *Social Finance*. Retrieved from https://socialfinance.org.uk/sites/default/files/news/final-press-release-pb-july-2017.pdf

Jackson, E. T. (2013). Evaluating social impact bonds: Questions, challenges, innovations, and possibilities in measuring outcomes in impact investing. *Community Development*, 44(5), 608–616.

Joseph, K. (2013, October 2). Social impact bonds [infographic]. Retrieved from www.rockefellerfoundation.org/uploads/files/a39e8cdf-494f-486e-a8c2- 1170c7ffc5c6-rockefeller.pdf

Katz, A. S., Brisbois, B., Zerger, S., & Hwang, S. (2018). Social impact bonds as a funding method for health and social programs: Potential areas of concern. *American Journal of Public Health*, 108(2), 210–215.

Kohli, J., Besharov, D. J., & Costa, K. (2012, March). *Social impact bonds 101: Defining an innovative new financing tool for social programs*. Center for American Progress. Retrieved from https://www.americanprogress.org/issues/general/news/2012/03/22/11238/social-impact-bonds-101/

Krasner, S. D. (1983). Structural causes and regime consequences: Regimes as intervening variables. In *International regimes* (pp. 1–22). Ithaca, NY: Cornell University Press.

Mandell, M. P., & Keast, R. (2008). Evaluating the effectiveness of interorganizational relations through networks. *Public Management Review*, 10(6), 715–731.

Misner, K. (2013, June). *Bringing social impact bonds to New York City*. Presentation, Baltimore, MD. Retrieved from http://www.aisp.upenn.edu/wp-content/uploads/2015/11/Kristin-Misner-1.pdf

Murray, S. (2018, Summer). A new form of capitalism. *Stanford Social Innovation Review*, 16(2).

NCSL. (2016, September 22). Social impact bonds. *National Conference of State Legislatures*. Retrieved from www.ncsl.org/research/labor-and-employment/social-impact-bonds.aspx

Roy, M. J., McHugh, N., & Sinclair, S. (2018, May 1). A critical reflection on social impact bonds. *Stanford Social Innovation Review*.

Salamon, L. (2013, July). *Towards a new era of social purpose finance*. Presentation, Baltimore, MD. Retrieved from https://earlychildhood.marylandpublicschools.org/system/files/filedepot/20/sibreport2013.pdf

Sanders, B., Teixeira, L., & Truder, J. (2013). *Dashed hopes, lives on hold: Single homeless people's experiences of the work programme*. London: Crisis.

Schinckus, C. (2017). Financial innovation as a potential force for a positive social change: The challenging future of social impact bonds. *Research in International Business and Finance*, 39(B), 727–736.

Social Finance. (2018). *Impact bond global database*. Retrieved from https://sibdatabase.socialfinance.org.uk/

Spectrum Health Newsroom. (2016, September). *Government Snyder: New pay-for-success pilot program launches today, aims to improve birth and health outcomes for high-risk women in West Michigan*. Retrieved from https://newsroom.spectrumhealth.org/gov-snyder-new-pay-for-success-pilot-program-launches-today-aims-to-improve-birth-and-health-outcomes-for-high-risk-women-in-west-michigan/

Spectrum Health Newsroom. (2018). *New support expands reach of strong beginnings women and children's health initiative*. Retrieved from https://newsroom.spectrumhealth.org/new-support-expands-reach-of-strong-beginnings-women-and-childrens-health-initiative/

Third Sector Capital Partners. (2013). *Preparing for a pay for success opportunity*. Retrieved from www.thirdsectorcap.org/wp-content/uploads/2013/04/Third-Sector_Roca_Preparingfor-Pay-for-Success-in-MA.pdf

Welch, S. (2017, April). Michigan tests pay-for-success model for diabetes prevention. *Crain's Detroit Business*. Retrieved from www.crainsdetroit.com/article/20170423/NEWS/170429950/michigan-tests-pay-for-success-model-for-diabetes-prevention

W. K. Kellogg Foundation. (2016, September). *State of Michigan expands WKKF-supported program aimed at improving healthy birth outcomes*. Retrieved from www.wkkf.org/news-and-media/article/2016/09/state-of-michigan-expands-wkkf-supported-program-aimed-at-improving-healthy-birth-outcomes

4 Collaboration among informal organizations to manage informal urban transport in Indian cities

Arindam Biswas and Mohit Dev

Introduction

Individuals sometime must act collectively to achieve their goals. Once individuals with common interests collectively work in groups, the possibility to achieve those goals become more realistic (Olson, 1965). The common goal can be very elementary (i.e., to get equal pay, to work for equal hours, and so on) or advanced (i.e., to achieve social reform, to fight against corruption, etc.) in nature. The collaboration to disburse common goals, public goods, and services may happen within government organizations, private organizations, or a combination of both. Various aspects from diverse realms of practice lead to collaboration and ultimately create these organizations for collaboration.

An organization can be assumed to be a set of institutional arrangements and participants who have a common set of goals and purposes, and who must interact across multiple action situations at different levels of activity (Polski & Ostrom, 1999). North (1992) visualized organization as a group of individuals engaged in a purposive activity. The constraints imposed by the institutional framework define the opportunity set and therefore the kind of organizations that will come into existence (North, 1992). The formal organizations operate through a set of structured norms and rules, whereas the informal organizations create norms independently that are mutually agreed upon and understood among the related stakeholders. Thus, collaboration takes place in a cross-boundary domain consisting of institutions from public and private domains (Emerson, Nabatchi, & Balogh 2012).

It is particularly interesting to explore the pattern of collaboration for extending public services within and across informal organizations or unorganized sectors.[1] The term "informal sector" refers to the group of all informal enterprises, and "informal economy" refers to a more generalized term comprising both informal employment in informal enterprises and informal employment outside informal enterprises (International Labor Organization, 2002; Moreno-Monroy, 2012). The International Labor Organization (ILO, 1972) and British anthropologist Keith Hart (1973) are credited with first use of the term "informal sector" to characterize unaccounted employment opportunities in Africa (Hart, 1973; ILO, 1972). Defiance from rules and norms is not intrinsic to these informal settings, which depend on other institutional responses for their operation (Biswas & Maurya, 2018). The informal sector provides necessary opportunities for earning a livelihood to the economically disadvantaged and socially reclusive people, migrants, and people with less skill or education. Experts argue that the informal sector is too big to be easily formalized and developing countries lack the institutional capacity to adequately monitor informal activities (Mukhija & Loukaitou-Sideris, 2014). Even though this vast extent of the informal economy in developing countries is unregulated, it is very much integrated with the larger formal economy. Therefore, it is particularly fascinating to explore the collaboration of different actors within an informal organization and its collaborative networking with other formal and informal organizations to facilitate public services.

This book chapter does not argue in favor of formalizing this "informal sector" or investigating the reasons for such informality, but puts forward a research agenda that investigates the role of collaboration in managing the collective action from different organizations that manage informal urban transport in Indian cities. It primarily focuses on the institutional dynamics of such informality and its contribution to form collaboration within informal private operators. This chapter investigates the organizational complexity within an informal organization, its networking with other formal and informal organizations, and institutional arrangements through multiple inputs from diverse disciplines, including markets, hierarchies, firms, families, voluntary associations, national governments, and international regimes (Ostrom, 2010). This chapter considers smaller metropolitan cities like Lucknow, Kanpur, Surat, Ahmedabad, etc. In these cities, various forms of informal transport like human or animal-driven vehicles to motorized minibuses operate. This chapter will corroborate inputs from diverse disciplines to develop a compelling argument.

It is structured in six sections that starts with a detailed discussion of the informal organization and labor market in Section 2. It briefly discusses the correlation between the labor market and the genesis of the informal organization in the emerging economies. It further discusses the role of the informal organization to manage informal transport from empirical evidence of Indian cities.

Section 3 further extends this argument with a theoretical underpinning of studying informal transport organizations. It invokes the popular methods of organizational studies and establishes the network between formal and informal transit networks. The section also proposes a framework of collaborative governance for the informal sector that connects between "starting condition," "facilitative leadership," and "collaborative process."

Section 4 discusses about the functioning of informal urban transport and its relation with the formal institutional settings. This discussion corroborates with the proposed framework of collaborative governance in Section 2.

Section 5 presents a discussion and insight on the collaborative process and collective action of informal transport organization in Indian cities. Finally, Section 6 concludes the book chapter with its final arguments.

Informal labor market and its nexus with the informal transport organization

Institutions are likely to be organizations: the physical embodiment of an institution, where people carry out particular sets of activities. The success of any sector, be it transport, education, health, or energy, depends critically on its institutions and its functioning irrespective of any country (Dhingra, 2014). The labor market is a key attribute of this functioning. The labor market is the outcome of interactions between suppliers of labor (individuals, differentiated by skill, education, training, experience, location, and mobility) and consumers of labor (organizations, public and private, differentiated by needs for particular skills, experience, training, and location) (Pratt, 1996). The informal sector constitutes a significant proportion of the total labor force. Contrary to the conventional notion, both the developed and developing economy experiences the presence of the informal sector in their labor market. However, informality in the labor market is more predominant in the emerging economies (Mukhija & Loukaitou-Sideris, 2015). To understand informality, one must not only consider its producers and consumers, but also those who record, analyze, penalize, encourage, and more broadly define an activity as being informal (Bureau & Fendt, 2011). Although all transactions in informal economy may be termed *stricto sensu* illegal, the degree of illegality does not originate from the activity itself, but from the societal perception, revealed through formal rules and their enforcement (Becker, 1963).

There is no denial that formal and informal economies are complementary to each other. The formal economy is seemingly more rigid, taxed, and structured whereas the informal economy is more complex and intricately connected to the formal economy (Webster et al., 2008). People who are poorly trained or less educated face major hindrances of getting a job in the formal economy. For them, the informal economy is a palliative to the problems raised by an excessively rigid, taxed, and unwelcoming formal economy (Cebula, 1997). People excluded from the formal economy can get a livelihood opportunity and keep their morale in place. Bureau and Fendt (2011) classified five forms of informal economy – household economy, alternative economy, underground economy, the criminal economy, and white color criminal economy (Bureau & Fendt, 2011). Among them, the underground informal sector touches all readily apparent manifestations of urban life between employment, housing, and transportation. Within the underground informal sector, the Organization for Economic Cooperation and Development (OECD) includes all illegal production activities that are purposefully hidden from the authorities for reasons such as tax and social security evasion and skirting regulations regarding the minimum wage, maximum working hours, hygiene, and security (Arkell, 2007). The urban workforce in the developing economies is mostly constituted of the informal economy. Sixty-eight percent of Mumbai's urban workforce is employed in the informal sector (Micro Housing Finance Corporation, 2012). Theoretically, such urban informality is characterized by four broad approaches – structuralist approach, neoliberal approach, reformist approach, and critical governance approach. The structuralist approach argues that informal activities are linked to the deepening of global capitalism, the abundant supply of labor, the weakening of government enforced regulations, employers' interest to avoid state's regulations on workplace governance, and wages. The neoliberal approach argues that the underlying problem of urban informality is too much regulation, which increases the costs of doing business, and unrealistic standards for growth in the informal economy. The reformist approach sees structural reasons for the existence of informality. It does not expect informality to disappear and advocates an active role by the government and civil society in supporting and upgrading informal activities. The critical governance approach is critical and skeptical of the state's role of the arbitrary use of state power in the enforcement of regulations. It includes the government agencies' method of hiring informal workers and uses informality for their economic advantages (Mukhija & Loukaitou-Sideris, 2015). Sometimes, people serving through informality receive partial acknowledgment either in the form of license or registration.

Engagement of informal workers in the organized and unorganized sector has different reasons. The same is true for the modern urban transport services in cities. Mobility is required to bridge the "gaps" between activities and the sites where they take place (Pratt, 1996). Today, the private operators operate informal sector fleets consisting of low-performance vehicles to provide mobility services in cities. These privately operated, small-scale services are varyingly referred to para-transit/low-cost transport/intermediate technologies/third-world transport (Cervero, 2000). The reasons for the informal sector's growth in transportation is attributed to the voids left unfilled by the formal public transport operators, poor road facilities, inability to strategically plan first and last mile connectivity, cost of doing business due to protected monopolies, and the institutional bottlenecks. It is particularly prevalent in developing countries, e.g., 79%, 63%, and 83% of all transport workers in India, Mexico, and the Philippines are categorized as informal workers (Spooner, 2011). Few other attributes, like the level of education of the workforce, accessibility to transit modes, regulation and its enactment, transit infrastructure, and mobility bottlenecks contribute to the extent of informal urban transportation. The role of collaboration to operate informal transport is seemingly prevalent because of the constant conflict of the informal sector with the formal actors. The absence of appropriate rules and norms often results in the undue exploitation of informal transport operators. In this situation, a strong personal and organizational collaboration safeguards informal transport operators from frequent exploitation. Collaboration not only strengthens a collective power but also increases wisdom among the informal transport operators by frequent information and knowledge exchange.

Theoretical underpinning of studying informal transport organization – a typical model of collaboration

Organization and institution are often used interchangeably. Institutions have multiple definitions. Ostrom (1990) defined institution as the set of working rules that are used to determine who is eligible to make decisions in some arena, including actions that are allowed or prohibited, aggregation rules to be used, procedures to follow, information that must or must not be provided, and payoffs assigned to individuals dependent on their actions (Ostrom, 1990). Coase (1937) argued that various forms of internal economic organization can be effective in minimizing the production cost and hence improve efficiency (Coase, 1937). Arrow (1951, 1974) applied his complex, abstract theory to comprehend social realities in a series of contributions outlining social choices and individual values, which further investigates the organizational limits of a society (Arrow, 1951, 1974). Williamson (1985) established a typology of organizational forms ranging from market to hierarchy (Williamson, 1985). North (1990) described institutions as providing rules of the game that determine incentives for individuals to engage in growth-enhancing or redistributive activities in the society (North, 1990). Groenewegen, Spithoven, and Berg (2010) termed institutions as man-made rules and their accompanying sanctions that are intended to make interactions less risky and more predictable. Institutions consist of established, durable, and stable rules, and vary from social values through norms and ensuing specific rules. Institutions are foundational elements of the social contexts in which organizations are embedded within (Baba, Blomberg, LaBond, & Adams, 2013). Institutional relationships (i.e., the type of relationship, interaction, and communication between different actors within an institution) assume great importance and must be well understood while carrying out institutional analysis.

In this chapter, the term organization appears close to North's description that refers to organization as a set of actors who cooperate or act jointly in production output that ranges from commodities, services, and statutes whereas institutions in a society provide the rules of the game that determine the incentives for individuals to engage in growth-enhancing or redistributive activities (North, 1990). The group of actors that constitutes organizations may share common interest, but it may also happen that organizations work for their own benefits prior to the social or overall benefits. The popular methods of organizational study are many e.g., analytical narrative, institutional mapping, historical institutional analysis, path dependence analysis, operational analysis, legal analysis, distributional analysis, participatory approaches, regulatory analysis, case studies, etc. (Dhingra, 2015). This book chapter uses narration[2] and institutional mapping[3] to discuss collaboration and institutional dynamics of the urban informal transport sector in India. In its process of narration, the study of the informal organization may seem to be conflictual. However, this conflict is not necessarily inimical. It can promote adaptation and cooperation, establish group boundaries, unite social factions, and engage new thought and agency patterns that can lead to paradigmatic changes beneficial to societies (Bureau & Fendt, 2011).

There might be criticisms about this institutionalist approach to theorizing informal sector functioning and exploring networking between organizations and actors. But there is no denial that the actual practice of institutional forms of informal sector grows out of specific conditions and possesses a collaborative pattern in management of its functioning. The literature on informal institutional design stresses the importance of homogeneity in interests and cultures, and of clear boundaries as to who belongs in an organizing community, if such institutions are to survive over time (Ostrom, 1990). Ostrom, Gardner, and Walker (1994) identified that collaboration in small and local communities creates informal organizations that manage shared natural resources, such as pastures, fishing waters, and forests. North (1993) argued that informal constraints will be altered in the course of interaction, evolve new informal means of exchange, and hence develop new social norms, conventions, and codes of conduct. In this process "obsolete" informal constraints will gradually wither away to be replaced by the new ones (North, 1993).

The informal sector coexists within an established formal sector. It is true for informal transport, which is fragmented between multiple informal organizations and provides transport service primarily known as "last mile" service. It means that passengers ride one mode as far as it goes and then switch to another mode to complete their travel (Cities Development Initiative for Asia, 2011). Generally, this switchover takes place from a formal public transport mode like public bus or mass transit mode (i.e., metro rail). The term "fragmented" refers to the extreme conflict between informal transport service providers who are competing against each other. Most of the time, multiple travel modes operate on the same route to provide the last mile connectivity (Figure 4.1).

The informal sector is less policy-driven and knowledge-rich like the traditional forms of formal governance. This approach to governance is expressed by emphasis on the "social networks weave," through which collective affairs are managed. It is largely out of the formal institution of governance (Healey, 1997). Governance can be seen as the process to exercise power by including the civil society (Biswas, Kidokoro, & Onishi, 2012). The collective interest and values of these entities do not always have a territorial restriction that is prevalent in the cases of the informal transport system. Thus, a cohesive consensus building between actors and organization goes through a social learning process. It engages in building up trust

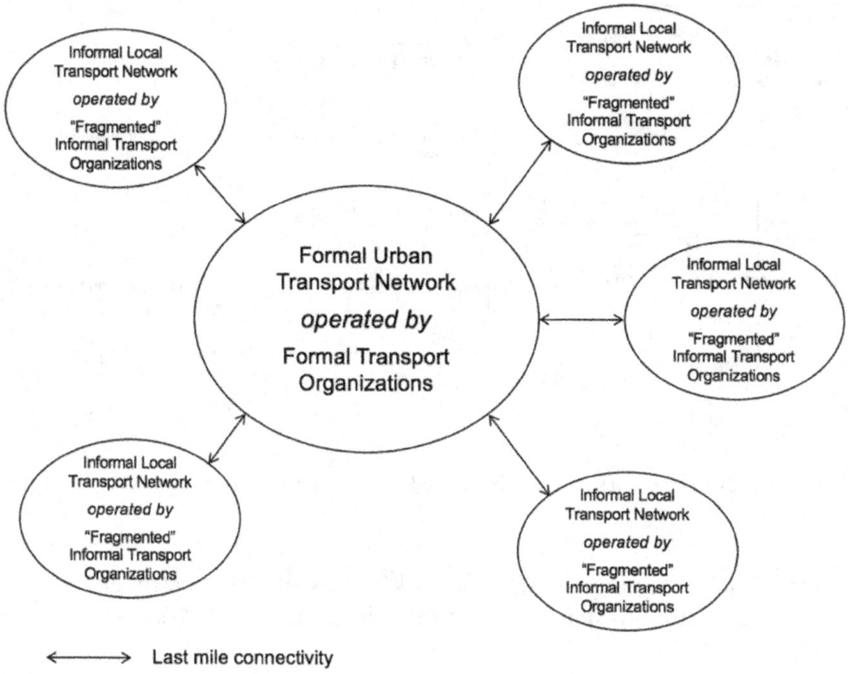

Figure 4.1 Network between Formal and Informal Transit Network

and confidence among each other. It emphasizes practical consciousness and local knowledge with its own reasoning process. Problem-solving with consensus follows specific steps, which happen with communication and dialogues among fragmented individuals. It creates confidence among each other, new systems of meaning, new cultures, new organizing routines, and new social networks. Instinctively, such activities build institutional capacity, not only through participation but through the way institutional capital creates and flows through the social relation and webs of participants (Heikkila & Gerlak, 2005).

One needs to adapt an evaluative framework to convey a structured analytical discussion on collaborative governance and organization. Ansell and Gash (2008) proposed a generalized framework of collaborative governance containing four broad variables – starting conditions, institutional design, leadership, and collaborative process. Following Ansell and Gash (2008), Emerson and her colleagues proposed an integrative framework for evaluating collaborative governance (Emerson et al., 2012; Emerson & Nabatchi, 2015). While drivers, actions, and collaborative dynamics are key aspects of informal sectors, the institutional setup is not applicable convincingly. (Figure 4.2). The chapter uses an adaptation of Emerson and

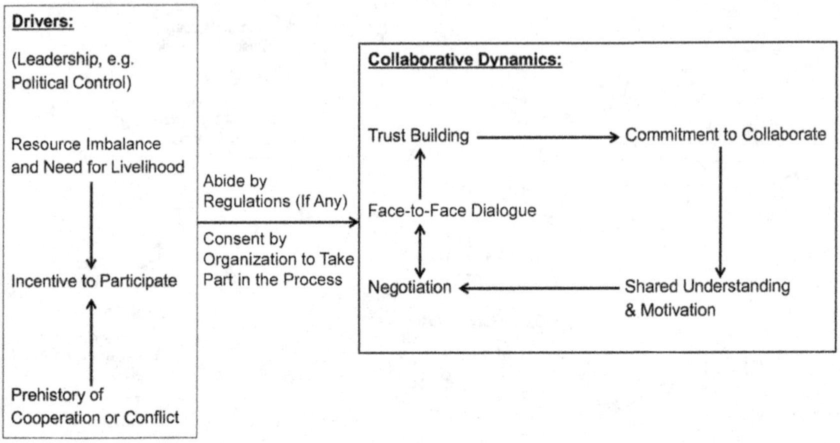

Figure 4.2 A Framework of Collaborative Governance for Informal Sector

Nabatchi's (2015) integrative framework to present an impactful discussion on India's urban informal transport organizations (Figure 4.2).

Drivers

The framework starts with "Drivers," or the reasons for the genesis of the informal sector. The informal transport sector exists due to a wide array of systematic limitations in an economy. In 2007, the Latin America Division of the World Bank published a book where the co-authors proposed a holistic framework of the composition and causes of informality. The authors specified different forms of causal theories – voluntary informality and involuntary informality (Perry et al., 2007). Two theories are presented in the Table 4.1.

Informal transport is a lucrative sector that attracts many individuals who are unable to access a permanent livelihood opportunity in the formal sector. However, it is not easy to get into informal transport which is a part of a system or a syndicate that manages informal activities. The number of willing participants is always much more than the eventual absorption in the syndicate. Generally, the syndicate decides an aspirant's absorption in the organization based on her/his perception of antagonism or cooperation. Mostly, the decision to include an aspirant is colluded with kickbacks and reverse benefits rather than a transparent selection process.

The next driver for a collaborative governance process is facilitative leadership. It is particularly important for informal transportation. Leadership can be directive or indirective – either way, the purposes of leadership in collaborative governance are maintaining rules, developing trust,

Table 4.1 Framework of Informality: Composition & Causes

Causal Theory 1	*Causal Theory 2*
Opportunistic evasion: – tax-evasion – illegal activities – avoidance of labor codes – unprotected workforce – subcontracted production	Labor market segmentation: – prevents workers from getting formal jobs
Defensive evasion: – burdensome state – captured state – weak state	Burdensome entry regulations: – prevents enterprises from formalizing
Passive evasion and state irrelevance: – pre-modern or bazaar economy – informal or non-state institutions	Hiring practices of firms – in response to excessive tax and regulatory burdens

facilitating dialogue, negotiating conflicts, and exploring mutual benefits. The informal sector does not have formal rules or manuals of functioning. As a result, conflicts are more frequent and extensive. The conflicts may arise within or between informal organizations. Therefore, the arbitration process is crucial in facilitating the appropriate functioning of the informal processes. In addition to the traditional leadership skills, a leader of the informal sector organization must possess wider acceptability or access to outside mediators like political patronages. The political parties mediate with informal organizations by putting their party worker or closest aide as the leader.

Collaborative dynamics

The collaborative dynamics work together in an interactive and iterative way to produce collaborative actions or the steps taken in order to implement the shared purpose (Emerson et al., 2012). Commitment to collaborate by participating actors depends on the original motivation and desire to benefit from participation. For informal activity, continuous engagement with this livelihood opportunity is the basic motivation. Once within the organization, most of the collaborative process in the informal sector builds on face-to-face dialogue between the stakeholders. As a consensus-oriented process, the "thick communication" facilitated by direct dialogue is necessary for stakeholders to identify opportunities for mutual gain. Hence, the face-to-face dialogue in informal transport is more than merely the medium of negotiation (Ansell & Gash, 2008). Trust between each actor and with the organizations is very important for the appropriate functioning of an organization that oversees informal activity. Many informal organizations are well managed due to an established set of rules and strong leadership that efficiently arbitrates during conflicts. Many times, conflict arises between two adjacent informal organizations that operate on the same route and wish to maximize profit in the cutthroat competitive market. In that scenario, the local political control functions as an arbitrator. This arbitration takes place without the direct or indirect involvement of the administrative and legislative functionaries.

Over time, people also develop networking and personal bonding within the organization that starts mostly because of the necessity for a livelihood opportunity. In a multicultural and fragmented society, collaboration occurs where individuals develop their own identities through potentially multiple webs of relationships. Knowledge and understanding are produced through this collaborative social learning process, not by the manipulation of abstract techniques by autonomous actors but through the prevalence of collaborative governance in local resource management disputes (Heikkila & Gerlak, 2005). An intensive level of conflict may actually create an incentive for collaboration when stakeholders are highly individualistic. Intensive conflict per se is not necessarily a barrier to collaboration. In many successful collaborations, the stakeholders cannot achieve their goals without engaging in a debate or conflict. Mediation increases the role of third-party intervention in the substantive details of the negotiation when stakeholders are ineffective in exploring possible win-win gains. Thus, leadership is crucial for informal organizations for setting and maintaining clear ground rules, building trust, facilitating dialogue, and exploring mutual gains. Leadership is also important for empowering and representing weaker stakeholders. At some point during the collaborative process, stakeholders must develop a shared understanding of what they can collectively achieve together. Shared understanding in the informal sector deals with the understanding about the domains and boundaries of its functioning. In informal transport, these boundaries can be manifold; e.g., determining routes or physical boundaries within which one organization operates, maintaining appropriate cues between the actors, negotiation with formal institutions like police and the local government, and maintaining harmony with the local communities. There might be several routes operated by several organizations or syndicates. A mutual recognition of each other's boundary and coexistence is a part of a shared understanding between two organizations. Feiock (2007) viewed shared understanding through transaction cost. He suggested that the cooperative governance arrangements emerge when contexts and institutional configurations reduce the transaction costs of cooperation for local actors. Transaction costs are reduced by formal and informal institutional arrangements that increase the availability of information, reduce obstacles to bargaining, and reinforce social capital (Feiock, 2007).

The chapter will examine collaboration of India's urban informal sector based on the derived framework from the above discussion. However, prior to the discussion based on this derived framework, one needs to get a grasp of India's informal urban transport organization. The next section presents a glimpse of India's informal urban transport system.

Informality and organizational setting of India's urban transport system

Both the organized and unorganized sectors offer urban transport services in India. The informal urban transport usually consists of a range of informal organizations and informal jobs. Jobs in informal transport are of two types – self-employment (owner and operator, employer, etc.) and wage employment (employees of informal enterprises). The earning gap between an employer and employees or operators is significant. However, if the employer is self-employed and operates the vehicle, the earning gap reduces significantly. The general belief is that the informal sector operates within an unregistered and unregulated environment (Chen, 2006). However, informality also saves money since the service providers avoid paying any duties and taxes and do not comply with labor protection laws. By skirting formal regulations, the operators have more freedom to provide services and respond to market shifts. The desire to exploit cheap labor, however, is not a prime motive for informality. Most informal workers are self-employed and do not hire employees (Poapongsakorn, 1991). Many of them work illegally or semi-legally due to the punitive nature of regulation or complete absence of it. If an employer hires operators in informal transport, originally the employer avoids tax and registration and not the operators (Chen, 2006). In India, informal transport is connected with the formal sector by regulations like driving authorization of the operators, vehicle registration and license, pollution control certificate, etc. However, it is completely independent and informal in its operation. Flexibility is a trademark of informal services, i.e., spatial flexibility (e.g., variable routing), temporal flexibility (e.g., variable schedules), and monetary flexibility (e.g., variable prices). Some of the core traits of informal transport compared to the formal transport are provided in Table 4.2.

The flexibility of informal transport services, which is advantageous in certain aspects, creates problems for organizational arrangements and setting up the institutional rules. In contrast to the regional transport authorities and formal organizational arrangements, the informal transport sector is held together in a loose, horizontal network, dependent upon carefully cultivated linkages and nurtured relationships among stakeholders, including fellow operators, parts suppliers, local police, trade unions, operator's associations, creditors, vendors, and street hustlers, among others. The informal transport sector depends upon the interpersonal and inter-operator network rather relying upon intra-firm relationships and collaborations for the production of services (Cervero, 2000).

A person's decision to join informal transport depends on its demand and the person's financial resources to start the operation. An entry fee is a compulsory prerequisite for membership of the route operator organization. In addition to the entry fee, the organization also decides membership fees and its necessary increment. The person may start operation only

Table 4.2 Contrasting Dimensions of Formal Versus Informal Transport Sectors

	Dimension	*Formal*	*Informal*
	Supply:		
1	Service structure	Fixed route, standardized	Variable route, adaptive
2	Delivery	Line-haul, trunk line	Distribution, feeder
3	Scheduling	Fixed timetable	Market-driven, adaptive
4	Reliability	Reasonably dependable	Inconsistent
5	Vehicle type	Large	Small to medium
6	Ownership	Public and private	Private
7	Market perspective	Monopolist	Entrepreneurial
8	Labor	Semi-skilled	Semi- to non-skilled
9	Organization	Bureaucracy	Route associations
	Demand & Price:		
10	Market focus	Mixed	Niche
11	Main trip purposes	Work, school, shop	Mode access
12	Trip distances	Medium to long	Short to medium
13	Customer relations	Impersonal	Interpersonal
14	Socio-demographics	Low to moderate income	Low income
15	Fare structures	Fixed, uniform	Variable, differentiated

Source: Adapted from Cervero 2000.

after the due registration process under the informal transport organization. A person may own multiple vehicles and arrange a leased contract with operators who do not own a vehicle. The owner and operators function as a profit-share arrangement or on rent per day basis. Contrary to the formal transport, the informal transport plies on feeder or distribution networks and supports public transportation. Route assignment between different transit modes is crucial for mutual benefits of individuals involved in informal transport service. Negotiations for routes take place between different service providers' organizations. Sometimes, intense negotiation precedes before routes assignment. Routes that yield more profits are subject to intense negotiation between associations. A vehicle once registered with a route remains in that route forever, unless some exceptional situation occurs like the relocation of the owner to a new city. The organization makes sure that nonmembers stay away from any possible route intrusions. In profitable routes, the entry fee is extremely high, which sometimes exceeds the gross cost of the vehicle. It enables the route operator organization to meet the expenses of its costs.

The route operators' organizations follow certain rules to maximize their members' profit and achieve fairness in vehicle operation. Generally, the route operating organization determines the fare. Maintaining the number of trips and order of trips is a very important vehicle operation rule. Eventually, the cumulative number of trips per day determines the quantum of revenue and profit of a vehicle operator. The purposes of route assignments are to bring in order and avoid extreme conflicts within spatially defined service areas. The leaders of operators' organizations are democratically elected among their members or nominated by the maximum number of members. Invariably, a senior person or a member who is respected among all is chosen. Informal transport organizations are closely connected with the political parties through trade unions. Lobbying for the organization's recognition and due support from among the political parties is crucial for its functioning (Arora et al., 2016). The organizations and their members use public places for many activities such as parking, passenger load and unload, amenities without paying any service fees. Therefore, the organizations indulge in a cordial relationship with the local communities and police to operate their business smoothly. In some places, organizations take care of passenger amenities and relationship building measures. This happens in places where competition among different travel modes is very high. The organization also assists its members in developing a business relationship with related stakeholders and support during any possible concerns that hurt its members' personal or business interests.

Transportation and environmental regulation impact the informal transport sector immensely. However, the informal transport operators are mostly unaware and skeptical about the prevailing regulatory environments. The informal transport operators are required to conform to the environmental clearance and traffic regulations. Frequent violation of traffic rules by public and private vehicles is very common in India (Institute of Urban Transport (IUT), 2014). Sometimes the operators manage to get away, and sometimes they pay a penalty or bribe the traffic police. Environmental regulation is generally better monitored and implemented. However, the operators also violate environmental regulations and fail to maintain the required standard of emission. Thus, frequent conflict takes place between regulatory authorities and informal transport operators. The organization plays a crucial role in mitigating such conflict and enlightening operators on measures to avoid such conflicts.

Even though the urban informal transport sector largely operates within the domain of informality, it has a strong connection with the formal sector. The Ministry of Housing and Urban Affairs (MoHUA), Government of India indexed informal urban transportation as para-transit index (number of intermediate public transport or IPT vehicles per 10,000 population), and revealed that para-transit is higher in cities without public transport and lower in cities with public transport (Ghosh & Kalra, 2016). The next section elaborates on the linkages between the informal and formal organizations.

Functioning of informal urban transport and its' relation with the formal institutional settings

Informal transport in India can be categorized as non-motorized three-wheeler (cycle rickshaw), motorized three-wheeler (auto rickshaw, battery powered e-rickshaw), and four-wheeler (taxi, share cab, mini bus). The extent of urban informality in the Indian transport sector shows a wide array of intermediate public transports like cycle rickshaw, auto rickshaw, bus, taxi, share cab, and mini bus (Figure 4.3).

The formal public and private organizations play crucial roles in connecting these public transports with the "collaborative process" of the informal transport organizations. In India, these organizations, which perform different activities, belong to different orders of the administrative hierarchy. These organizations are responsible for delegating various transport functions. Formal or institutional interaction with informal transport operators starts during the permit approval period and continues throughout the entire transit operation phase. Table 4.3 provides generalized information about the functions that connect the informal transport sector with formal organizations.

The Central Government enacts national legislation, ratifies policy, and decides associated financial allocations. The Regional Transport Authority or RTA (established under each State Government's legislative framework) issues permits and licenses to the drivers. Whereas, the traffic police are responsible for the enforcement of rules and regulations on roads. The documents required to obtain permits are application forms, residence proof, driving license, fitness certificate, pollution under control (PUC) certificate,

Figure 4.3 The Nature of Informal Sector or Intermediate Public Transport near Charbagh Railway Station of the Indian City of Lucknow

Table 4.3 Organizations and Urban Transport Functions Connecting "Starting Conditions" and "Collaborative Process"

Urban transport functions	*Organizations under different governance hierarchy*		
	Central	*State*	*Local*
Policy	Ministry of Housing and Urban Affairs (MoHUA)	Ministry/Department of Urban Development, Development Authority	–
Transport planning	–	Ministry/Department of Urban Development, Development Authority	Municipal Corporation
Road investment infrastructure	Ministry of Road Transport & Highways (MoRTH), National Highway Authority of India (NHAI)	Public Works Department (PWD)	Municipal Corporation
Road infrastructure (O & M)	Ministry of Road Transport & Highways (MoRTH), National Highway Authority of India (NHAI)	Public Works Department (PWD)	Municipal Corporation
Suburban rail system	Indian Railways	–	–
Metro rail system	–	Special Purpose Vehicle (SPV), Metro rail corporation, Development Authority	–
Bus transport (city)	–	State Road Transport Corporation (SRTC)	Bus Corporation, Municipal Corporation
Bus transport service operations (regional)	–	State Road Transport Corporation (SRTC)	Bus Corporation, Municipal Corporation
Bus regulation and licensing	Ministry of Road Transport & Highways (MoRTH)	State Transport Authority (STA)	–
Bus terminals and depot operations	–	–	Bus Corporation, Municipal Corporation
Traffic management	–	Police	Municipal Corporation
Traffic engineering	–	Public Works Department (PWD)	Municipal Corporation
Traffic enforcement	–	Police	–
Motor vehicle registration, safety, and emission regulation	–	State Transport Authority (STA)	–

Source: Adapted from Dhingra, Urban transport institution (2014).

etc. (IUT, 2014). RTA regulates permits for motorized informal transport (e.g., auto rickshaw, taxi, share cab, and minicab) whereas the local government (municipal corporation) regulates permits for non-motorized three-wheelers (e.g., cycle rickshaw). There are two kinds of permit systems, which vary by the city: open permit and closed permit. The number of permits is not capped for an open permit that allows complete freedom for entry of a vehicle operator in the market. The closed permit is not freely available at all times, and their numbers are capped and controlled by the regulating authorities (Arora et al., 2016). Most permits are renewable in nature and vary between one year to five years, depending on the regulatory authority and vehicle type. An example about different actors and organizations in determining route that enhances the understanding of the networking between "starting conditions" and "collaborative process" is given below (Figure 4.4).

Determination of a route depends on three attributes – permit, actual route identification, and vehicle operation. The political establishment influences route distribution between different transport organizations through trade unions. It happens by four different facets of operations – the operators, the parking stand, the route, and the fare (Arora et al., 2016). The role of trade unions is in sharp contrast to the existing Central Motor Vehicle

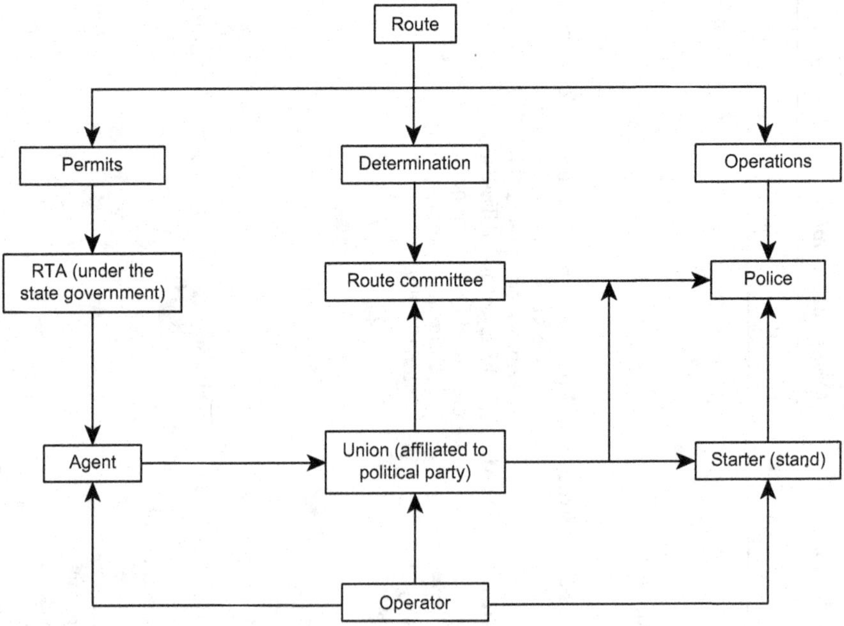

Figure 4.4 Actors and Organizations Map of IPT in Kolkata
Source: Arora et al., 2016.

Rules (MVA) 1989 and its subsequent rules. The MVA 1989 Rules do not recognize the trade unions for discharging its function and responsibility towards the informal transport. It recognizes the RTA for issuing permits and traffic police for ensuring adherence of rules (IUT, 2014).

The Ministry of Road Transport and Highways (MoRTH, Government of India), notified the Central Motor Vehicle Rules (CMVR) 1989. Several states implemented these regulations in coherence with the act and the rules. Chapter 66 of the MVA articulates that an operator can only start a public transport operation if the State Transport Authority (STA) or the RTA approve its permit (MoRTH, 1989). However, there are many ambiguities in the act and discrete decision-making for permit approval. This leads to frequent legislative conflict between the operators and the state. The Motor Vehicle (Amendment) Bill (MVAB) 2016 and the proposed Road Transport and Safety Bill (RTSB) 2015 are still pending in the Parliament for its approval. RTSB 2015 proposes to create a national regulatory authority to oversee regulation presently overseen by the ministry itself. Two major findings from the bill might be important for discussion – it proposes an exemption of transport vehicles, operating with a license from further permit, and quashes any requirement to renew the license for transit right. It empowers the RTA to waive off any permit condition to promote low-cost, last mile connectivity within its jurisdiction (Arora et al., 2016). The National Transport Development Committee (NTDC), Government of India has recommended creating state-level offices of transport strategy in collaboration with the agencies for urban development. The NTDC has also recommended a comprehensive urban transport law in each state and setting up of the roles and responsibilities of multiple cities and state-level entities for integration of public transport, land use, multi-modal integration, safety, facilities for the walk and non-motorized transport (NMT) (National Transport Development Policy Committee, 2014). Yet, there is no clear ideas to integrate informal transport organizations along with formal transportation.

From the institutional perspective, the evolution of informal transport may not be attributed only to address first or last mile connectivity but also to fill in the voids created by the absence or minimal presence of an institutional framework and a regulatory mechanism. The extent of many informal modes of travel options expanded only after the 1980s. Prior to it, Indian cities were served by fewer public transport options and mostly managed by the state government's institutions. But the increased supply of different modes of mobility resulted in an informal transport that is managed by a collaborative process and supported by various stakeholders of the society. In organizational settings, authority belongs to an individual or group of individuals who exercise the authoritative power (refer to Figure 4.2) to control the organization and its output. These organizations might vary in scale and outreach, e.g., government, corporate, religious institution, and cooperative. But, people or groups of people who administer authoritative power generally have certain responsibilities. Authoritative power is required to achieve coordination of activities of the members of organizations and control output (Arrow, 1974). It leads to the following section of this chapter that discusses insights on collaborative process and collective action of informal transport organization.

Insight on the collaborative process and collective action of informal transport organization in Indian cities

The informal sector facilitates transport service levels (i.e., door-to-door) and serves as an employment source, but often cripples a government sponsored transit service and system management (e.g., Mexico City). Studying an organization that is outside the formal institutional authority is complex and an interesting case for organizational study. Ambivalence towards supporting informal sector transport services has further complicated the problem (Zegras & Gakenheimer, 2006). An organization which is largely informal in nature needs to establish rules that are part of the operational strategy and that are flexible for maximum support from its members. The rules depend on individual(s) advocating authoritative power and the organization's aim in optimally functioning its business, combining market demand, adhering to rules and regulations, and judicial directives. In order to understand the processes of structural change of a particular situation, one has to open up and overtly include one or more of the underlying "exogenous" sets of variables (Ostrom, 2005). For informal transport operation, the exogenous organizations like the RTA, agents (route committee), and (traffic) police determine rules. The rules affected by various external organizations are clustered in two broad groups with at least three levels of networking. These two broad groups are rules and permits. The action arena can be referred to as the arena of collective actions, and it consists of operator, route committee, and the trade union. The first level underlies operational situations where individuals interact directly with the society or community members (e.g., passenger travels, financial transaction, local economic exchange, and social intimacy with a certain community). The second level underlies collective-choice situations where individuals interact to choose some of the rules that are in effect at operational levels (e.g., traffic regulations, pollution level determined by legislation and enforced by exogenous organizations). The institution process develops a collaborative and self-organizing governing mechanism that relies on collective actions from all of its operators. The third level includes a legislative process that creates the rules used by the exogenous organizations (Figure 4.5) (Ostrom, 2005).

Local community and other attributes also play crucial roles in determining the collaborative process in the action arena. Empirical research showed that individuals who systematically engage in collective action provide local public goods without an external authority to offer inducements

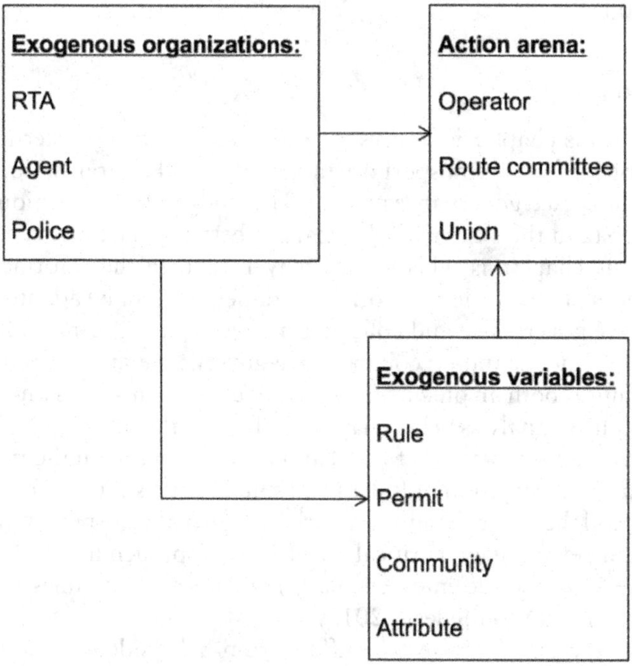

Figure 4.5 Actors in Informal Institutions and Their Collaboration

(Ostrom, 1998). The operators are an individual entity and facilitated by the organizational behavior of informal transport organizations to enable the collective action. Various actors, including the customers and service providers, interact with each other and benefit by the interactions (Flanagin, Stohl, & Bimber, 2006).

There is not much literature available to bridge a nexus between informal organizations and the theories of collaborative efforts and collective action in informal transport organizations. But it is very fascinating to learn the order of collective actions among the informal transport operators. While the operators join this informal sector operation for individual interest from the unorganized action, their action increasingly supports greater organizational benefit. Olson (1965) suggested that organizations can, therefore, support common or group interests through organizations that also serve individual interests. Their characteristic and primary function is to advance the common interests of groups of individuals (Olson, 1965). The informal transport organization constitutes the operator, route committee, and union. In the absence of authoritative power from the operator, the trade union takes a leading role in managing activity and governing the organization. This collaborative process offers the potential to enrich the social learning, the creativity, and the effectiveness of this coevolution (Innes & Booher, 2003)

Conclusion

The aim of this chapter is to present a discussion on the pattern of governance among informal transport organizations and their translation towards an institutionalized governance process. The study of the institutions enables us to understand the system and/or make it better. In fact, the central argument of this chapter is whether we may recognize the informal sector's operations as an institution or not! This framework can be adapted into the collaborative governance and collective action of the informal urban transport system. Understanding collaborative governance and collective action usually requires both an outsider's perspective and an insider's knowledge to ensure a holistic analysis. This chapter highlights the collaborative process and collective action between formal and informal actors in the functioning of informal transportation in Indian cities. It describes the legislative procedures and collaborative dynamics of urban informal transport in India. It is an interesting example of a critical governance approach in which arbitrary use of state power in the enforcement of regulations determines informality (Mukhija & Loukaitou-Sideris, 2015).

In India, the transport sector suffers from a lopsided demand against supply constraints. The informal sector thrives within this kind of environment. Providing public service by a group of extremely diverse people in a non-regulatory and unruly environment is a risky proposition. However, the informal transport organizations are able to perform the task with the help of various actors of the formal and informal sector. The operators and the owners are key to this collaboration, whereas travel route determination and distribution strengthen this collaboration. The huge population number and mass unemployment in the formal sector result in a persistent labor supply to informal urban transportation. It somehow justifies the commitment of collaboration and shared understanding among the operators, owners, and the organization to undertake the relevant collective actions. Eventually, actors within an informal urban transport organization develop trust among each other and with the organization. It creates a lifelong network and personal relationship.

This collaborative process of functioning is not evolving much with time or technological innovation. The mode of transit is changing from manually operated rickshaw to battery operated rickshaw and so on, but the nature of collaboration remains the same. It is perhaps due to the muted competition (for whatever reasons), where organizations have less incentive to invest in new knowledge and in consequence, do not induce rapid institutional change. As a result, we experience a stable organizational structure (North, 1993). Formal organizations like the RTA, the STA, political parties, police, and local administrations influence the informal transport sector's operation. Vigorous organizational competition accelerates the process of institutional change (North, 1993). At this moment, all of these organizations are working towards a similar goal and benefit from this collaboration. Hence, the collaborative process of operation of informal sector transportation seems to continue for some time in the future.

Notes

1 In organized sectors, employment terms are fixed. Employees are protected under various schemes like the minimum wages act, factories act, etc. However, in unorganized sectors, there are no such employment terms. The unorganized sector consists of all unincorporated private enterprises owned by individuals or households engaged in the sale and production of goods and services operated on a proprietary or partnership basis.
2 A narrative analysis seeks to understand institutional formation and change. It is used to investigate questions of political economy, such as political and economic governance and inter/intra-state relations (Dhingra, 2015).
3 An institutional mapping helps lay out who the actors are and what their motivations are. This method is usually employed to completely understand the characteristics of a particular infrastructure. This is also called "Institutional Relationship Analysis" (Dhingra, 2015).

References

Ansell, C., & Gash, A. (2008). Collaborative governance in theory and practice. *Journal of Public Administration Research and Theory*, 18(4), 543–571.

Arkell, J. (2007). *New developments and perspectives [power point slides]*. Retrieved from www.oecd.org/sti/ieconomy/36929397.pdf

Arora, A., Anand, A., Banerjee-Ghosh, S., Baraya, D., Chakrabarty, J. Chatterjee, M., . . . Taraporevala, P. (2016). *Integrating intermediate public transport within transport regulation in a megacity: A Kolkata case study*. New Delhi, India: Centre for Policy Research.

Arrow, K. J. (1951). *Social choice and individual values*. John Wiley & Sons.

Arrow, K. J. (1974). *The limits of organization*. New York, NY: Norton & Company.

Baba, M. L., Blomberg, J., LaBond, C., & Adams, I. (2013). New institutional approaches to formal organizations. In D. Caulkins, & A. T. Jordan (Eds.), *A companion to organizational anthropology* (pp. 74–97). West Sussex, UK: Blackwell Publishing Ltd.

Becker, H. S. (1963). *Outsiders: Studies in the sociology of deviance*. New York, NY: The Free Press.

Biswas, A., & Maurya, K. K. (2018). Governance and institutional framework for smart cities in India. In J. Mugambwa, & M. W. Katusiimeh (Eds.), *Handbook of research on urban governance and management in the developing world* (pp. 50–83). Lucknow, PA: IGI Global.

Biswas, A., Kidokoro, T., & Onishi, T. (2012). An insight of metropolitan planning and governance in India. *10th conference of Asian city planning* (pp. 1–9). Tokyo: The City Planning Institute of Japan.

Bureau, S., & Fendt, J. (2011). Entrepreneurship in the informal economy: Why it matters. *The International Journal of Entrepreneurship and Innovation*, 12(2), 85–94.

Cebula, R. J. (1997). An empirical analysis of the impact of government tax and auditing policies on the size of the underground economy: The case of the United States. *The American Journal of Economics and Sociology*, 56(2), 173–185.
Cervero, R. (2000). *Informal transport in the developing world*. Nairobi: UN-Habitat, United Nations Centre for Human Settlements (Habitat).
Chen, M. A. (2006). Rethinking the informal economy: Linkages with the formal economy and the formal regulatory environment. In B. Guha-Khasnobis, R. Kanbur, & E. Ostrom (Eds.), *Linking the formal and informal economy: Concepts and policies* (pp. 75–92). Oxford: Oxford University Press.
Cities Development Initiative for Asia. (2011). *Informal public transportation netowrks in three Indonesian cities*. Metro Manila: Asian Development Bank.
Coase, R. H. (1937). The nature of the firm. *Economica*, 4(16), 386–405.
Dhingra, C. (2014). *Urban transport institution*. Retrieved May 27, 2018, from A World Resource Institute website https://wricitieshub.org/sites/default/files/Urban%20Transport%20Institutions_1.pdf
Dhingra, C. (2015). *Urban transport institutions*. EMBARQ – Sustainable Urban Mobility. Mumbai: World Resource Institute.
Emerson, K., & Nabatchi, T. (2015). Evaluating the productivity of collaborative governance regimes: A performance matrix. *Public Performance & Management Review*, 38(4), 717–747.
Emerson, K., Nabatchi, T., & Balogh, S. (2012). An integrative framework for collaborative governance. *Journal of Public Administration Research and Theory*, 22(1), 1–29.
Feiock, R. C. (2007). Rational choice and regional governance. *Journal of Urban Affairs*, 29(1), 47–63.
Flanagin, A. J., Stohl, C., & Bimber, B. (2006). Modeling the structure of collective action. *Communication Monographs*, 73(1), 29–54.
Ghosh, A., & Kalra, K. (2016). Institutional and financial strengthening of intermediate public transport services in Indian cities. *Transportation Research Procedia*, 14, 263–272.
Groenewegen, J., Spithoven, A., & Berg, A. V. (2010). *Institutional economics: An introduction*. Basingstoke: Palgrave Macmillan.
Hart, K. (1973). Informal income opportunities and urban employment in Ghana. *The Journal of Modern African Studies*, 11(1), 61–89.
Healey, P. (1997). *Collaborative planning: Shaping places in fragmented societies*. Vancouver: UBC Press.
Heikkila, T., & Gerlak, A. K. (2005). The formation of large-scale collaborative resource management institutions: Clarifying the roles of stakeholders, science, and institutions. *Policy Studies Journal*, 33, 583–612.
Innes, J. E., & Booher, D. E. (2003). Collaborative policymaking: Governance through dialogue. In M. Hajer, & H. Wagenaar (Eds.), *Deliberative policy analysis: Understanding governance in the networked society* (pp. 33–59). Cambridge: Cambridge University Press.
Institute of Urban Transport. (2014). *Improving and upgrading IPT vehicles and services*. Delhi: Institute of Urban Transport.
International Labor Organization. (1972). *Employment, income and inequality: A strategy for increasing productive employment in Kenya*. (A Report of an Inter-Agency Team Financed by the United Nations Development Programme and Organized by the International Labour Office). Geneva, Switzerland.

International Labor Organization. (2002). *Women and men in the informal economy: A statistical picture*. Geneva: UN.

Micro Housing Finance Corporation. (2012). *Informal sector: Customer profile in Mumbai*. Mumbai: Micro Housing Finance Corporation.

Ministry of Road Transport and Highways. (1989). *The central motor vehicles rules*. New Delhi: Government of India.

Moreno-Monroy, A. (2012). Critical commentary: Informality in space: Understanding agglomeration economies during economic development. *Urban Studies*, 49(10), 2019–2030.

Mukhija, V., & Loukaitou-Sideris, A. (Eds.). (2014). *The informal American city: Beyond taco trucks and day labor*. Cambridge, MA: The MIT Press.

Mukhija, V., & Loukaitou-Sideris, A. (2015). Reading the informal city: Why and how to deepen planners' understanding of informality. *Journal of Planning Education and Research*, 35(4), 444–454.

National Transport Development Policy Committee. (2014). *India transport report: Moving India to 2032*. New Delhi: Routledge.

North, D. C. (1990). *Institutions, institutional change, and economic performance*. Cambridge, UK: Cambridge University Press.

North, D. C. (1992). *Transaction costs, institutions, and economic performance*. San Francisco, CA: ICS Press.

North, D. C. (1993). Five propositions about institutional change. *Economics Working Paper Archive at WUSTL*. Stanford University, USA.

Olson, M. (1965). *The logic of collective action: Public goods and the theory of groups*. Cambridge, UK: Harvard University Press.

Ostrom, E. (1990). *Governing the commons: The evolutions on institution for collective actions*. Cambridge, UK: Cambridge University Press.

Ostrom, E. (1998). A behavioral approach to the rational choice theory of collective action: Presidential address. *The American Political Science Review*, 92(1), 1–22.

Ostrom, E. (2005). Developing a method for analyzing institutional change. *Workshop in political theory and policy analysis*. Indiana University.

Ostrom, E. (2010). Institutional analysis and development: Elements of the framework in historical perspective. *Historical Developments and Theoretical Approaches in Sociology*, 2, 261–288.

Ostrom, E., Gardner, R., & Walker, J. (1994). *Rules, games, and common-pool resources*. Ann Arbor, MI: University of Michigan Press.

Perry, G. E., Maloney, W. F., Arias, O. S., Fajnzylber, P., Mason, A. D., & Saavedra-Chanduvi, J. (2007). *Informality: Exit and exclusion*. Washington, DC: The World Bank.

Poapongsakorn, N. (1991). The informal sector in Thailand. In A. L. Chickering, & M. Salahdine (Eds.), *The Silent revolution: The informal sector in five Asian and near eastern countries*. San Francisco: ICS Press.

Polski, M. M., & Ostrom, E. (1999). An institutional framework for policy analysis and design. *Workshop in political theory and policy analysis*. Indiana University.

Pratt, A. C. (1996). Coordinating employment, transport and housing in cities: An institutional perspective. *Urban Studies*, 33(8), 1357–1375.

Spooner, D. (2011). *Transport workers in the urban informal economy: Livelihood profile*. Retrieved from http://global-labour.net/wp-content/uploads/2011/07/Spooner-D.-2011.-Urban-Informal-Transport-Livelihood-Profile.pdf

Webster, E., Benya, A., Dilata, X., Joynt, C., Ngoepe, K., & Tsoeu, M. (2008). *Making visible the invisble: Confronting South Africa's decent work deficit*. Johannesburg: University of the Witwatersrand.

Williamson, O. E. (1985). *The economic institutions of capitalism*. New York: Free Press.

Zegras, P. C., & Gakenheimer, R. (2006). *Driving forces in developing cities' transportation systems: Insights from selected cases*. Boston: MIT Press.

5 Collaborative networks for regional economic development

An examination of the Mega-Economic Regions (MERs) in South Korea

Eunok Im and So Hee Jeon[1,2]

Introduction

Although local economic development as a policy arena has traditionally been perceived as competitive rather than as cooperative or collaborative, recent years have observed an increasing number of collaborative economic development efforts among localities in many countries around the world (Lee, Feiock, & Lee, 2012a). Collaborative governance among localities is defined as the process in which "two or more local governments seek to accomplish a desirable outcome through coordination or cooperation" (Lee et al., 2012a, p. 253). Scholars have explained the possible reasons of collaborative networks from different theoretical perspectives. First, according to resource dependence theory, which argues that organizations cannot produce all critical resources for its survival by themselves and thus are dependent on their external environment, organizations may collaborate with one another in order to better acquire scarce resources for their survival and competitiveness (Pfeffer & Salancik, 2003). In addition, organizations may form collaborative relationships for stability and legitimacy reasons (Esparza & Jeon, 2013; Lee, Lee, & Feiock, 2012b; Uzzi, 1997; Zucker, 1991). Collaborative networks help an organization enjoy more stable relationships with other organizations, which can help the organization to better cope with challenges from the external environment (Uzzi, 1997; Lee et al., 2012b). Through networking with other organizations, an organization, especially a younger and smaller organization, can also increase its legitimacy (Esparza & Jeon, 2013; Zucker, 1991).

Existing research on collaborative governance has accumulated much knowledge over the past few decades. Some scholars have focused on understanding what factors influence the formation of collaborative governance (e.g., Andersen & Pierre, 2010; Feiock, Steinacker, & Park, 2009; Fleishman, 2009; Lee et al., 2012a). Others have examined why some organizations collaborate more than others (e.g., Im, Jeon, & Kim, 2017). Still others have explored what factors influence the success of collaborative governance (e.g., Ansell & Gash, 2008). However, as Emerson, Nabatchi, and Balogh (2012) point out, much less research has been done about actual collaborative actions and their impacts. To address this gap in the literature, the present research examines not only the context and drivers but also actions and outcomes of collaborative networks. Specifically, this study focuses on collaborative governance for economic development during the Lee Myung-bak Administration in South Korea (Korea, hereafter, for short) – particularly, mega-economic regions (MERs) – and analyzes the Korean MERs using Emerson and Nabatchi's (2015) integrative framework for collaborative governance. Although there are other frameworks for collaborative governance (e.g., Ansell & Gash, 2008; Thomson & Perry, 2006), we use Emerson and Nabatchi's (2015) framework for analysis because their framework is more integrative in the sense that it includes a comprehensive set of factors that are critical to understanding collaborative governance.

Our case from a Korean context may interest the international audience who seek effective collaborative processes in countries where such processes are hard to be facilitated. Our study provides a case about how a central government can promote local governments' collaboration. Local governments are likely to engage in collaborative processes on a voluntary basis. This, however, might not hold in countries where local governments lack the capacity to develop, initiate, and run effective collaborative governance. The Korean context provides an ideal setting to test the effect of a central government's top-down approach to facilitate collaborative governance among local governments. In Korea, due to limited autonomy, local governments are dependent upon a central government for both financial and administrative resources. The central government drives a strong push to promote collaborative local governance for regional economic development.

To this end, the Korean central government first established MERs within each of which local governments were provided with strong financial incentives to collaborate with others. Given the institutional background, we analyze how the central government's top-down or central-driven approach (i.e., the establishment of MERs and financial incentives for collaboration) would affect interlocal collaboration and regional economic development. Our findings from the setting provide meaningful policy implications about the central government's role in promoting collaboration among local governments.

By analyzing the processes and outcomes of the Korean MERs, this study contributes to both literature and practice. While there has been much research on collaborative governance, relatively little research has explored the performance or outcomes of collaborative governance (Emerson et al., 2012). By exploring not only the processes and dynamics of the MERs but also its effectiveness, this study contributes to fill the gap in the literature. In addition, by thoroughly analyzing a regionally based collaborative governance which was initiated and enforced by the central government, this study could provide some lessons and guidelines to other countries which may consider adopting a similar strategy for their economic development.

The structure of this paper is as follows: The next section provides a brief description of the history of economic development policies in Korea and explains the MERs initiatives. Then, based on Emerson and Nabatchi's (2015) integrative framework for collaborative governance, we analyze the context, drivers, operation, and outcomes of the Korean MERs. Finally, we discuss contributions and limitations of the study and suggest directions for future research.

Regional cooperative development in Korea

In the 1960s, for the pursuit of rapid economic growth, the Korean government placed a particular emphasis in its economic development strategies on "the selection of optimum location and the expansion of physical infrastructure for industrial and urban development" (Seo, 2009, p. 650). The efficiency-oriented spatial policy contributed to the heavy concentration of industries and population in the Seoul Metropolitan area (Kim, 1995).

In the 1980s, in an attempt to address the uneven regional development between Seoul and the rest of the country, the Korean government initiated measures for devolution of economic power and balanced regional development. The new policy approach accomplished meaningful improvements in ameliorating the intense concentration in Seoul. However, entering the late 1980s, the strategic focus gradually reverted to concentration as the nation encountered substantial industrial restructuring into information technology industries. The central government reconsidered the potential positive functions of the Seoul Metropolitan area as a national economic growth engine for knowledge-based and high-tech industries. The policy reversion aggravated the economic gap between Seoul and the rest again (Park, 2005), which eventually led to another shift in the government's development policy.

Getting into the new century, the Korean government acknowledged the widening regional economic disparities that likely harm the nation's global competitiveness, and its spatial plans re-emphasized the importance of peripheral areas' economic competitiveness and focused on nurturing regional capabilities (Seo, 2009, p. 651). Since 2008, with the inauguration of President Lee Myung-bak (2008–2013), the government consistently developed and implemented policies for interlocal/regional cooperation to promote competitive regional economies and to increase local governments' economic capabilities.

The strategic focus on interlocal cooperation has been fueled mainly by two factors (Im et al., 2017). First, the introduction of a local autonomous system in 1995 has led to the excessive competition among local governments, incentivizing them to maximize their authorities and profits as an economic agent (Kang, 2009). The competition often resulted in redundant investments, other negative external effects, and accordingly inefficient development. To cope with the inefficiencies arising from excess competition, the central government encouraged regional cooperation. Second, the deficiency of local revenue sources motivated local governments to voluntarily seek external resources either from the central government or other neighboring local governments for their local economic development. In sum, the Korean government's interlocal/regional cooperative plans have been developed as policy measures against the widening regional economic disparities (Seo, 2009).

In particular, the Lee Myung-bak Administration amended the Special Act for Promoting Balanced National Development (SAPBND) in 2009 in support of the regional development policy of establishing MERs as a cooperative strategy over the territory of the country (Ahn, 2011; Cho, 2013). As stated clearly in Article 1 of the amended SAPBND, the central government aimed to promote regional competitiveness through collaboration among local institutions within the region and through regional characteristics-based development.

The establishment of the MERs is considered "a noticeable turn" and "a radical change" in Korean regional development history, because "no forms of regionally based governance has come into existence throughout the entire history of regional development in Korea" until the establishment of seven MERs (Cho, 2013, p. 247). Focusing on this new and radical strategy for regional economic development, the present research explores the context and drivers of the MERs and collaborative actions in the MERs. This study also examines the outcomes of MERs by assessing if and to what extent the spatial strategy of the MERs accomplished its intended results.

The establishment of the Mega-Economic Regions (MERs)

The MER scheme is designed "for integrated regional development at the mega-region scale by encouraging, cooperation and coordination among local governments within each ER." (Choe, 2011, p. 11). In 2009, the Korean Government established the MERs based on the industries of regional specialization for affiliated localities' common economic prosperity. Considering geographic proximity and economic interdependence and complementarity of localities (Ahn, 2011), the Korean central government partitioned the entire nation into seven MERs: Capital Region, Chungcheong Region, Honam Region, Daegyeong Region, Dongnam Region, Gangwon Region, and Jeju Region. Each MER has a population of more than five million people except the last two MERs (i.e., Gangwon Region and Jeju Region), with a population of about one million people each (Choe, 2011). Each of the former five MERs is composed of at least two upper-level local governments,[3] while each of the latter two MERs are identical with an administrative area (i.e., Province, or *Do*).

The MER initiative was implemented as part of the five-year Economic Regional Development Plan (ERDP) for 2009 to 2013 under the direction of the Presidential Committee on Regional Development (PCRD), which was launched to set up new regional development policies. The ERDP set four clear goals for regional policy; 1) regional development based on specialized industries, 2) decentralization and regional autonomy, 3) establishment of mega-economic regions (MERs), and 4) interregional cooperation for reciprocal development (PCRD, 2009). In other words, the MERs spatial strategy was designed to strengthen the industrial specialization of a region and eliminate, if any, inefficiencies in the regional development. The Korean central government expected that the collaboration among provinces and municipalities in each MER would allow for economies of scale in specialized industries and ultimately improve the nation's overall economic competitiveness (Ahn, 2011).

According to the ERDP, the collaborative economic development projects in the MERs are centered around four key sectors: science and technology, infrastructure, culture and tourism, and water and environment. First, for the promotion of high-tech businesses, the MERs make the best of regional hub-universities, research institutes, and industrial complexes. For example, Chungcheong Region has attracted information technology companies to build an IT industry cluster, also known as the "Silicon Valley of Korea." The cluster settled in the Chungcheong MER's central metropolitan city (i.e., Daejeon) and four cities in two affiliated provinces (Cheonan and Asan in South Chungcheong, and Chungju and Chungwon in North Chungcheong) where a few research universities and several key manufacturing facility complexes are located (Im et al., 2017). Second, in order to increase physical and social networks for balanced national development, infrastructure construction projects, such as inter-provincial highways and railroads, were actively pursued at both the intra- and inter-MER levels. Third, MERs also developed projects in the culture and tourism sector. For example, Daegyeong Region and Gangwon Region are engaged in an inter-provincial river development project and health-care tour project, respectively. Lastly, in the area of water and environment, local governments collaborate for water quality management projects and green energy projects. Table 5.1 summarizes the leading industries of each MER and the size and number of collaborative economic projects in the MERs implemented from 2010 to 2012.

Within each MER, local governments develop collaborative economic projects that fit into the boundary of the leading industries in their own ER. As a governance system, an Economic Regional Development Committee (ERDC) is formed in each MER to manage and consult MERs' projects (Jang, 2011). Consisting of affiliated metropolitan mayors, provincial governors, and relevant civilian experts, the committee coordinates and directs a MER's policy and programs. Once it is formed, participating local governments develop a regional project plan together in consultation with the ERDC and apply for the financial supports from the central government. Responding to the call for support, the central government plays a coordinating role to provide a packaged grant for the interlocal cooperative projects. This allows avoiding any inefficiencies arising from the project-based budget allocation from each ministry, and eliminates individual local governments' redundant investments (Kim, 2013). For example, in 2010, more than 200 local projects were filed, and they were classified into 24

Table 5.1 Leading Industries and the Size and Number of Collaborative Projects in Each MER (2010–2012)

MER	*Participating Metro-Cities/ Provinces*	*Leading Industries*	*2010*		*2011*		*2012*	
			Size	*Number of Projects*	*Size*	*Number of Projects*	*Size*	*Number of Projects*
Capital Region	Seoul Incheon Gyeonggi	Information Technology	11.6 (12%)	13 (15%)	16.0 (7%)	25 (15%)	19.3 (8%)	22 (12%)
Chungcheong Region	Daejeon N. Chungcheong S. Chungcheong	Bio, Medical, Pharmaceuticals, New IT	17.2 (18%)	17 (20%)	37.3 (17%)	26 (16%)	42.2 (17%)	31 (17%)
Honam Region	Gwangju N. Jeollabuk S. Jeollanam	New Renewable Energy, Photonics	26.5 (27%)	23 (27%)	48.2 (22%)	35 (22%)	52.4 (21%)	38 (21%)
Daegyeong Region	Daegu North Gyeongsang	IT Conversion, Green Energy	18.7 (19%)	12 (14%)	49.7 (23%)	29 (18%)	56.9 (23%)	31 (17%)
Dongnam Region	Busan Ulsan S. Gyeongsang	Automobile & Components	13.7 (14%)	11 (13%)	37.1 (17%)	28 (17%)	40.5 (16%)	29 (16%)
Kwangwon Region	Kwangwon	Medical Conversion, Health Care Tourism	7.4 (8%)	7 (8%)	15.0 (7%)	11 (7%)	20.3 (8%)	15 (8%)
Jeju Region	Jeju	Water, Tourism, and Leisure	1.7 (2%)	2 (2%)	12.5 (6%)	8 (5%)	14.9 (6%)	12 (7%)
Total			96.8 (100%)	85 (100%)	215.8 (100%)	162 (100%)	246.5 (100%)	178 (100%)

Note: The size of projects is shown in million dollars. For simplicity, one thousand Korean won was converted into one U.S. dollar. Project type – that is, whether they are an umbrella project that is composed of sub-projects or if they are a single project – was not considered in counting the number of projects.

Source: Choe (2011, p. 11) and KIAT (2013, p. 34, Table 3–2); modified and reorganized by the authors.

categories for which block grants were considered for the local applicant governments (Jang, 2011). Then, the Ministry of Trade, Industry, and Energy of the central government and its affiliated organization, Korean Institute for Advancement of Technology (KIAT), assessed the collaborative project plans prepared by local governments and made decisions about subsidy on a highly selective basis. Thus, strictly speaking, the regional partnerships at the MER level were not established entirely voluntarily by local government. Rather, those interlocal collaborations were strongly encouraged or to some extent coerced by the central government.

MERs were a central part of the economic development policy implemented in President Lee's government. The policy was abolished in 2014 during the Park Geun-hye Administration as the new administration sought an alternative plan.[4] As such, policies may hold valid only for a particular period but not in other times. Nonetheless, the findings from our study deliver policy implications that are not time-specific. This is because our study explores a context where local governments lack capacities and/or incentives to voluntarily form and maintain interlocal collaborative governance, and examines whether or not and how a central government can promote collaborations among local governments. Such mitigating conditions may arise anytime (i.e., not time-specific) and need to be overcome. For example, after several years of abolishment, the current Moon Jaein Administration stresses the importance of strengthened autonomy, capacity, and competitiveness of local governments. It does not necessarily take the exact same policy measures as illustrated in our study. However, the findings of this study may provide some implications for the development and implementation of a new regional policy.

Collaborative governance in the MERs: application of Emerson and Nabatchi's (2015) integrative framework

The system context

According to Emerson and Nabatchi (2015), collaborative governance regimes emerge within a dynamic system context comprised of such factors as "policy and legal frameworks," "political dynamics and power relations," socioeconomic characteristics, and so on (p. 41). It is evident that those dynamics in the system context influenced the emergence and evolvement of the Korean region-based governance. The MERs were initiated and created by the central government, which historically has had greater power over local governments (Cho, 2013; Im et al., 2017). The Lee Myung-bak Administration amended the SAPBND in 2009 in ways that the law supports the presidential regional policy directions that emphasize regional economic competitiveness. In addition to having the amended 2009 SAPBND as the legal framework, the central government also had the PCRD develop a five-year ERDP, which served as the practical ground and policy guides for the creation of the seven MERs. Despite the revision of the Local Autonomy Act in 1988 to strengthen the autonomy of local governments, the central government has still played strong influence over local governments, and its steering role has reinforced (Lee, 2009). In sum, the MERs emerged as the result of a strong top-down push from the central government.

Drivers and formation of collaborative networks for economic development

Then what propels local governments in the MERs to collaborate with one another and with other institutions? Emerson and Nabatchi (2015) suggest the following four factors as the drivers for collaboration: uncertainty, interdependence, consequential incentives, and initiating leadership (p. 44). Organizations are faced with uncertainty due to such factors as limited information, scarce resources, and changing political environments. Under such uncertainty, an organization may compete with other organizations in order to acquire more information and resources critical to its survival and success (Pfeffer & Salancik, 2003). However, when an organization realizes that it cannot solve the problem alone and/or it can better acquire information and resources when working with others – that is, when an organization realizes the interdependence with others – then the organization likely turns from competition to collaboration (Emerson & Nabatchi, 2015). When it comes to local economic development in Korea, the past local economic development strategies that focused on each administrative district/city resulted in excessive competition among local governments and inefficiencies in resource utilization, which did not help accomplish the intended local economic development/growth (Ahn, 2011, p. 646). Thus, in order to overcome the problems associated with overly intense competition among local governments, to accomplish the economy of scale and the economy of networks, and thus ultimately to promote regional economic development, the Korean local governments had the motivations to collaborate with others (Ahn, 2011). In addition to economic interdependence, geographical proximity also matters for collaborations because it enables organizations to reduce transaction costs, to better share information and knowledge, and to better utilize resources (Bang, 2011). The MERs were created based on the consideration of both economic interdependence and geographical proximity of localities (PCRD, 2009).

The third factor identified by Emerson and Nabatchi (2015) as a driver of collaboration is consequential incentives. Korean local governments in the MERs also had consequential incentives to collaborate with others within the same MER. Arguably, one of the most explicit incentives is the financial support or grant for regional collaboration projects from the central government. As previously mentioned, local governments in the MERs can develop a regional economic development project in consultation with the ERDC and apply for a grant provided by the central government. Korean local governments in general do not enjoy a high level of financial independence from the central government. According to the 2015 report published by the Ministry of Security and Public Administration (MOSPA), the average financial independence of Korean local governments, calculated by dividing the total local tax and non-tax revenues by the total local budget, is only about 50% (MOSPA, 2015). The insufficient local revenues and low budgetary independence serve as a great motivator for Korean local governments to seek collaboration with others and to pursue financial support from the central government (Im et al., 2017).

Finally, initiating leadership also matters to initiating collaborations (Emerson & Nabatchi, 2015). Initiating leadership is defined as "the presence and actions of a person or core group that stimulates interest in and instigates preliminary discussions about creating a collaborative endeavor" (Emerson & Nabatchi, 2015, p. 47). In each MER, the ERDC was established as "the formal institution of regional governance" (Cho, 2013, p. 251). The ERDC played an important role as the governing mechanism in the MERs. The ERDC developed the overall plans for the MER's regional development, and consulted and managed interlocal collaborative regional projects within the MER. The creation of ERDC was led by the PCRD (Cho, 2013), which again shows that the creation of MERs and interlocal collaborations in the MERs were initiated by the top-down push from the central government. However, the ERDC creation also shows that although the Korean central government may still have had strong power over local governments and played a role as the steerer, it encouraged each MER to row toward the goal of regional development through the regional governing institution of the ERDC (Lee, 2009; PCRD, 2008).

Collaborative actions

The previous sections discussed what dynamics in the Korean system context influenced the emergence of the regionally based governance for economic development, and what factors worked as the drivers for the creation of collaborative governance in the MERs. Then how many local governments participated in collaborative governance for economic development? Table 5.2 below shows the number of participating local governments in each MER for the period of 2010–2012. The table also presents the number of nongovernmental participants – e.g., private companies, universities, research institutions, etc.

The number of governmental and nongovernmental participants in collaborative projects has increased over the period from 2010 to 2012. Together with Table 5.1 above, the data suggest that the idea of collaborative governance for economic development has attained growing interest and support over time in terms of the number of participating organizations, the number of collaborative projects, and the amount of revenue invested.

Table 5.2 The Number of Collaboration Participants in Each MER (2010–2012)

MER	*2010*			*2011*			*2012*		
	Governmental Participants		*Nongovernmental Participants*	*Governmental Participants*		*Nongovernmental Participants*	*Governmental Participants*		*Nongovernmental Participants*
	Si/Do	*Si/Gun/Gu*		*Si/Do*	*Si/Gun/Gu*		*Si/Do*	*Si/Gun/Gu*	
Capital Region	7	2	52	11	4	133	14	5	143
Chungcheong Region	18	6	40	24	6	100	32	6	119
Honam Region	17	9	65	25	10	108	28	14	124
Daegyeong Region	13	11	44	24	24	145	28	29	157
Dongnam Region	9	3	30	22	3	112	25	5	119
Kwangwon Region	2	10	11	5	15	30	6	20	37
Jeju Region	2	4	4	3	4	15	5	4	25
Total	68	45	246	114	66	643	138	83	724

Note: Si/Do refers to metro-cities/provinces. Si/Gun/Gu means cities/counties/autonomous districts.

Source: KIAT (2013) p. 35 Table 3–3 and p. 42 Table 3–11; reorganized by the authors.

Once created, collaborative governance operates based on interactions among participating institutions. Given the high number of collaborative projects conducted in the MERs, it is not possible to analyze in detail how participants in each collaborative governance interacted with one another. However, collaboration participants' responses to the 2013 survey by the Korea Institute for Advancement of Technology (KIAT) help to glimpse the perceived collaboration dynamics to some extent. The questions that the KIAT asked collaboration participants include: to what extent the collaboration participant thinks that it understands its and other collaboration participants' roles and responsibilities in the collaborative project, to what extent the collaboration participant understands the process and system of issue resolution in the collaborative governance, and the collaboration participant's perception of effective communication among collaborators (KIAT, 2013, pp. 92–94). All questions were asked on five-point Likert scales.

Regarding the roles and responsibilities, 61.6% of respondents answered that the organization very well understands its role and responsibilities as collaboration participants, and 35.9% answered that it has a good understanding (KIAT, 2013, p. 92). When it comes to other participating organizations' roles and responsibilities, 45.2% responded to have a very good understanding, and 46.3% reported to have a good understanding (KIAT, 2013, p. 92). Regarding the process of issue resolution, 42.9% of respondents answered that they are very well aware of with whom they should discuss and coordinate an issue, and 50.1% answered that they are well aware of it (KIAT, 2013, p. 93). Finally, regarding communication among collaborators, 34.8% of respondents strongly agreed and 47.8% of respondents agreed that they actively communicate with collaborators via on- and off-line communications (KIAT, 2013, p. 94). Although it does not provide detailed information about interactions in each collaborative governance, however, the survey results suggest, at least to some extent, that collaboration participants generally had positive perceptions about the collaborative projects that they participated in.

Collaboration outcomes

The purpose of the creation of regionally based governance or the MERs was to promote regional economic development. Then a subsequent question is whether or not the collaborative efforts brought their intended results – that is, regional economic (re)development. This study examines the impact of collaborative governance in the MERs in two ways. First, this research explores to what extent the collaborative projects in the MERs have accomplished economic outcomes measured by participant perceptions and project-produced profits in each MER. Second, this study also reviews the macroeconomic impact of the MER scheme, examining the population movements and Gross Regional Domestic Production (GRDP) across regions.

In order to examine the direct economic outcomes of collaborative regional development projects in each MER, this study used information offered by the Korea Institute for Advancement of Technology (KIAT). Specifically, this study used the 2013 KIAT report as its primary source of information in exploring the direct economic outcomes of collaborative projects in each MER. In March 2013, in an effort to understand the performance outcomes of collaborative regional economic development projects in the MERs, the KIAT distributed via e-mail a survey questionnaire to the leading agency of each collaborative project, and the leading agency redistributed the survey questionnaire to every participating organization (KIAT, 2013). At the time of the survey, there were a total 56 collaborative projects, and the number of participating organizations that received the survey was 739 (KIAT, 2013). The survey was composed of project outcome-related questions, and the KIAT asked respondents to provide answers for each year that the project was performed. For instance, if a project was performed during the period of 2010 through 2012, the respondent was asked to provide answers for each year of 2010, 2011, and 2012. In short, the survey questions were primarily to measure the performance outcomes of MER collaborative projects on a yearly basis. As performance outcomes, the KIAT used such measures such as profits, number of new hires, and cost reduction in manufacturing. Out of 739 organizations that received the survey, 529 organizations responded to the survey, yielding a response rate of 71.6% (KIAT, 2013).

One of the survey questions also asked respondents their perceptions of the effectiveness of the collaborative projects. The question asked, "By collaborating for this project with agencies that are in complementary relationships with my organization, we were able to produce synergy effects that each organization alone would not be able to accomplish" (KIAT, 2013, p. 97). The response options were measured by a five-point Likert scale, ranging from "strongly disagree" to "strongly agree." Among the 529 respondents, 33.5% respondents answered that they strongly agree with the statement; 52.7% agreed with the statement; 12.3% neither agreed nor disagreed; the percent of respondents that disagree or strongly disagree was 0.9% and 0.4%, respectively (KIAT, 2013, p. 97). The results suggest that the majority of respondents, or 86.2% of the respondents, have positive perceptions about the effects of collaborative economic development projects.

While it is encouraging that the players in collaborative governance positively perceive the collaborative efforts and their effectiveness, perceptions and actual performance/achievements can differ. Thus, in order to more objectively evaluate the effectiveness of collaborative governance for economic development, this study takes into account project-produced profits in the MERs. Profits produced through collaborative projects could serve as a good indicator of whether or not and how much regional collaborative governance contributed to the economic growth of a region.

Figure 5.1 presents the total profits earned per a million dollars of project expenditures in each of the seven MERs in the years of 2010, 2011, and

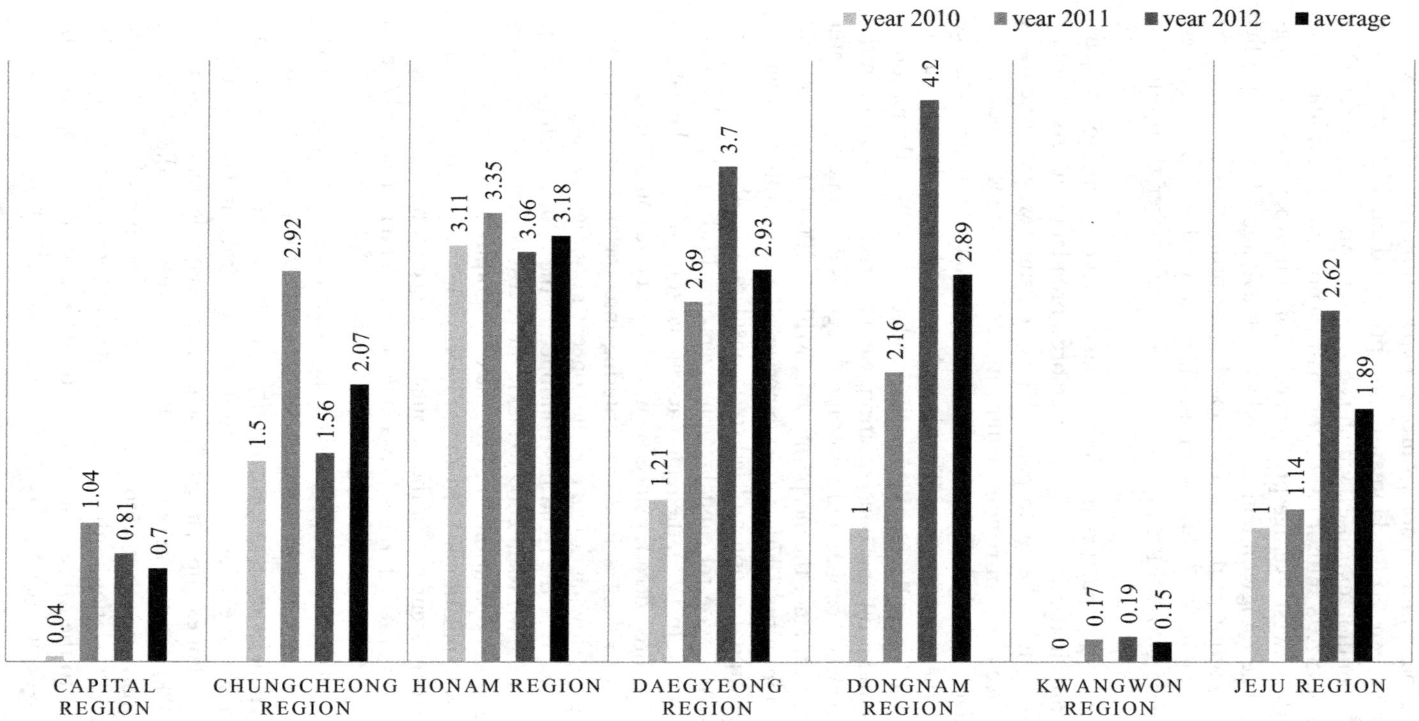

Figure 5.1 Profits Generated per a Million Dollar Project Expenditures in Each MER (2010–2012)

Note: Total profits per one million dollars of project expenditures are shown in million dollars.

Source: The figure was created by using data presented in Table 4-50 of the KIAT (2013) report (p. 75). Specifically, the total amount of project-produced profits was divided by total project expenses. In the KIAT report, the project expenses and project-produced profits were suggested in Korean won. In this study, 1,000 Korean won was converted into one U.S. dollar.

2012. The figure also presents the average profits over the period of 2010 through 2012 per a million dollars project expenditures for each MER.

Among the seven MERs, Homan region produced the highest average profits per $1-million expenses, which is $3.18 million, followed by Daegyeong region ($2.98 million) and Dongnam region ($2.83 million). The MER with the lowest average profit per $1-million expenses was Kangwon region. The Kangwon region produced an average $150,000 profits per every $1-million expenses. The next lowest profit was produced by the Capital region, $0.7 million profits per every $1-million expenses. Thus, for these two MERs, inputs/expenses were greater than outputs/profits.

In addition to the participant perceptions and the amount of project-produced profits in the MERs, we also explore a broader or macroeconomic impact of the MER scheme. In particular, we examine whether the MER scheme improved local or regional competitiveness, achieving one of its primary objectives of the balanced growth of non-capital regions in accordance with that of the capital region. To this end, we look into the population movements and Gross Regional Domestic Product (GRDP) in the nation.

To understand economic concentration, we first track the changes in the population between capital and non-capital regions overtime with greater interest in the time since the inception of the MER in 2009. During its rapid industrialization in the 1970s, Korea experienced a huge influx of population into the capital region and led to a considerably high concentration (Park, 2009). Area-wise, the capital region covers only 11.8% (11,818 km^2) of the entire country. In 1970, the region accounted for 28.3% of the nation's population. In three decades since then, the concentration ratio substantially increased to 46.3% in 2000. Entering into the new millennia, the rate of change is slowing down, but the concentration has still aggravated. Figure 5.2 shows that the trend has continued in the 2000s, even after the introduction of the MERs in 2009 to tackle the excess concentration of economic power and population. In 2015, the demography shows that 49.4% of the nation's population lives in and/or nearby the capital city of Seoul.

Unlike the consistent rise in the population concentration in the region, GRDP displays a different trend. The GRDP of the capital region has hovered below 50%, making ups and downs between years. In 2008 and 2009, at the introduction of the MER policy, the degrees of concentration in the capital region are 48.4% and 49% respectively for both population and GRDP. Later, between 2010 and 2014, we identify a gap between these two concentration metrics where a lower concentration is observed in GRDP than in the population. For example, in 2011 the proportion of the population is the highest (49.3%), but the share of GRDP is the lowest (48.2%). Although it is yet inconclusive that the temporary drop in the proportion of GRDP in the capital region in relation to that of the population between 2010 and 2014 is attributable to the MER policy, the figure suggests that the proportion of GRDP of non-capital regions has increased during that period.

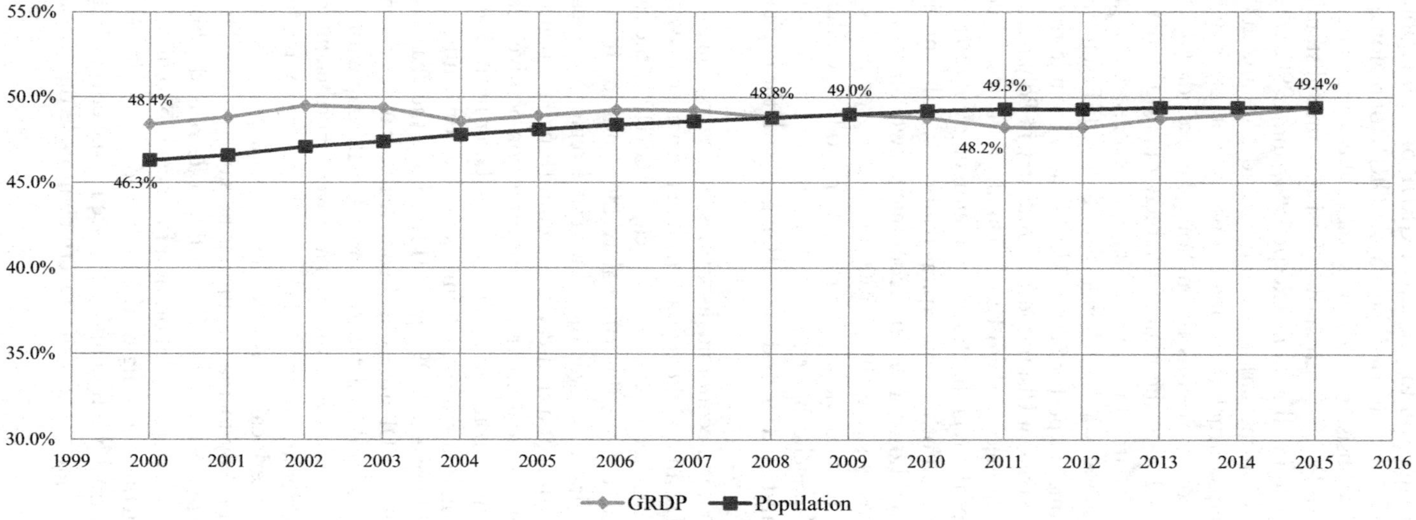

Figure 5.2 The Ratio of GRDP and Population of the Capital Region

Source: Data collected from the website of Statistics Korea (January 10, 2018), http://kostat.go.kr/portal/korea/index.action

To tease out the effect of growing population on economic performance, we now turn our attention to per capita GRDP of each region. Figure 5.3 presents the U.S. dollar-converted[5] per capita GRDP of regional segments in Korea since 1985. Consistent with the successful economic development in the past several decades, the figure shows consistent and substantial economic growth in the metric in all regions except 1997 and 1998, when a nationwide financial crisis hit the national economy, and 2008 and 2009, when the U.S. financial collapse struck the global economy. Notably, Dongnam region outperformed the other regions throughout the period. The considerably high per capita GRDP of the region is largely due to the development of industrial clusters located in several of its major cities. The region's heavy-industry clusters were established even before the MER scheme and drove the strong economic outperformance. The clusters include the automobile and chemical industries in Ulsan, the steel industry in Pohang, and the shipbuilding industry in Geojedo and Ulsan. Thanks to a strong economic and production base of the region, Dongnam region enjoyed more considerable economic wealth than other non-capital regions. We also note that Chungcheong region has shown a drastic economic growth since the late 2000s, which was due to its successful attraction of fast-growing high-tech and biotech industry firms to the area during the period. Since the late 2000s, Dongnam and Chungcheong regions have been ahead of the capital region in terms of per capita GRDP and the GRDP gap with the capital region has been growing.

To better understand economic disparities, we make a direct comparison of per capita GRDP among the regions, having the national average per capita GRDP set as 100 (see Figure 5.4). Per capita GRDP in the capital region had been the highest above the national average until the financial crisis in 1997. It was the first time ever that the capital region's per capita GRDP was surpassed by that of a non-capital region. Dongnam region, thanks to the solid economic foundation arising from the competitive heavy-industry clusters, suffered little from the financial crisis. Later in the 2000s, per capita GRDP in Dongnam region, Chungcheong region, and Honam region sharply increased between 2009 and 2011. Among the changes, we should note that per capita GRDP in Chungcheong region has been increasing since the MER policy was established in 2009 and then the gap with that of Dongnam (capital) region has been reduced (narrowed). Further, interestingly, per capita GRDP in Honam region, where the MER policy made the largest expenditures for interlocal economic development projects between 2010 and 2012, continuously increased during the same period. However, since 2013, which was the last year of MER policy, it decreased. This implies that the investment in interlocal collaboration for local economic growth indeed made fruitful outcomes leading to the improved economic performance in this region. In contrast, we find little evidence for the effect of the MER policy in Daegyeong region where the government made the massive spending

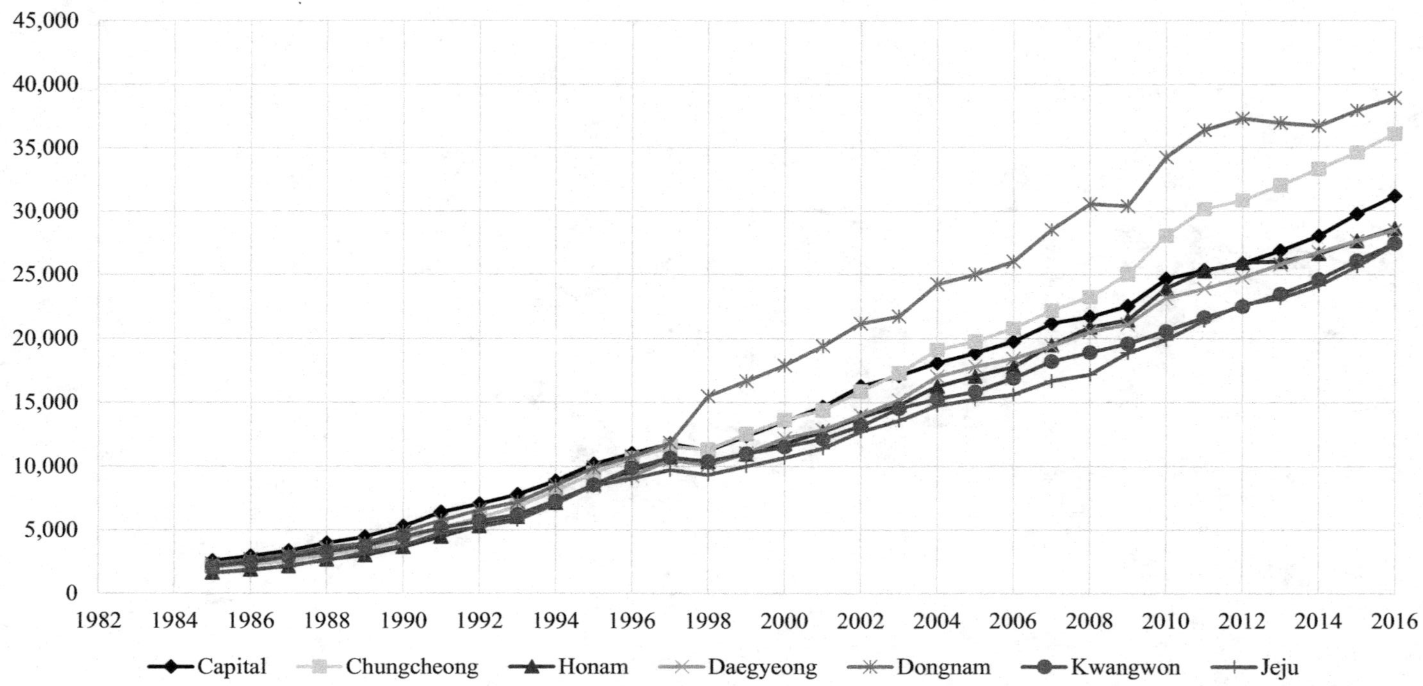

Figure 5.3 Changes in Per Capita GRDP in the MERs

Note: GRDP is shown in U.S. dollars. For simplicity, 1,000 Korean won was converted into one U.S. dollar.

Source: Data collected from the website of Statistics Korea (January 10, 2018), http://kostat.go.kr/portal/korea/index.action

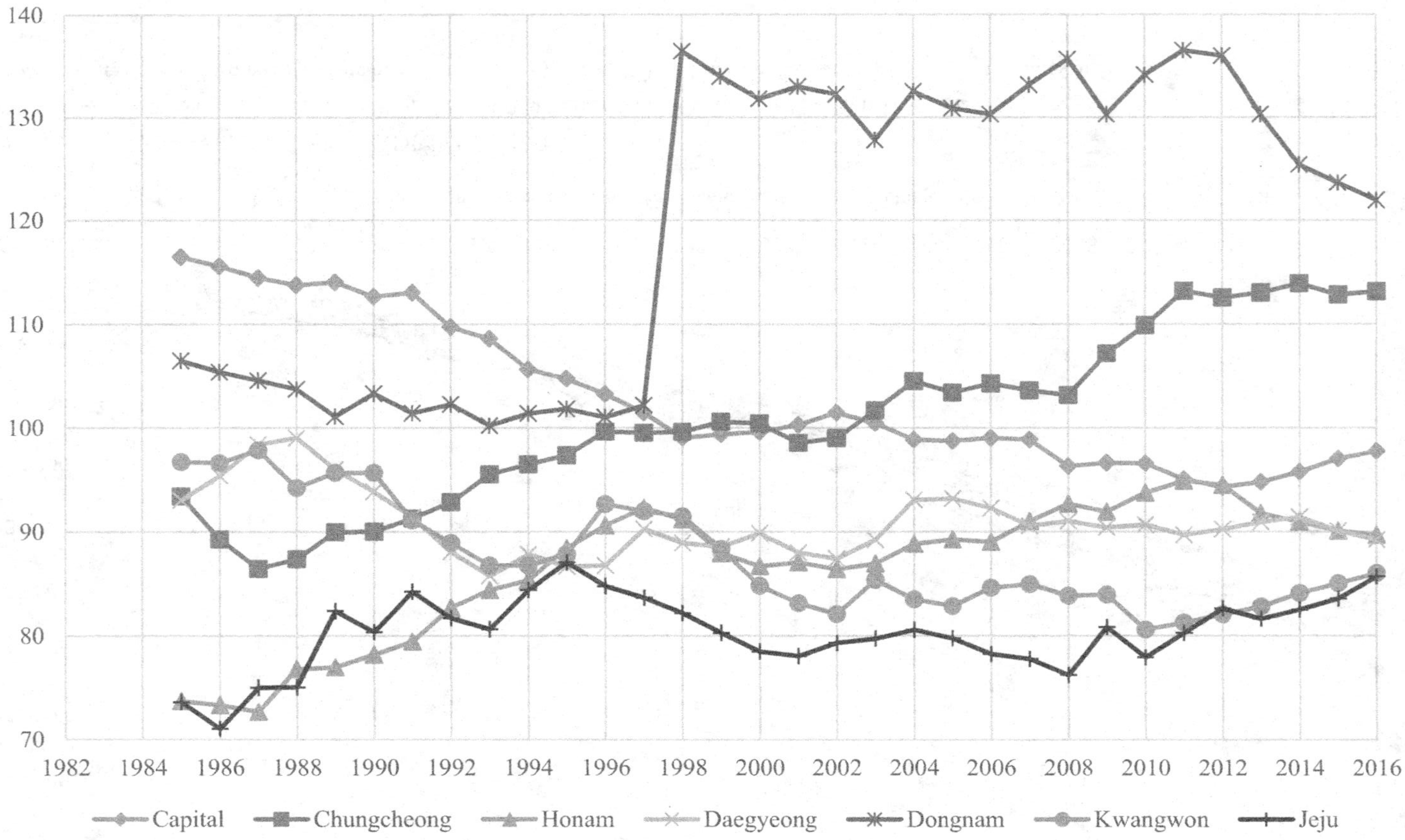

Figure 5.4 Changes in Per Capita GRDP in the MERs (the National Average GDRP in Each Year = 100)

Source: Data collected from the website of Statistics Korea (January 10, 2018), http://kostat.go.kr/portal/korea/index.action

in the interlocal collaboration only second to that of Honam region from 2010 to 2012.

Conclusion

By using Emerson and Nabatchi's (2015) integrative framework for collaborative governance as the foundation of analysis, this study analyzed regional economic development collaborations in the Korean MERs. The analysis of the MERs suggests that the regionally based governance emerged as the result of a strong top-down push from the central government (Cho, 2013). The central government, which historically has had stronger power over local governments (Im et al., 2017), initiated the MERs scheme through the revision of the SAPBND in 2009 and through the creation of a five-year ERDP by the PCRD.

In addition, several factors worked as the drivers of collaborative governance for regional development. The uncertainty combined with economic interdependence propelled local governments to collaborate with one another rather than compete (Ahn, 2011; Emerson & Nabatchi, 2015). Grants from the central government for regional collaboration projects were great financial incentives for local governments to collaborate, especially in the Korean context where local governments often suffer from insufficient local revenues and low budgetary independence (Im et al., 2017). Finally, the initiating leadership by the ERDC in each MER also helped to propel collaborations in the MERs. By developing overall plans for an MER's regional development and managing collaborative regional projects in the MER, the ERDC served as "the formal institution of regional governance" (Cho, 2013, p. 251) in each MER and contributed to propel collaborative governance for regional economic development.

The analyses of collaborative governance in the MERs show that collaborations for regional economic development have grown over time. The yearly analysis suggests that the number of collaborative projects, the number of participating organizations, and the amount of investments in the collaborative projects have all increased over the period of 2010 to 2012. Regarding collaboration experiences, the majority of collaboration participants reported positive interactions with other participants (KIAT, 2013).

The effectiveness of collaborative regional development projects in the MERs was analyzed from two different angles of the direct outcomes of collaborations and the macroeconomic impact of the MERs scheme. Regarding the direct outcomes, the majority of collaboration participants who responded to the KIAT survey, or 86.2% of respondents, reported positive perceptions about the effectiveness of collaborative projects. In addition, objective measures of outcomes such as project-produced profits suggested that most MERs, except the Capital Region and Kwangwon Region, experienced positive net profits and thus benefited from collaborative regional development projects. At the macro-level, the correlation between investment in collaborative projects and per capita GRDP seems to vary across different MERs. Per capita GRDP in Dongnam region, Chungcheong region, and Honam region sharply increased between 2009 and 2011. Further, per capita GRDP in Honam region, where the government made the largest expenditures for collaborative projects, continuously increased between 2010 and 2012 and has decreased since 2013, which was the last year of the MER policy. However, we find little change in per capita GRDP in Daegyeong region from 2010 to 2012, where the government made the massive investment in collaborative projects only second to that of Honam region during the same period.

By analyzing the impact of a regionally based governance for economic development, or the MERs, this study contributes to the literature on collaborative governance. Although much knowledge has been accumulated on collaborative governance, as Emerson et al. (2012) pointed out, relatively little research has focused on understanding the performance of collaborative governance. By investigating if and to what extent collaborative governance for regional economic development has brought its intended effects, this study contributes to fill the gap in the literature. The present study may also help the Korean government with its future directions and policies by suggesting to what extent the radical spatial strategy of MERs has worked for regional development. Finally, recent global trends in regional development show that a number of countries such as Japan, France, and the United Kingdom have adopted or have started to adopt regionally based governance as their development strategies, especially for their global city-region (Ahn, 2011; Ahn & Cho, 2009; Scott, 2001; Yun & Woo, 2017). For instance, the regional development policy for Tokyo, Japan has shifted away "from a multipolar regional pattern towards that of a ringed metropolis" (Kikuchi et al., 2014, p. 161). Thus, this research may also shed some light for other countries that implement or consider implementing similar strategies for their regional development.

This study is not without limitations. First, while providing useful analysis of the system context, drivers, and outcomes of collaborative governance in Korean MERs, this study presents only limited information on the interactive processes of collaborative governance. A few factors made it challenging to look into the detailed collaborative dynamics. As described above, there were a number of collaborative projects implemented in each MER, and furthermore, the MERs were abolished in 2014 shortly after the start of the Park Geun-hye Administration. For these reasons, it was not feasible to examine collaborative interactions of each individual collaboration project in the MERs. Future research should more thoroughly investigate the interactive processes of collaborative governance. By so doing, and when such information is combined and simultaneously analyzed with performance data, future research will be able to better assess the relationship between the nature and quality of collaborative interactions and collaborative outcomes.

Next, this study used a publicly available document published by KIAT as a source of information when exploring the direct economic outcomes of collaborative governance in the ERs. Given that the MERs were initiated for a large-scale nationwide regional economic development and that the MERs were abolished in 2014 with the start of a new administration, it was not possible for the researchers of the present study to independently estimate the economic outcomes of collaborative projects for each ER. However, the use of a secondary data source limited our ability to identify and consider other possible measures to examine the effects of collaborative governance in the MERs. If possible, future research should develop a multi-dimensional measure of economic outcomes of collaborative governance, and collect and analyze various performance data based on the multi-dimensional measure.

The final limitation of this study relates to the difficulty in accurately measuring the macro-level effects of the MERs. As a way to explore if the MERs scheme improved regional competitiveness and decreased regional economic disparities, this study looked into the per capita GRDP across different regions. While our analysis might suggest some seeming contributions of the MERs scheme to decreasing regional economic disparities, it does not provide any definite correlation or causal relation between the two factors. This study recommends future research to examine the macro-level impact of the MERs in a more systematic, quantifiable manner.

Notes

1 Both authors contributed equally to this research and thus share first co-authorship. The author names are listed in alphabetical order.

2 Corresponding author: So Hee Jeon, Department of Political Science and Public Administration, Central Michigan University, e-mail: jeon1s@cmich.edu

3 South Korean local governments are structured in two tiers. The upper (or regional) tier includes Seoul Special City, six Metropolitan Cities, nine Provinces (*Do*), one Special Autonomous City, and one Special Autonomous Province. The lower (or basic local) tier is composed of 227 Municipalities, including 74 cities (*si*), 84 counties (*Gun*), 69 autonomous districts (*Gu*).

4 Shortly after the Park Geun-hye Administration took over in 2013, the central government abolished MERs in 2014. Accordingly, after the MER abolishment, cooperative projects at regional levels that local governments voluntarily form (with little intervention from an MER or the central government) have gained more significance in the government's policy effort for further economic devolution to locals.

5 We use a simple conversion rate: 1,000 Korean Won (KRW) to 1 U.S. Dollar (USD). The use of simple conversion helps general (non-Korean) readers to gauge the monetary value originally represented in KRW. More precisely, the historical average exchange rate between the two currencies is 1,004.50 KRW/USD for the period between January 1, 1985, and December 31, 2016. To compute the average rate, we use the historical monthly rates from www.investing.com/currencies/usd-krw-historical-data. There have been substantial variations during the three-decade period, with the highest 1,995.00 and the lowest 668.90. However, it does not invalidate our finding in Figure 5.3 as our focus is on the relative size and the trend overtime.

References

Ahn, Y. J. (2011). Development policy of macro-economic region in Korea: Review and prospect. *Journal of the Korean Association of Regional Geographers*, 17(5), 638–647. (in Korean)

Ahn, Y. J., & Cho, Y. K. (2009). Development policy of 'Metropolregionen' as mega economic regions in Germany. *Journal of the Economic Geographical Society of Korea*, 12(4), 557–575. (in Korean)

Andersen, O. J., & Pierre, J. (2010). Exploring the strategic region: Rationality, context, and institutional collective action. *Urban Affairs Review*, 46(2), 218–240.

Ansell, C., & Gash, A. (2008). Collaborative governance in theory and practice. *Journal of Public Administration Research and Theory*, 18(4), 543–571.

Bang, M. S. (2011). A study on intergovernmental relations of mega economic region establishment: Based on the view of institutionalism. *Journal of the Korean Urban Management Association*, 24(4), 3–34 (in Korean)

Cho, C. J. (2013). The area-wide economic regions in Korea: Orthodox new regionalism or politically-inflicted regionalism? *World Technopolis Review*, 1(4), 240–255.

Choe, S. C. (2011). Introduction: Reshaping regional policy in Korea. In H. W. Richardson, H. C. Bae, & S. C. Choe (Eds.), *Reshaping regional policy*. Cheltenham, UK: Edward Elgar.

Emerson, K., & Nabatchi, T. (2015). *Collaborative governance regimes*. Washington, DC: Georgetown University Press.

Emerson, K., Nabatchi, T., & Balogh, S. (2012). An integrative framework for collaborative governance. *Journal of Public Administration Research and Theory*, 22(1), 1–29.

Esparza, N., & Jeon, S. H. (2013). Interlocking boards of trustees and grant acquisition among homeless service organizations. *Public Performance & Management Review*, 36(4), 637–664.

Feiock, R. C., Steinacker, A., & Park, H. J. (2009). Institutional collective action and economic development joint ventures. *Public Administration Review*, 69(2), 256–270.

Fleishman, R. (2009). To participate or not to participate? Incentives and obstacles for collaboration. In R. O'Leary, & L. B. Bingham (Eds.), *The collaborative public manager: New ideas for the twenty-first century*, Washington, DC: Georgetown University Press.

Im, E, Jeon, S. H., & Kim, J. (2017). Which local self-governments seek more collaboration? Evidence from interlocal collaboration for economic development in South Korea. *Lex Localis-Journal of Local Self-Government*, 15(2), 155–172.

Jang, J. H. (2011). Regional development policy in Korea: Past, present, and future. *Journal of the Economic Geographical Society of Korea*, 12(4), 576–596.

Kang, M. H. (2009). *Interlocal collaboration strategies for successful regional development*. Paper presented at the Conference of the Korean Association for Local Government Studies. Seoul, Korea.

Kikuchi, T., Maruyama, S., Inazaki. T., Kumaki, Y., Kureha, M., Sano, O., . . . & Marui, A. (2014). Introduction to the special issue on 'Tokyo: Past, present, and future (part II)'. *Journal of Geography (Chigaku Zasshi)*, 123(2), 159–162.

Kim, D. J. (2013). *Metropolitan development in Korea: Experiences and policy issues [power point slides]*. Retrieved from www.scag.ca.gov/programs/Documents/Partners/015_DevelopmentKorea.pdf

Kim, Y. W. (1995). Spatial changes and regional development. In G. Y. Lee, & H. S. Kim (Eds.), *Cities and nation: Planning issues and policies of Korea* (pp. 53–78). Seoul, Korea: Nanam Publishing House. (in Korean)

Korean Institute for Advancement of Technology (KIAT). (2013). *Performance evaluation of the mega-economic regions collaboration projects and the establishment of performance management system*. Seoul, Korea: KIAT. (in Korean)

Lee, I. W., Feiock, R. C., & Lee, Y. (2012a). Competitors and cooperators: A micro-level analysis of regional economic development collaboration networks. *Public Administration Review*, 72(2), 253–262.

Lee, Y., Lee, I. W., & Feiock, R. C. (2012b). Interorganizational collaboration networks in economic development policy: An exponential random graph model analysis. *Policy Studies Journal*, 40(3), 547–573.

Lee, Y. S. (2009). A comparative study on the regional development policies between the Roh and the Lee administrations. *Korean Local government Review*, 10, 25–46. (in Korean)

Ministry of Security and Public Administration (MOSPA) (2015). *A comprehensive overview of 2015 local government sinance*. Retrieved from www.index.go.kr/. (in Korean)

Park, B. G. (2005). Spatially selective liberalization and graduated sovereignty: Politics of neo-liberalism and 'special economic zones' in South Korea. *Political Geography*, 24(7), 850–873.

Park, S. O. (2009). A history of Korea's industrial structural transformation and spatial development. In Y. Huang, & A. M. Bocchi (Eds.), *Reshaping economic geography in East Asia* (pp. 319–337), Washington DC: The World Bank.

Pfeffer, J., & Salancik, G. (2003). *The external control of organizations: A resource dependence perspective*. Stanford, CA: Stanford University Press.

Presidential Committee on Regional Development (PCRD). (2008). *Annual report of regional development for the Lee Myung-bak government*. Seoul, Korea: PCRD. (in Korean).

Presidential Committee on Regional Development (PCRD). (2009). *Paradigm shift in regional policy and new regional development policy*. Seoul, Korea: PCRD.

Scott, A. J. (2001). Globalization and the rise of city-regions. *European Planning Studies*, 9(7), 813–826.

Seo, J. K. (2009). Balanced national development strategies: The construction of innovation cities in Korea. *Land Use Policy*, 26(3), 649–661.

Thomson, A. M., & Perry, J. (2006). Collaboration processes: Inside the black box. *Public Administration Review*, 66, 20–32.

Uzzi, B. (1997). Social structure and competition in interfirm networks: The paradox of embeddedness. *Administrative Science Quarterly*, 42(1), 35–67.

Yun, J., & Woo, M. (2017). Functional interdependence and employment growth of mega-economic regions: Implications for regional planning. *Journal of Korea Planning Association*, 52(2), 117–136. (in Korean)

Zucker, L. G. (1991). The role of institutionalization in cultural persistence. In W. W. Powell, & P. J. DiMaggio (Eds.), *The new institutionalism in organizational analysis* (pp. 83–107). Chicago, IL: University of Chicago.

6 Urban regeneration as a collaborative effort – strategic responses to decline in East Germany

Nebojša Čamprag

Introduction

After decades of growth, many prosperous economies started to face multidimensional consequences of rapid deindustrialisation. The phenomenon was particularly widespread in Europe, where nearly one third of all cities underwent at least one decade of population decline since the 1960s (Turok & Mykhnenko, 2007). The so-called "downward spiral" that a number of cities got into most commonly commenced with loss of employment opportunities, which further lead to urban decline and outmigration, usually with alarming rates. For some years now, this phenomenon has been in the focus of both urban studies and planning practice. Although a vast body of literature dealt with experiences from declining industrial cities from the perspective of the Global North, the extreme downfall of the former industrial giants in the context of the U.S.A. has attracted major attention.

Based on the research undertaken so far, early responses to urban decline usually involved pragmatic physical redevelopments of some exposed inner-city brownfields and derelict infrastructures (Moulaert, Rodriguez, & Swyngedouw, 2004). More knowledge on the phenomenon helped in the formulation of some more comprehensive strategies, while a number of cities shifted towards the tertiary sector and high-tech industries, and even reached significant growth. However, the majority of others haven't coped that successfully with the situation, which in such cases often has led to even more dramatic downfalls and further declines in population. Different impacts on socio-economic and political restructuration, on the one hand, highlighted origins and advancements of the phenomenon of urban decline as highly context and location specific. Furthermore, often associated with combating the trend in decline were diverse interests and preferences of a number of actors. Dealing with such comprehensive urban phenomena thus necessarily required constructive engagements across the boundaries of different spheres in order to bring stakeholders together and trigger innovative solutions.

As Emerson et al. pointed out, the principle of collaborative, cross-boundary governance has the potential not only to "generate impacts and adaptations across the systems" (Emerson, Nabatchi, & Balogh, 2012, p. 1), but also "to carry out a public purpose that could not otherwise be accomplished" (Emerson et al., 2012, p. 2). However, in spite of the rising scholarly interest for collaborative governance on all levels, "its definition remains amorphous and its use inconsistent" (Emerson et al., 2012, p. 1), while evidence remains scarce when it comes to the performance and impact of such frameworks for managing the complexity of urban decline in practice (Martinez-Fernandez, Audirac, Fol, & Cunningham-Sabot, 2012). Furthermore, considering thereby a misbalance in the geographical representation of cases, this chapter focuses on the former German Democratic Republic (GDR) as a rather specific case that allows plenty of opportunities for testing collaborative governance frameworks in practice. This case is rather particular considering that nearly all of its cities experienced rapid depopulation following the fall of state socialism and the "shock therapy" of socio-economic restructuring after German reunification (Bontje, 2004).

In contrast to other western countries where the state traditionally played a less important role in urban planning, since the early 2000s, the German Federal government has actively dealt with the problem of extreme population loss and urban decline in accordance with the specifics of its planning system. These experiences were largely based on setting integrative frameworks for encouraging collaborative governance on a local level, finally making the German approach particularly interesting for broadening scholarly knowledge on understanding both the phenomenon of decline itself, along with finding effective and innovative ways for achieving economic redevelopment. On the other hand, despite a number of innovative mechanisms for collective action that collaborative governance has provided in the case of East German cities, its efficiency showed it would be hard to reach in practice, as collaborative action is difficult to accomplish in situations when "shared goals and operating rationale for taking action are not made explicit" (Emerson et al., 2012, p. 17). This chapter thus aims at highlighting practical implications of collaborative-based strategic frameworks using the outcomes of national and local government initiatives in Germany to manage the complexity of the urban decline phenomenon. Special attention is paid to Leipzig and Dresden, as these cities are considered to be the most advanced in reaching economic (re)development in the former GDR.

In order to formulate appropriate frameworks for achieving economic redevelopment, acknowledging and fully understanding the complexity behind the phenomenon of urban decline seems to be of crucial importance. The following section thus summarizes the most relevant perspectives on this phenomenon.

Current perspectives on the phenomenon of urban decline

The debates on urban decline started at the end of the 1990s; however, the concept was formulated way before. The term "shrinking cities" (*schrumpfende Städte*) was introduced by Häußermann and Siebel in the late 1980s, when they described both decline in population and economic performance in some German cities resulting from deindustrialisation (Häußermann & Siebel, 1988). The U.S. American perspective on the same phenomenon referred to urban decline of its industrial cities (Pallagst, Wiechmann, & Martinez-Fernandez, 2011), although a number of authors also used alternative terms, such as urban decay or simply depopulation. Despite different terminology and the fact that there is still no general definition adopted to fully describe the phenomenon, a consensus was reached on its major causes in de-industrialisation, suburbanisation, and demographic changes (Fritsche et al., 2007). As these phenomena were by no means restricted to German, U.S., or U.K. contexts, the discourse on urban decline spread to the international arena, with enormous potential of cross-national knowledge still to be exploited (Großmann, Bontje, Haase, & Mykhnenko, 2013).

Despite its multidimensional effects, the more extensive knowledge on the phenomenon of urban decline for establishing effective strategic frameworks in strategies for economic redevelopment has caught international attention relatively recently. The reasons for this should be found in the dominant paradigm among planners and policymakers exclusively set on growth since early industrialisation (Logan & Molotch, 1987; Martinez-Fernandez & Wu, 2009; Oswalt & Rieniets, 2006). The course of economic and population expansion was previously not only the aim, but also the imperative, with an underlying assumption that all cities and towns could achieve such universal development goals. These objectives, and their many associated taboos, started to change since the turn of the millennia. First, the process of urban decline was recognized as much more complex than it had been seen before. Instead of population loss as its most visible and measurable effect that has often been used as a relevant parameter to quantitatively encompass and measure shrinkage (Beauregard, 2007), the phenomenon was acknowledged as a multidimensional process, including its effects on the socioeconomic potentials of a city or a region in question. Second, as the topic got more broadly discussed, the focus gradually shifted away from growth-oriented approaches. Hidden potentials of the phenomenon became the focus of discussions after a number of researchers called for innovative alternatives, (Frazier & Bagchi-Sen, 2015; Haase, Athanasopoulu, & Rink, 2013; Ringel, 2014), along with considerations of new action schemes to relate shrinkage with urban sustainability and liveability (Delken, 2008; Endlicher & Langner, 2007; Schetke & Haase, 2008). After the debate finally spread to praxis, planners and policymakers even started to consider implementation of policies for the so-called "managed" or "smart" decline (Frazier & Bagchi-Sen, 2015; Frazier, Bagchi-Sen, & Knight, 2013).

Considering a concept described by Emerson et al. (Emerson et al., 2012), acknowledgment of urban decline as a comprehensive and multidimensional process, in which affected communities rely on their local resources to deal with the causes and consequences of long-term decline, could be considered as one of the major prerequisites for establishing collaborative arrangements for economic redevelopment in practice. Nevertheless, although an increasing number of scholars argued that collaborative initiatives could enhance capacities of cities to combat the causes and consequences of decline, there was also evodemce showing that local decision-makers were often confronted with many difficulties in practice to engage their communities in the process of coproduction (Schlappa, 2015; Wirth, Elis, Müller, & Yamamoto, 2016). In spite of many recent advances, urban research still faces the challenge to not only investigate trajectories and hardly predictable overall trends of urban decline, but also to examine solutions to deal with this phenomenon in greater depth (Martinez-Fernandez et al., 2012; Steinführer et al., 2010).

Before illustrating the above-elaborated issues using the case of East German cities, the following section provides a brief overview of the most relevant initiatives at the level of the European Union (EU) that fostered and largely influenced integration of collaborative models into a governance framework across the European declining cityscape.

Integrated approach to urban regeneration in European policy framework

Concerning the fact that a large part of the former GDR was structurally significantly weaker and more rural than its western counterpart, its cities and communities were generally more prone to demographic changes and development problems after the reunification in the year 1990. However, urban decline was not an exclusive problem for reunified Germany. Some recent research demonstrated that nearly 40% of all European cities with more than 200,000 inhabitants have been experiencing a population decline over the last few decades (EU, 2016; Turok & Mykhnenko, 2007), with a major pole of shrinkage situated in post-socialist countries[1] (Figure 6.1). Aside from the exceptional conditions for massive outmigration, many of these countries have also been facing decades of declining fertility rates. Although such a situation necessarily would require a cross-boundary approach, the general lack of direct responses to urban decline at the EU policy level resulted from planning and development remaining a matter of national governments (Haase et al., 2013). An alternative to create a more even ratio between population and employment opportunities among the EU countries were thus various schemes for financing local projects that would foster the engagement of local communities and collaboration between public, private, and third-sector organizations (Soto, Houk, & Ramsden, 2012).

The recently introduced strategy "Europe 2020" proposed by the European Commission (EC) advocates for smart, sustainable, and inclusive development, aiming to foster cohesion among highly diverse European regions (EU, 2012; EC, 2014). These core principles were also present in a number of programs and initiatives dealing with urban regeneration issues. The EC previously set up the integrated approach "URBAN Community Initiative"

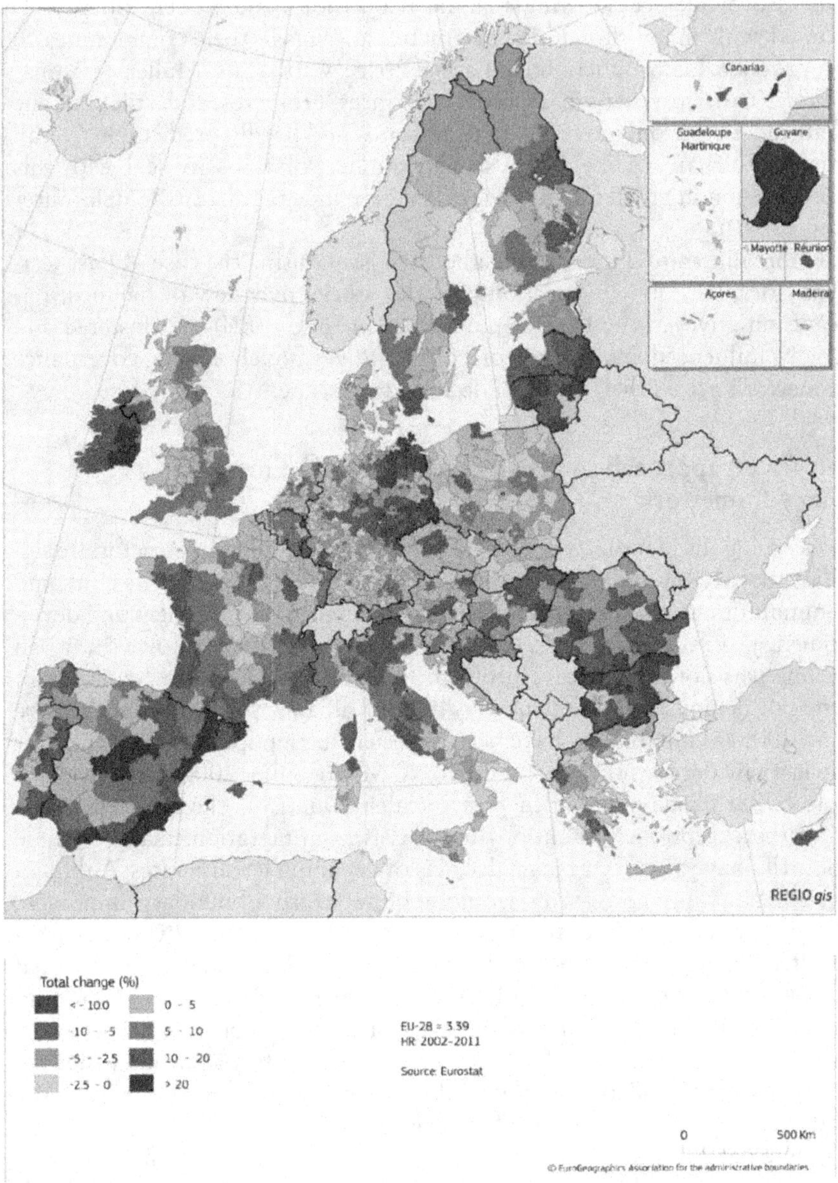

Figure 6.1 Change in European population 2001–2011.

Source: European Commission, 2014: 85.

in 1994, which started as URBAN I (1994–1999), and prolonged to its second phase as URBAN II (2000–2006). Aside from the partnership principle in urban regeneration contexts, the general aim was to support innovation as part of the broader policy for promoting economic and social cohesion (EU, 2011). The project targeted neighbourhoods in extreme deprivation, in which the solutions were to be found at grassroots levels, through inclusion of local citizens in development and implementation phases. The programs were mostly financed through the European Regional Development Fund (EFRE),[2] which equally aimed at strengthening economic and social cohesion in the EU by correcting imbalances between its regions. More recently, the bottom-up policy initiatives, such as the Acquis Urban, the Leipzig Charter, and the Toledo Declaration firmly incorporated the concepts of "partnership" and "integrated approach" into local, national, and European urban policy (Schlappa, 2015).

Although the importance of collaborative approaches to deal with urban decline was on the increase, implementation of such strategies was associated with many challenges. While the EU policy instruments indeed supported and enabled many cities to advance bottom-up, integrated, and sustainable development approaches, it remained somewhat unclear how declining communities should have benefited from them (Schlappa, 2015). In Germany alone, twelve cities – including Leipzig – participated in each of the two URBAN programs, and their experience revealed that for the local municipalities with tight budgets in greater need of external resources, accessing the funds was not always an easy task. First, they required a sound institutional and organizational basis to get engaged in the complex tasks of lobbying and negotiation, besides project formulation and implementation (Swyngedouw, Moulaert, & Arantxa, 2002). Second, participation would often get conditioned by co-financing (Haase et al., 2013). This finally illustrated the major contradiction of the EU cohesion policy set around the growth paradigm, and the real conditions for development that often resulted from exclusion of the most affected communities. Lack of skills, access to centers of power, or simply financial resources thus made reliance either on alternative solutions or on national policy frameworks more realistic, as was the case in the particular German context.

Urban decline and integrative response in East Germany

After the reunification in the year 1990, industrial production in the cities of the former GDR went down to a third of its original level, while their economic performance has remained persistently low, accompanied by significant decreases in population. In contrast to the significant shrinkage occurring in the Eastern states, the most economically prosperous centres, like Cologne, Munich, or Hamburg, have shown a continuously growing trend since 1991 (EU, 2016; Harms, 2009). They performed as magnets for new investments and inward migration, however, at the expense of less

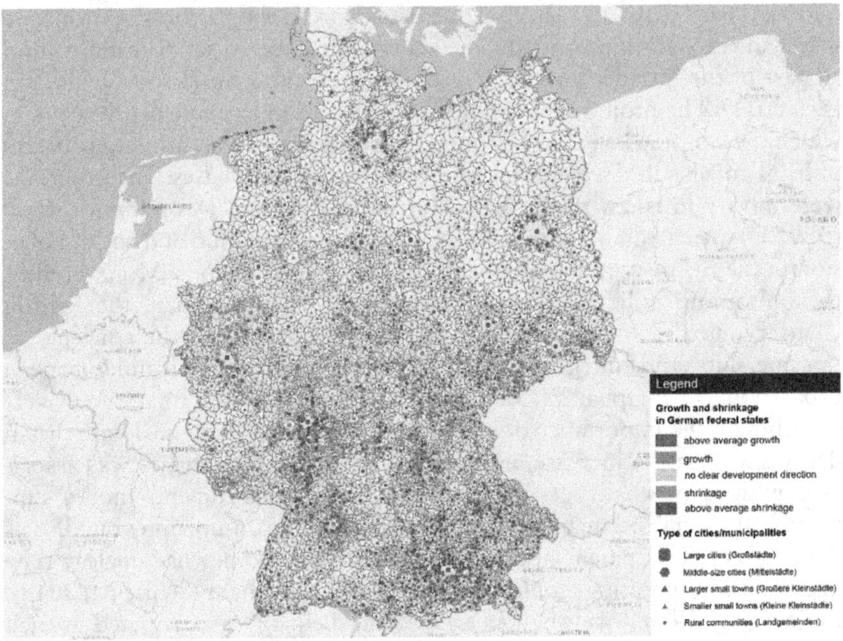

Figure 6.2 Growth and shrinkage in German federal states.

Notes: According to the database for comparative analysis of cities "Urban Audit," out of 125 German cities – 102 from the western part and 23 from the eastern part of the country – a total of 58 experienced population loss during the monitoring period between 2006 and 2015, 14 of which from the former GDR (EU, 2016). Although since 2012 some shrinking cities in Germany experienced slight increases in population, 23 of them were on a continuous drop – 8 in the eastern part,[1] 8 in the former industrial Ruhr region,[2] and 7 in other parts of the West Germany.[3]

[1]Frankfurt an der Oder, Brandenburg, Neubrandenburg, Gorlitz, Dessau, Gera, Cottbus and Zwickau.
[2]Moers, Bochum, Iserlohn, Duisburg, Oberhausen, Recklinghausen, Bottrop and Witten.
[3]Mulheim, Saarbrucken, Esslingen and Neckar, Wilhelmshaven, Celle, Schweinfurt and Hildesheim.

Source: (BBSR [Federal Office for Building and Regional Planning], 2014. Retrieved February 22, 2017, from https://gis.uba.de/maps/resources/apps/bbsr/index.html?lang=de).

economically developed medium-order centres, most of which were located in the former GDR (Domhardt & Troeger-Weiß, 2009).

As forerunners of massive demographic and economic decline, East German cities have been under the researchers' focus, and still represent a highly current topic in urban studies. The process of their decline since the 1990s has been characterized as a multi-dimensional demographic eclipse, associated with physical and structural processes (Gatzweiler, 2012) and causing the so-called urban perforation pattern (Daldrup, 2003; Schetke & Haase, 2008). Many researches agreed that there were three main causes for slow-burn shrinkage of cities occurring in the context of reunified Germany (Domhardt & Troeger-Weiß, 2009; Großmann et al., 2013; Kühn & Liebmann, 2012; Oswalt, 2006; Schetke & Haase, 2008). First, deindustrialisation and underuse of industrial infrastructure caused a decrease in the number of jobs that triggered the downward spiral scenario, especially affecting mono-structural industrial cities. Second, suburbanisation and urban sprawl had a significant impact as well, occurring either from the core city towards more peripheral locations of the city region, or from smaller and structurally weaker towns to economically powerful urban agglomerations. Lastly, the shrinkage also resulted from natural demographic changes, with mortality levels exceeding both fertility and immigration rates.

Stabilisation of the rapid population loss in the former GDR required simultaneous management of its growing economic, infrastructure, and social problems. Management of the perforating urban fabric was particularly challenging, due to the loss of population that caused extreme difficulties for the maintenance of urban infrastructure, in some cases even resulting in their abandonment. Deteriorating urban infrastructure further reflected on the quality of local living conditions, which contributed to massive outmigration. Equally important was the situation in which the declining number of urban populations meant not only low economic performance and consequently bad taxing opportunities, but also increasing needs for social services – all of which had direct effects on available public budgets. With lowered revenues and limited resources, local government became even more powerless to cope with the rising difficulties. As a result, development directions of East German cities largely depended on a particular set of local circumstances that required an individual approach in the formulation of proper responses. Small towns in vicinities of economically prosperous agglomerations could thus profit from the effects of suburbanization, but peripheral towns in structurally weaker rural regions faced serious consequences of demographic change. For such communities, there were no alternatives for economic (re)development, but to rely on external funding opportunities as the very last solution to cope with decline.

Strategic responses to urban decline in Germany

Although local municipalities all over East Germany have previously undertaken most of the well-known strategies to oppose the deterioration trend (Eisinger, 1989), these interventions showed rather limited effects. First, rising local taxes to offset growing expenditures was considered legal in Germany only up to limited and often minor amounts. Second, downsizing public services became difficult as it contradicted municipal legal responsibilities at a certain point. Finally, vigorous engagement in economic development activities had a highly uncertain outcome and often produced additional costs without providing the required results (Bernt, 2009). In addition to these basic ways of reducing dependence on the local tax base, local governments in East Germany also aimed at shifting responsibilities towards the upper levels of government. This was technically possible because the German Federal government took concrete measures regarding the problem of extreme population loss and urban decline – contrary to the U.K. and U.S., where the state traditionally played a less important role in urban planning. However, mobilization of taxing power of the federal state through a system of intergovernmental grants was not a guarantee for success. Federal allocations did not provide a total compensation for economic and population losses because fiscal equalizations were calculated on the basis of population figures (Bernt, 2009). For municipalities that have lost population, this meant loss of resources as well. Alternative solutions were necessary, however, they also needed to take into consideration that in both cases of reliance on either national or supranational levels, there was a risk of obtaining a form of dependency, in which cities could become driven by political and planning directives negotiated elsewhere (Bernt, 2009; Großmann, Beauregard, Dewar, & Haase, 2012). In order to avoid as many unfortunate governance scenarios as possible, the access to German federal funds was strategically conditioned. Drawing the parallel with the integrating framework for collaborative governance as defined by Emerson et al. (2012, p. 6), the national policy in Germany provided a "system context" based on subsidy programs, aiming to motivate affected communities to set a collaborative governance regime at the local level. Collaborative dynamics established through local efforts therefore became of crucial importance for reaching the objectives of the federal policy to make a desired impact.

The integrated approach to urban regeneration in Germany advocated for inclusion of a variety of important development aspects – such as social, economic, and ecological – through several programs. Initiated in 1999, the "Social City" program (*Soziale Stadt*) was the first major step to tackle both physical and social rehabilitation at the same time. The government aimed to support municipalities caught up in long-term decline through provision of important investments, prioritizing neither competitiveness nor growth any longer (BMUB, 2014). Instead, it was based on the principle of enhancing the capacity of local actors to deal with the immediate socio-economic and environmental problems resulting from decline. This complex task required an integrated approach that enforced close collaboration at different levels between various departments and administrative levels.[3] Until the end of the program in 2011, there were 715 interventions to resist social and spatial marginalization in 418 cities and municipalities (BMUB, 2013).

Shortly after the launch of the "Social City" program, a broader political answer to demographic shrinkage appeared in the form of the seven-years action program, "Urban Restructuring East" (*Stadtumbau Ost, 2001–2009*). As a successor of the former traditional renewal initiatives, the program was jointly directed by the Federal Ministry of Transport, Building, and Urban Affairs along with six East German Federal States; it had a significant budget and offered quite comfortable funding conditions. Led by the idea of housing market consolidation, the *Stadtumbau Ost* program aimed at establishing a more optimal balance between housing demand and housing supply. However, the strategy had much broader focus spanning from upgrading old buildings, over valuable quarters, finally to the whole inner-city areas. Its main objectives were to contribute to future viability of municipalities, stabilize structural deterioration and social erosion of the affected districts, preserve buildings in the urban centers, and, finally, improve attractiveness of East German municipalities from both residential and economic perspectives.[4] Participation in the program would ensure provision of subsidies for a variety of urban development projects, which made it highly attractive for many municipalities to participate, including Leipzig and Dresden. Until 2014, the program secured 1.48 billion euros through the Federal Government to support urban development measures in 483 municipalities from the eastern parts of the Federation (BMUB, 2013). In ten years of the program, approximately 300,000 empty dwellings were destroyed (BMVBS, 2012; Bernt, 2009).

Considering the most important results of the *Stadtumbau Ost* program, the major shift of German policies was surely the most outstanding one. With advancements of the strategy, political and planning agendas set their aims at achieving necessary adjustments to real conditions, rather than unrealistic growth. Its equally important feature was that it supported collaboration between municipalities, citizens, and housing companies, which, as a result, intensified efforts towards partnership building in most of the participating municipalities. Formation of public-private partnerships was secured through strategic requirements, such as for comprehensive urban development plans (*integrierte Stadtentwicklungspläne*) that were supposed to be developed in collaboration between local authorities and housing enterprises, as the prerequisite for acquiring funds (BMVBS, 2012). The plans addressed the problems of vacancies and abandonment through involvement of both local administrators and local property owners to evaluate present conditions and define future development steps. This approach was supposed to enable communities to determine their policy guides according to their own priorities, which was basically a political decision in each individual case. In contrast to a well-established system context, the national policy framework still demonstrated results with varied success in practice.

In the focus of the following section are the specific cases of Leipzig and Dresden, along with their contextualization in the broader context of the former GDR, to demonstrate the major opportunities of collaborative the governance framework and its implementation challenges in dealing with urban decline.

Leipzig and Dresden in the context of strategic responses to decline

As the biggest cities in the former GDR after the capital Berlin, the case of "shrinking" Dresden and Leipzig showed that struggle with urban decline was not only a matter of small and marginalized communities. Following the common scenario of rapid economic decline, Dresden was facing industrial regression and high unemployment rates that initiated significant outmigration. Coupled with decreasing birth rates, the number of its inhabitants decreased by 60,000 people in a single decade from 1989 to 1999 (Wiechmann, 2007). Also, Leipzig was for a long time one of the symbols of urban decline, both in post-war and post-reunification Germany. After the unemployment rate reached 20% in the mid-1990s, the city was already facing rapid population decline, growing house vacancies, and underused urban infrastructure. During the early post-unification years, the federal government at first stimulated urban regeneration through new construction in both of these cities.[5] However, driven by the growth-oriented national investment incentives, dynamic construction only further contributed to the problem of housing and office vacancies, as well as to the advancements of suburbanization. Until the turn of the millennia, urban policies in both of the cities were not adapted to the new circumstances. Dramatically rising housing vacancies initiated intensive lobbying by the large housing companies, which finally made the problem get the public attention (Bernt et al., 2014).

Applying the concept of integrated framework for collaborative governance developed by Emerson et al. (2012), a general system context to oppose the extreme population loss and urban decline set at the federal level involved the cross-boundary dimension of collaborative governance regime, established between federal state governments, local governments, civil society, the community, and the private sector. In such a system set around a common goal to reach economic redevelopment, the local governments in both of the cities in focus played the driving role in setting the framework' regime, clearly demonstrating a number of relevant advancements. This long journey started after the federal funding program *Stadtumbau Ost* was introduced in 2001.

Considering the case of Dresden, the launch of federal initiatives finally encouraged its local government to establish the Integrated City Development Concept (*Integriertes Stadtentwicklugskonzept INSEK*) that necessarily required the involvement of collaborative action in the decision-making process. The newly designed strategic plan, developed in close cooperation with thousands of involved citizens, was no longer growth oriented, but instead envisioned a compact European city with a stable population, reduced land consumption, and an attractive urban center (Wiechmann, 2007). The prognoses were thus generally based on the premises of a stable population development, enabling nearly 6,000 housing units to get pulled down and reused as green spaces or potential sites for single-family housing. The simultaneous quest for finding alternative development directions largely followed the principle of cross-boundary governance with profound support by the government of the state of Saxony. This implied a major turn towards the legacy and potential of university education and research, which represented a solid basis for growth of high-tech regional clusters of innovative enterprises under market economic conditions (Röhl, 2000). It also enabled the constitution of the necessary "innovative milieu," linked to socioeconomic conditions and a culture of joint cooperative learning at the regional level.

Sternberg's (1995) perspective on the concept of innovative milieu implies that it could be developed "through labour mobility, input-output-relations and face-to-face contacts, which are encouraged by spatial proximity" (p. 199). Besides the utilization of local resources and synergies between local actors, this concept also highly relies on necessary external networks and collective learning, enabling a sustained process of innovation (Camagni, 1995). However, the establishment of the innovative milieu in Dresden became successful as it comprised not only high technology, but also all sectors of the economy. Because of the strategic shift towards smart technologies, its reliance on close cooperation with officials of the state and district, and creation of an innovative milieu, the local government in Dresden has managed to attract a large number of subsidies for co-financing new industrial establishments as well as new investments. In spite of serious population losses in the surrounding regions, the region of Dresden regained growth since the 1990s, becoming one of the first in East Germany to initiate a self-enforcing path of economic development. In spite of remarkable success, such a sudden shift also implied necessary revisions of the previously defined long-term urban planning objectives that largely surpassed the concept of a compact European city with a stable population.

In contrast to this example, the local government in Leipzig never officially declared a policy that would acknowledge shrinkage. Instead, a growth-oriented strategy was followed from the very beginning, with the clear aim to attract large investors in industrial and service sectors (Rink, Couch, Haase, Krzysztofik, & Nadolu, 2014). Although an alternative plan was developed, it only briefly addressed management of a way too pessimistic scenario of decline.

Economic and urban recovery of Leipzig commenced after determined city leadership brought together a number of local stakeholders to produce strategies that emphasized urban renewal, economic development, social integration, and environmental reclamation. This strategic approach was supposed to attract vital funds from the German federal government and the EU. Both demolitions of excessive buildings and urban restructuring were carried out through the integrated strategy (*Stadtentwicklungsplan*; German abbreviation STEP), enacted in the year 2000 (Stadt Leipzig, 2000). The plan was drafted during a comprehensive, interdisciplinary procedure of the so-called "inter-departmental integrated management handling" (Stadt Leipzig, 2009, p. 67) that required two years of participatory efforts of local stakeholders, experts, and public input. Besides concrete steps towards consolidation of the housing market through demolition and refurbishment, the main objectives of the plan have also considered renovation and rehabilitation of the main qualities of the city center, establishment of a new hierarchy of the urban center, as well as an increase of competitiveness of the selected key areas. The plan also laid out large green areas at the site of urban perforations, supported temporary use of private green spaces, and promoted integrated neighbourhood development strategies, while the local government subsidized the acquisition of owner-occupied flats in listed historic buildings. Besides, due to large public subsidies, the local government in Leipzig managed to attract investments from a range of international players and important urban mega events, which finally triggered significant population and economic increases. After quite satisfactory results, the forthcoming edition of the plan from 2009 foresaw neither demolition measures, nor addressed shrinkage any longer.

Considering the major outcomes, the initiatives in Dresden and Leipzig could be considered as generally successful in coping with the problem of decline in East Germany. However, there were also some less favourable outcomes to be determined. The most evident was the lack of an appropriate forward-looking approach to manage the forthcoming sudden regrowth (Čamprag, 2018). The deficiency of comprehensive and long-term considerations of possible scenarios resulted in a significant shortage in schools and kindergartens, necessary adaptations of transport infrastructure, or inefficient wastewater disposal to satisfy the growing needs. Furthermore, restructuring of the social makeup along with the ongoing physical fragmentation of the urban fabric also triggered the sudden rise of the demand for affordable housing, which came, ironically, after years of demolishing excessive housing stock (MDR Sachsen, 2017).

The issue of rising demand for housing was particularly emphasized in Leipzig. The city officials thus advocated for strategic cooperation with all the actors with potential interest, from self-organized groups to powerful entrepreneurs. The responsibilities for successful management of this issue were divided between many stakeholders, including the city-owned housing construction company LWB (Wohnungsbaugesellschaft LWB), several housing cooperatives, as well as the network for housing projects "Netzwerk Leipziger Freiheit," founded by the city of Leipzig to strengthen the integrative approach towards finding solutions (Sauerwein, 2017). Within the frame of this specific network of various construction groups, the stakeholders with common interests were given the freedom to determine their own interventions, including the particular decisions about whether to construct new buildings or renovate existing ones. In spite of such an innovative and inclusive approach to the issue, the provision of affordable housing remained highly dependent on market rules. This raised the question whether the newly adopted role of the city administration in consulting and coordination services could be considered effective in achieving desired results while navigating potential pitfalls. However, conversely, the freedom in decision-making that the construction groups gained also raised questions regarding selective historic preservation, and all the potential consequences that the phenomenon could have, namely increasing urban fragmentation resulting from upgrading and renewal running next to dilapidation and vacancies.

The smart and well-intended strategic approach coming from the federal level to deal with urban decline in other cities of the former GDR equally demonstrated some vulnerabilities, with many difficulties associated with its implementation. First, their outcomes largely failed to address a great diversity of implications of the declining phenomenon. Considering that derelict housing had extraordinary visibility in cities, the strategic frameworks were commonly based on demolition of excessive housing stock and intentions to improve open spaces and recreational areas that would allow cities to recover and attract new population and investments (Martinez-Fernandez et al., 2012; Oswalt, 2006). The resources were almost exclusively granted in relation to managing housing stock, while other aims had less relevance. More than 270 municipalities thus adapted their planning schemes to meet these criteria (Bernt, 2009). Demolition of vacant buildings thus largely became the prime urban development goal, often failing to address the specific local constellation of problems, but rather aiming at the provision of necessary federal funds. Second, the task of demolition and upgrading on the local level itself proved to be extremely difficult to achieve in cases of big numbers of owners involved. The problem of lack of ownerships in unrenovated multi-storey buildings in the inner-city areas was equally problematic, as well as situations in which owners refused to sell their property for a low price out of speculative reasons. Third, these initiatives were also highly costly, and some cities remained unable to apply for federal funds, as they couldn't afford to co-finance the upgrading measures. The final result of the federal strategic frameworks to deal with urban decline in different communities of East Germany could therefore be primarily characterized by the one-sided focus and extreme variations of their success rates. These features represent a solid ground for the following evaluation of the overall performance of collaborative governance in Germany.

Collaborative efforts as strategic response: from path dependency to new development perspectives

Many authors argued that collaborative action in the form of partnerships between public, private, and civic sectors could be a reasonable instrument in urban development and revitalisation strategies. While demonstrating significant potential for finding innovative and inclusive approaches, such collaborations in the former GDR also demonstrated vulnerability and some undesired effects in practice. First, partnerships between the public and private sector generally showed that they were particularly unstable and short lasting. On the one hand, they would adopt a rather artificial character, which made the special scope of partnerships often get fragmented towards far-reaching reductions in planning options (Bernt, 2009). On the other hand, instead of anticipated collaborative efforts to define a common strategic framework for action, an agreement between many stakeholders on policy priorities was extremely difficult to reach, even including the decision which neighbourhoods should be preserved (Glock & Häußermann, 2004). Second, collaboration and proper development of integrated plans was a matter of resources, both financial as well as in competent staff. Many municipalities had difficulties properly designing plans on their own, as they were either poor or understaffed. It often resulted with other, more powerful actors taking over support of the process, which was critical as they often had particular interests in the plans realization (Bernt et al., 2014; Glock & Häußermann, 2004). Finally, as the general shift from government to governance imposed various dilemmas for success of participatory planning in general, it also got reflected in the context of East German cities. These were, according to Feuerbach (2010), heavy dependency of the local initiatives on external findings, community organizations having limited influence that depended on their institutionalization, and demographic and socioeconomic homogenization of the affected neighbourhoods that made empowering the local residents rather difficult. All these general outcomes largely opposed one of the major prerequisites for establishing successful collaborative action in clearly defined, shared goals and operating rationale for taking action, as suggested by Emerson et al. (2012, p. 17).

There are several particular reasons for many communities in East Germany to face difficulties with institutional change towards the creation of new development paths that need to be highlighted. The most remarkable example is in the phenomenon that Liebmann and Kuder named "institutional path dependency" (Liebmann & Kuder, 2012). Such communities suffered from a general lack of strategies that could initiate alternative approaches to regeneration, and thus help overcome problems associated with historically grounded directives. A large number of cities even avoided setting up new development paths as long as possible. The reasons for this should not only be found in a long tradition of unquestioned singular development orientation, but also in the high costs of path change, additional investments necessary to establish conditions for a new start, as well as in the persistence of industrial mentality among old industrial elite and workers (Kühn, 2008; Liebmann & Kuder, 2012). Although many strategies turned out to be unsuccessful due to the strong local egoism (Domhardt & Troeger-Weiß, 2009) and deeply rooted path dependencies (Liebmann & Kuder, 2012), the equally important reason was that local partnerships for urban regeneration in German cities were generally carried out with a lack of tradition and experience in the field (Friesecke, 2007). Comprehensive and hardly predictable effects associated with the phenomenon were another significant challenge for successful implementation of advanced collaborative strategies to oppose urban decline.

Strategic approaches adopted in Dresden and Leipzig showed urban development patterns characterized by legitimation through the political system and a rather consequent imposition of integrated development concepts. Although system context was the same, collaboration dynamics set by the local governments was actually not based on the same regimes. In both of the cases, the regimes were set by the integrated urban development strategies, showing plenty of diversities – from the approaches to urban decline, to the adopted theories of action, to the share of stakeholders. Nevertheless, both were subordinated to changes and updates depending on the nature and level of impacts resulting from their joint actions, which, according to a proposition by Emerson et al. (2012, p. 19), leads towards a more sustainability over time. The case of Dresden particularly supports this claim, demonstrating that in the face of a greater uncertainty of future developments, flexibility of a strategy is even more important than its consistence. This further builds up on the argument of Emerson et al. (2012, p. 5) regarding the driver of uncertainty and its importance in setting up direction for collaborative governance regimes, as well as of interdependence through cross-boundary cooperation that in Dresden included both federal and state support, as well as the adopted strategy having regional resonance. On the other hand, Leipzig, on its way to regrowth, demonstrated the importance of the strategic vision and initial determination of the local government, but also reminded one of the necessity of long-term planning objectives for managed regrowth. This case particularly emphasized the importance of leadership as the essential driver for collaborative governance (Emerson et al., 2012, p. 5), since the local government in Leipzig never officially abandoned the growth-oriented objectives.

Although many achievements in Dresden and Leipzig resulted from collaborative governance efforts, their success also heavily depended on generally favorable circumstances that also involved a high potential for reliance on development alternatives. This could explain relatively quickly achieved regrowth, although a coherent urban development strategy that would comprehensively address the problem has never been fully achieved in both of the cities. Lobbying of the most powerful actors gathered around real-estate business and banking interests made the issue of shrinkage get tackled primarily as a housing problem, while other issues were less privileged and addressed with slower progress. This largely contradicts the propositions suggested by Emerson et al. (2012), particularly the ones recommending shared motivation to sustain principle engagement; stressing the importance of collaborative identification of shared theories of action; and relating targeted outcomes with shared theory of action. Besides from some success, local governance in both of the cities thus also demonstrated challenges in defining and managing shared goals and stakeholders' participation to foster the ideal of collaborative approach in its full capacity. This provides evidence that although collaborative governance could be considered as an important tool to strategically combat urban decline, it is far from being a panacea for its many implications.

After nearly two decades since the first federal initiatives to oppose the shrinking trend in the former GDR have appeared, prosperous West German cities like Munich, Frankfurt, or Hamburg are still far ahead of the national average. However, compared to other East German cities, Leipzig and Dresden demonstrated significant progress (Bontje, 2004; Liebmann & Kuder, 2012; Wiechmann, 2007). Also, cities like Potsdam, Jena, or Erfurt, with more or less success, found their ways out of the post-socialist and post-industrial pasts, in which collaborative development strategies based on either historic or alternative potentials, such as culture or research, had a significant role. Many other East German communities still have difficulties with institutional change towards the creation of new development paths, which illustrates high polarization in Germany remaining a bitter reality. It resulted from a variety of local conditions, as well as the fact that economic performance of a large number of cities in East Germany has been based on singular orientation. In times of crisis and economic difficulties, such firm dependencies on former development paths often got under a heavy influence of powerful and conservative local actors. Unevenly distributed across participants, the power thus "can enable or disable subsequent agreements or collective courses of action" (Emerson et al., 2012, p. 11). Strong commercial-industrial development paths additionally restricted both mobilisation and performance of innovative collaborative efforts. Especially vulnerable were peripheral locations, which have been under continuous and significant shrinkage, mostly due to either loss of significance as administrative or service centre, or simply as less attractive residential places. In such cases, communities failed adequately or on time collaboratively to formulate replies to deindustrialization processes on the local level – neither through innovative growth-oriented strategies, nor through the ones to manage shrinkage. Continuous loss of population and prosperity, along with a generally low alternative potential for development, classified cities like Gera, Magdeburg, Cottbus, or Hoyerswerda in the "loser cities" category, where decline even turned into a permanent state (Bertelsmann Stifftung, 2006; Glock & Häußermann, 2004; Kühn & Liebmann, 2012). Referring to Emerson et al. (2012), these communities failed to "generate a new capacity for joint action that did not exist before and sustain or grow that capacity for the duration of the shared purpose" (p. 14). This finally provides evidence that the form of collaborative governance adopted in Germany to address the phenomenon of decline strongly depended on both capabilities and resources of affected localities.

Conclusion and final remarks

Shortly after the launch of the *Soziale Stadt* program, the new federal states in reunified Germany responded with the collaborative establishment of urban restructuring policies that aimed at revitalizing city centers and dealing with deconstructions and conversions in large housing areas. The strategies that followed, such as *Stadtumbau Ost*, further promoted the integrated citywide urban development approach, which became a precondition for funding the demolition of abandoned or unused buildings. Nevertheless, even such elaborated strategic policies were not able to change patterns of uneven development and disadvantage in each and every case, especially among smaller cities and communities losing the race for regional competitive advantage (Haase, Rink, & Grossmann, 2016; Pallagst et al., 2011; Schlappa, 2016). It turned out that public-private partnerships established under such conditions were severely complicated endeavors, and that local politics remained more dependent on national government resources than on private investments (Bernt, 2009). Glock and Häußermann (2004), in their analysis of policy implementation at the local level, even questioned the overall legitimacy of public interventions, due to implementation of demolitions at the expense of upgrading measures, as well as with their focus being far too narrowly set on housing market issues.

Following the common points of criticism of the initiatives in Germany in the academic literature so far, this study demonstrated that, first, managing urban decline is generally not an easy mission, neither on national nor on local governance levels. It often required unpopular reformulations of growth-oriented policies to ones that acknowledge decline, and a disparity that called for regional thinking but required responses embedded in particular localities. Furthermore, demands for the redefinition of perspectives to urban decline implied the development of innovative, flexible, and integrative solutions, but also finding more suitable and sustainable ways of their implementation at the local level. Second, the major governmental programs based on collaborative efforts in Germany have demonstrated similar challenges in praxis. Besides exclusively growth-oriented strategies that required reformulation, they mostly regarded the slowly changing negative connotation of shrinkage in urban development contexts, a number of small and economically weak communities in need of extensive support, and difficulties with predicting future population dynamics. Third, many problems in praxis of this well-intended and somewhat idealistic approach were usually in proportion to the number of involved interests and actors having varying degrees of power. The tradition of singular development orientation, along with a general lack of experience for proper set of collaborative frameworks to deal with the complexity of urban decline, often reflected on the capacities of local governments' adaptability to rapidly developing conditions. Finally, the success rate of collaborative, cross-boundary governance established in the cities of the former GDR strongly depended on both capabilities and resources of affected localities. Although the strategic frameworks have set common requirements for accessing the national government resources, they have generally failed to address significant disparities in development alternatives among the affected communities.

The outcomes of this study provide some important perspectives for other cities and regions facing similar challenges to reach economic redevelopment. The strategic frameworks based on collaborative action and cross-boundary cooperation in declining communities confirmed that the major challenge for ensuring successful implementation generally rests upon finding mechanisms to reconcile significant local disparities in the system context. Equally important is to balance power relations in the process of setting up shared goals and operating rationale for taking action. Finally, efficient and sustainable collaborative governance should also necessarily aim at reaching beyond its required prerequisite of reaching stakeholders' consensus. Such farsighted objectives should also consider anticipation of outcomes or some future trends on which successful implementation of development strategies may depend, even in cases when carrying out a public purpose would involve presently less desired or seemingly contradictory interventions.

Notes

1 According to the official statistics, during the period between 2008 and 2012 there were 117 regions in the EU where the population fell by more than 8.0 per thousand inhabitants on average (Eurostat, 2014). European database for comparative analysis of EU cities "Urban Audit," revealed that out of 950 large and medium-sized cities in 30 EU countries, 328 (35%) lost population in the period between 2006 and 2015 (EU, 2016). Much bigger number of cities, however, had significant fluctuations throughout the same period. Although the situation seems to be slightly improving, the biggest current loss of population still occurs in the cities of Central and Eastern Europe (Dijkstra, 2014), where 110 out of a total of 154 cities shrank (mostly in Bulgaria, Croatia, Slovakia, Poland, and Hungary), including the Baltic countries of the former Soviet Bloc (Latvia, Lithuania). Population loss could be traced in other parts of Europe as well, such as in decreasing rural areas in the southern countries of the continent, in Western European declining industrial agglomerations, as well as to peripheral areas in Northern Europe.
2 Projects Website: http://ec.europa.eu/regional_policy/en/funding/erdf/
3 On the national level, the collaboration was established between several ministries: the Ministry of Transport, Construction and Housing, the Ministry of Economy and the Ministry of Social Affairs (Vranken, 2007). Responsible for the program implementation was the Federal Ministry of Housing, which also worked in close cooperation with departments at the level of federal states in charge of housing, economy, and social affairs.
4 Concerning the fact that shrinking was not only affecting eastern states, only a few years after the *Stadtumbau Ost* another program was launched. "Urban Restructuring West" (*Stadtumbau West*, 2004-2015) was addressing cities and municipalities in the Western part of the country that faced economic and demographic changes. The program supported 496 municipalities. Until the end of 2015, around 846 million euros of federal financial assistance was spent for different urban measures. Common for both programs was the integrated urban development approach, as a prerequisite for successful urban redevelopment initiative (BMUB, 2015).
5 In the period between 1991 and 2012, 182.2 million euros was invested in the Leipzig redevelopment areas from the Federal program of Urban Renewal (Stadt Leipzig, 2017).

References

Beauregard, R. A. (2007). Shrinking cities in the United States in historical perspective : A research note. In K. Pallagst et al. (Eds.), *The future of shrinking cities: Problems, patterns and strategies of urban transformation in a global context* (pp. 61–68). Berkeley, CA: University of California, Center for Global Metropolitan Studies, Institute for Urban and Regional Development, and the Shrinking Cities International Research Network.

Bernt, M. (2009). Partnerships for demolition: The governance of urban renewal in East Germany's shrinking cities. *International Journal of Urban and Regional Research*, 33(3), 754–769.

Bernt, M., Haase, A., Großmann, K., Cocks, M., Couch, C., Cortese, C., & Krzysztofik, R. (2014). How does(n't) urban shrinkage get onto the agenda? Experiences from Leipzig, Liverpool, Genoa and Bytom. *International Journal of Urban and Regional Research*, 38(5), 1749–1766.

Bertelsmann Stifftung. (2006). *Deutschland zwischen Wachstum und Schrumpfung Wanderungsbewegung in Deutschland.* Retrieved March 1, 2017, from https://www.bertelsmann-stiftung.de/fileadmin/files/user_upload/Deutschland_zwischen_Wachstum_und_Schrumpfung.pdf

BMUB [Federal Ministry for the Environment, Nature Conservation and Nuclear Safety]. (2013). *Stadtumbau Ost*. Retrieved March 1, 2017, from http://www.nationale-stadtentwicklungspolitik.de/NSP/DE/Staedtebaufoerderung/StadtumbauOst/stadtumbauost_node.html

BMUB [Federal Ministry for the Environment, Nature Conservation and Nuclear Safety]. (2014). *10 Jahre Stadtumbau West*. Retrieved from http://www.staedtebaufoerderung.info/StBauF/SharedDocs/Publikationen/StBauF/StadtumbauWest/ZehnJahreSUW.pdf?__blob=publicationFile&v=6

BMUB [Federal Ministry for the Environment, Nature Conservation and Nuclear Safety]. (2015). *Stadtumbau West*. Retrieved March 3, 2017, from http://www.staedtebaufoerderung.info/StBauF/DE/Programm/Stadtumbau/StadtumbauWest/stadtumbau_west_node.html

BMVBS [German Federal Ministry of Transport, Building and Urban Development]. (2012). *10 Jahre Stadtumbau Ost-Berichte aus der Praxis*. Retrieved March 3, 2017, from https://leibniz-irs.de/fileadmin/user_upload/pure_files/385337/Statusbericht5.pdf

Bontje, M. (2004). Facing the challenge of shrinking cities in East Germany: The case of Leipzig. *Geo Journal*, 61(1), 13–21.

Camagni, R. (1995). The concept of innovative milieu and its relevance for public policies in European laging regions, *Papers in Regional Science*, 74(4), 317–340.

Čamprag, N. (2018). The trap within anticipated regrowth: Two sides of strategic response to urban decline in Leipzig. *Articulo: Journal of Urban Research* [Online], http://journals.openedition.org/articulo/3596

Daldrup, E. L. (2003). Die "perforierte Stadt" neue Räume im Leipziger Osten. *Informationen Zur Raumentwicklung*, (1), 55–67. Retrieved from http://www.architektur-baukultur.de/nn_23680/BBSR/DE/Veroeffentlichungen/IzR/2003/Downloads/1__2Daldrup,templateId=raw,property=publicationFile.pdf/1_2Daldrup.pdf

Delken, E. (2008). Happiness in shrinking cities in Germany: A research note. *Journal of Happiness Studies*, 9(2), 213–218.

Dijkstra, L. (2014). *Investment for jobs and growth: Promoting development and good governance in EU regions and cities*. Sixth report on economic, social and territorial cohesion. European Commission, Brussels.

Domhardt, H. -J., & Troeger-Weiß, G. (2009). Germany' s shrinkage on a small town scale. In K. Pallagst et al. (Eds.), *The future of shrinking cities: Problems, patterns and strategies of urban transformation in a global context* (pp. 161–168). Center for Global Metropolitan Studies, Institute for Urban and Regional Development, and the Shrinking Cities International Research Network. Berkeley, CA: University of California.

Eisinger, P. K. (1989). *The rise of the entrepreneurial state: State and local economic development policy in the United States*. Retrieved from http://books.google.com/books?hl=en&lr=&id=xW3xuiqdoYAC&oi=fnd&pg=PR11&dq=eisinger+the+entrepeneurial+state&ots=rC-LPJhGdp&sig=5zmTtTypYHFIBV67vF5J6R0PZKU%5Cnhttp://www.jstor.org/stable/144374%5Cnhttp://www.amazon.com/dp/0262550423%5Cnhttp://www.jstor.org

Emerson, K., Nabatchi, T., & Balogh, S. (2012). An integrative framework for collaborative governance. *Journal of Public Administration Research and Theory*, 22(1), 1–29.

Endlicher, W., & Langner, M. (Eds.). (2007). *Shrinking cities: Effects on urban ecology and challenges for urban development*. Frankfurt: Internationaler Verlag der Wissenschaften "Peter Lang".

European Union. (2011). *An introduction to the urban pilot programme*. Retrieved from http://ec.europa.eu/regional_policy/archive/urban2/urban/upp/src/frame1.htm
European Union. (2012). Europe 2020: Europe's growth strategy. Publications Office of the European Union, Luxembourg.
European Union. (2016). *Urban audit*. Retrieved from http://ec.europa.eu/eurostat/web/cities.
Eurostat. (2014). *Eurostat regional yearbook 2014*. Publications Office of the European Union, Luxembourg.
Feuerbach, F. (2010). Community planning in shrinking cities: Between top-down and bottom-up – the Case of reitbahnviertel in the city of Chemnitz, Germany. *Vulnerability, risk and complexity: Impacts of global change on human habitats (IAPS 21 Conference, Abstracts of Presentations)*. Leipzig, Germany: Helmholtz Centre for Environmental Research-UFZ.
Frazier, A. E., & Bagchi-Sen, S. (2015). Developing open space networks in shrinking cities. *Applied Geography*, 59, 1–9.
Frazier, A. E., Bagchi-Sen, S., & Knight, J. (2013). The spatio-temporal impacts of demolition land use policy and crime in a shrinking city. *Applied Geography*, 41, 55–64.
Friesecke, F. (2007). The role of partnerships in urban regeneration: Similarities and differences between Germany and United Kingdom. *FIG Working Week 2007 (Hong Kong SAR, China, May 13–17, 2007)*, 1–18.
Fritsche, M., Langner, M., Köhler, H., Ruckes, A., Schüler, D., Zakirova, B., . . . Westermann, J. (2007). Shrinking cities: A new urban challenge for research in urban ecology. In M. Langner, & W. Endlicher (Eds.), *Shrinking cities: Effects on urban ecology and challenges for urban development* (pp. 17–33). Bern, Switzerland: Internationaler Verlag der Wissenschaften "Peter Lang".
Gatzweiler, H. P. (2012). Regionale Disparitäten in Deutschland: Herausforderungen für die Raumentwicklungspolitik. *Geographische Rundschau*, 64(78), 54–60.
Glock, B., & Häußermann, H. (2004). New trends in urban development and public policy in eastern Germany: Dealing with the vacant housing problem at the local level. *International Journal of Urban and Regional Research*, 28(4), 919–929.
Großmann, K., Beauregard, R., Dewar, M., & Haase, A. (2012). European and US perspectives on shrinking cities. *Urban Research & Practice*, 5(3), 360–363.
Großmann, K., Bontje, M., Haase, A., & Mykhnenko, V. (2013). Shrinking cities: Notes for the further research agenda. *Cities*, 35, 221–225.
Haase, A., Athanasopoulou, A., & Rink, D. (2013). Urban shrinkage as an emerging concern for European policymaking. *European Urban and Regional Studies*, 23(1), 103–107.
Haase, A., Rink, D., & Grossmann, K. (2016). Shrinking cities in post-socialist Europe: what can we learn from their analysis for theory building today? *Geografiska Annaler: Series B, human geography*, 98(4), 305–319.
Harms, H. (2009). Changes on the waterfront: Transforming harbor areas. In K. Pallagst et al. (Eds.), *The future of shrinking Cities: Problems, patterns and strategies of urban transformation in a global context* (pp. 37–48). Center for Global Metropolitan Studies, Institute for Urban and Regional Development, and the Shrinking Cities International Research Network. Berkeley, CA: University of California.
Häußermann, H., & Siebel, W. (1988). Die Schrumpfende Stadt und die Stadtsoziologie. In J. Friedrichs (Ed.), *Soziologische Stadtforschung* (pp. 78–94). Wiesbaden: VS Verlag f{ü}r Sozialwissenschaften. https://doi.org/10.1007/978-3-322-83617-5_5.

Kühn, M. (2008). Wachstum und Schrumpfung der Industriestadt: Regenierungsstrategien in Brandenburg an der Havel. In A. Schild, & D. Schubert (Eds.), *Städte zwischen Wachstum und Schrumpfung (Dortmundter Beiträge zur Raumplannung 129)* (pp. 83–96). Dortmund: IRPUD-Institute for Spatial Planning, University of Dortmund.

Kühn, M., & Liebmann, H. (2012). Urban regeneration: Strategies of shrinking cities in Eastern Germany. *Erde*, 143(1–2), 135–152.

Liebmann, H., & Kuder, T. (2012). Pathways and strategies of urban regeneration: Deindustrialized cities in Eastern Germany. *European Planning Studies*, 20(7), 1155–1172.

Logan, J. R., & Molotch, H. L. (1987). The city as growth machine. In *Urban Fortunes: The Political Economy of Place* (pp. 50–98). Berkeley; Los Angeles; London: University of California Press.

Martinez-Fernandez, C., Audirac, I., Fol, S., & Cunningham-Sabot, E. (2012). Shrinking cities: Urban challenges of globalization. *International Journal of Urban and Regional Research*, 36(2), 213–225.

Martinez-Fernandez, C., & Wu, C. -T. (2009). Shrinking cities : A global overview and concerns about Australian mining cities cases. In K. Pallagst et al. (Eds.), *The future of shrinking cities: Problems, patterns and strategies of urban transformation in a global context* (pp. 29–36). Center for Global Metropolitan Studies, Institute for Urban and Regional Development, and the Shrinking Cities International Research Network. Berkeley, CA: University of California.

MDR Sachsen. (2017, June 6). Leipzig wächst, seine Aufgaben auch. *MDR Sachsen, Das Sachsenradio*. Retrieved from http://www.mdr.de/sachsen/leipzig/leipzig-waechst-und-damit-die-aufgaben-100.html

Moulaert, F., Rodriguez, A., & Swyngedouw, E. (2004). *The globalized city: Economic restructuring and social polarization in European cities*. Oxford, UK: Oxford University Press.

Oswalt, P. (2006). Shrinking cities, volume 1 international research. *Shrinking Cities*, 1, 1–17.

Oswalt, P., & Rieniets, T. (2006). Introduction. In *Atlas of Shrinking Cities*. Ostfildern-Ruit, Germany: Hatje Cantz Publishers.

Pallagst, K. M., Wiechmann, T., & Martinez-Fernández, C. (2011). *Shrinking cities: International perspectives and policy implications*. New York, NY: Routledge.

Ringel, F. (2014). Post-industrial times and the unexpected: Endurance and sustainability in Germany's fastest-shrinking city. *Journal of the Royal Anthropological Institute*, 20(S1), 52–70.

Rink, D., Couch, C., Haase, A., Krzysztofik, R., & Nadolu, B. (2014). The governance of urban shrinkage in cities of post-socialist Europe: policies, strategies and actors. *Urban Research & Practice*, 7(3), 258–277.

Röhl, K. (2000). *Saxony's capital dresden: On the way to become Eastern Germany's first "innovative milieu"?* Diskussionsbeiträge aus dem Institut für Wirtschaft und Verkehr, Nr. 5/2000, TU Dresden.

Sauerwein, U. (2017, June 20). Warum man in "Hypezig" noch gut und günstig wohnt. *WeltN24*. Retrieved from https://www.welt.de/sonderthemen/immobilienwirtschaft/article165705602/Warum-man-in-Hypezig-noch-gut-und-guenstig-wohnt.html

Schetke, S., & Haase, D. (2008). Multi-criteria assessment of socio-environmental aspects in shrinking cities: Experiences from eastern Germany. *Environmental Impact Assessment Review*, 28(7), 483–503.

Schlappa, H. (2015). Co-producing the cities of tomorrow: Fostering collaborative action to tackle decline in Europes shrinking cities. *European Urban and Regional Studies*, 24(2), 162–174.

Schlappa, H. (2016). Leading strategy in shrinking cities. *Hertfordshire business school working paper*. Retrieved from https://uhra.herts.ac.uk/bitstream/handle/2299/17277/S170.pdf?sequence=2&isAllowed=y

Soto, P., Houk, M., & Ramsden, P. (2012). *Implementing community-led local development in cities: Lessons from URBACT*. Paris: URBACT.

Stadt Leipzig. (2000). *Stadtentwicklungsplan Wohnungsbau und Stadterneuerung*. Koln: Dezernat Planung un Bau.

Stadt Leipzig. (2009). *Leipzig 2020: Integriertes Stadtentwicklungskonzept (SEKo)*. Koln: Dezernat Stadtentwicklung un Bau.

Stadt Leipzig. (2017). *Programm Städtebauliche Erneuerung*. Retrieved February 22, 2017, from http://www.leipzig.de/bauen-und-wohnen/stadterneuerung-in-leipzig/foerderprogramme/programm-staedtebauliche-erneuerung/

Steinführer, A., Bierzynski, A., Großmann, K., Haase, A., Kabisch, S., & Klusácek, P. (2010). Population decline in polish and czech cities during post-socialism? Looking behind the official statistics. *Urban studies*, 47(11), 2325–2346.

Sternberg, R. (1995). Innovative milieus in Frankreich. *Zeitschrift für Wirtschaftsgeographie*, 3/4, 199–218.

Swyngedouw, E., Moulaert, F., & Arantxa, R. (2002). Neoliberal urbanization in Europe: Large-scale urban development projects and the new urban policy. *Antipode*, 34, 542–577.

Turok, I., & Mykhnenko, V. (2007). The trajectories of European cities, 1960–2005. *Cities*, 24(3), 165–182.

Vranken, J. (2007). Changing forms of solidarity: Urban development programs in Europe. In Y. Kazepov (Eds.), *Cities of Europe: Changing contexts, local arrangements, and the challenge to urban cohesion* (pp. 255–276). Oxford: Blackwell Publishers Ltd.

Wiechmann, T. (2007). What are the problems of shrinking cities? Lessons learned from an international comparison. In K. Pallagst et al. (Eds.), *The future of shrinking cities: Problems, patterns and strategies of urban transformation in a global context* (pp. 5–16). Center for Global Metropolitan Studies, Institute for Urban and Regional Development, and the Shrinking Cities International Research Network, University of California, Berkeley, CA.

Wirth, P., Elis, V., Müller, B., & Yamamoto, K. (2016). Peripheralisation of small towns in Germany and Japan? Dealing with economic decline and population loss. *Journal of Rural Studies*, 47, 62–75.

7 Collaborative governance for urban regeneration in Italy

Denita Cepiku, Elona Guga, and Benedetta Marchese

Introduction

Italy, as most of the countries harshly hit by the 2008 financial crisis, has been left with high unemployment rates, a high public deficit, and a public debt that has risen above 130%. Nonetheless, citizens demand high-quality services, especially in health and education. The pressure and challenges that have emerged from the crisis have increased the complexity and costs of public policy, making impossible the proper design and implementation of reforms in the short run. Often, governments lack the capacities and financial resources to achieve their diverse and critical policy agendas. Given the complexity and costs of different tasks, these challenges cannot be solved by any single organization, be it public, nonprofit, business, or civil society association. Therefore, different actors collaborate together to achieve something that cannot be realized by a single actor (Huxham, 1996).

Nevertheless, opportunities may rise from turbulent times. Public officials tend to rescue the country from urgent threats and they also try to improve the governance. However, such improvement goes beyond the state boundaries, changing government roles and establishing collaboration with inter-institutional networks, public-private partnerships, joined-up government (horizontal coordination and integration between departments and agencies within government), and users' engagement through co-production. Under these circumstances, management mechanisms and systems are expected to change in collaborative settings compared to how they work in traditional organizations (Cepiku, 2017).

The chapter provides collaborative governance examples that are being implemented in Italy as a reaction to the financial and economic crisis of 2008. The aim is to understand the challenges and opportunities that these forms of collaboration face.

Method of research

Collaborative governance has been identified as one of the several strategies adopted by public administrations to address the effects of the global economic and financial crisis. Much has been written on networks and co-production in Anglo-Saxon countries, while the literature is less developed with reference to other contexts, such as the Mediterranean countries. In this regard, Italy represents an interesting case study considering both the harsh effects of the crisis and the creative responses.

Our chapter investigates cases that provide valuable insights on best and worst practices of collaborative governance. The emphasis on best practices has spread widely across all sectors of society. The term "best practice" implies that it is the best case compared to any other alternative action. Overman and Boyd (1994) define the best practice research as "the selective observation of a set of exemplars across different contexts in order to derive more generalizable principles and theories of management" (p. 69). Three main characteristics associated with a best practice have been identified by S. Bretschneider, Marc-Aurele, and Wu (2004): 1) a comparative process, 2) an action, and 3) a linkage between the action and some outcome or goal. The best practice research might be a new positive, practical, prescriptive, and innovative paradigm in research (Overman & Boyd, 1994). According to Altshuler (1992), "the best way scholars can help improve public management is to search out, observe, and think hard about "best practices" (p. xi).

Empirical research on collaborative governance has proven that designing and delivering healthcare services in such a way improved the implementation process and strengthened compliance (Bovaird, 2007; Cepiku & Giordano, 2014). An empirical research of Organization for Economic Cooperation and Development (OECD) (2011) proved that monitoring the quality of parks, urban streets, or lake water could be less expensive and more effective if residents and community are involved. Although the benefits of collaborative arrangements are well evidenced in the literature, their success will depend on adopted approaches and circumstances, such as the context, the value being produced, and/or the nature of the task (Alford & Hughes, 2008).

The use of best practices has been criticized by some as void of theory (Bardach, 2003; Overman & Boyd, 1994), as most best practice research begins with observation of practice, while little attention is devoted to understanding the underlying theoretical frameworks that may serve to explain what the researcher is attempting to observe. Another frequent criticism of best is the lack of methodological rigor (Bardach, 2000; Bretschneider, Choi, Nabatchi, & O'Leary, 2012; Myers, Smith, & Martin, 2006; Overman & Boyd, 1994). Moreover, best practices are relative, depending on region, context, and time. "Nothing is 'best' everywhere and forever" (General Accounting Office, 1990) and there is no evidence that best practices are transferable across contexts (Bretschneider et al., 2004; Overman & Boyd, 1994). As Patton (2015) argues, "'best' is a matter of perspective and criteria."

All of these problems highlight the need for dialogue about and deliberation on multiple interpretations and perspectives, instead of supporting the search for best-ness (Patton, 2015). In qualitative analysis, one should also look for and investigate the negative or deviant cases and try to understand why they occurred and what circumstances produced them (Gibbs, 2007). Considering an unsuccessful case might be useful because, where patterns and trends have been identified, our understanding of those patterns and trends is increased by considering the instances and cases that do not fit within the pattern. Dealing openly with the complexities and dilemmas posed by unsuccessful cases is both "intellectually honest and politically strategic" as "the human world is not perfectly ordered and human researchers are not omniscient" (Patton, 1990, p. 464). Accordingly, our case studies have been selected as representing novel approaches and solutions to the crisis. We adopt a public management perspective, focusing on the managerial challenges that are posed that determine, somehow, a good and a bad practice. The source of information is evidence obtained from official public reports, official NGOs' reports, and the media.

Italy's wicked problems

The global financial and economic crisis has been one of the most important international events of the last decade and it will profoundly shape the future of the European Union as well as that of Italy (Di Quirico, 2010). Administrative and institutional dualism, the different North-South speed in the modernization process, the relationship between institutional performance and civil society, and free-riding behaviors have influenced the adoption of different modernization tools and the implementation of different reforms (Cepiku & Meneguzzo, 2011; Lagravinese, 2015). Furthermore, the Italian public sector is characterized by implementation gaps; low economic competitiveness; wide-ranging reforms; the absence of continuity of reforms; downsizing reforms that did not have an impact on the size of public sector; and a variation of speed and degree of modernization in different geographical areas (Cepiku & Meneguzzo, 2007, 2011; Di Mascio & Natalini, 2015).

The Italian context shaped both exposure to financial pressure and the government's ability to react. Spending review efforts have targeted local governments and often, local governments have required central government intervention as they were unable to deliver basic services, increasing tensions between the central and local government (Cepiku, Mussari, & Giordano, 2016; Di Quirico, 2010). High levels of debt and deficit, European Union pressure to reform, and the country's context led Italy toward austerity measures, even though they did not produce the required results (Di Mascio & Natalini, 2015). They increased inequality in access to health care and deteriorated the overall health and well-being of the population, increasing the difference in the quality of care between regions (De Belvis et al., 2012). The crisis reduced economic activity, cutting the amount of financial resources collected. In addition, anti-crisis policies increased the budget deficit and public debt, preventing the public sector from being able to satisfy citizens' needs, deteriorating the trust of citizens in government. This statement is confirmed by the OECD, where only 43% of citizens trust their government in OECD countries (OECD, 2017).

Under these circumstances, innovative ideas, hybrid solutions, and collaboration between different actors become prominent. In fact, citizens' involvement and integration into policy and decision-making processes is a major challenge in the 21st century (Collaborative Democracy Network, 2006).

Some illustrative examples of collaborative governance in Italy

Shared administration

Shared Administration is a practice based on the cooperation between citizens and local administration for the regeneration and maintenance of urban common property. It has been promoted by Labsus – Laboratory for Subsidiarety (Labsus – Laboratorio per la sussidiarietà), which is a volunteer association that generates innovative ideas on how to better serve the community. The basic premise of this collaborative form is the principle of horizontal subsidiarity enshrined in Article 118 of the Italian Constitution, which demands all levels of governments to find ways to share their powers and cooperate with single or associated citizens willing to exercise their constitutional right to carry out activities of general interest. The local administration, as a level of government closer to the citizen, is the ideal place for the application of this innovative model, which makes it possible to multiply the resources by allying with citizens in order to respond to problems the administration cannot handle alone.

In 2014, Labsus proposed a new legal instrument that recognized the possibility of active citizens to participate in the care of common goods through a new collaborative form: The Regulation on Shared Administration was born with the purpose of giving a new legal form to the relationship between administrated and administrators.

The activity of private individuals, envisaged by the Regulation, is then carried out through collaboration agreements, i.e., the individual agreements with which citizens define the scope and the methods of interventions for the care and regeneration of the urban commons, while the administration undertakes to cooperate, supporting the initiative. Volunteers are autonomous and should offer their time, skills, and dedication based on their availability. They could offer technical, financial, and space-saving interventions on public buildings and areas. Civic interventions could both improve and maintain service standards offered by the municipality, or ensure collective use of public buildings or areas that are not included in municipal maintenance programs. The intensity of collaboration could be occasional, constant, or continuous for activities related to shared management and regeneration of common properties.

These collaboration agreements can be stipulated between a municipality and citizens, individuals or in groups, as well as associations, cooperatives, and companies. A new type of administration has been proposed, which no longer considers the citizen merely as a recipient of the services provided by the administration. Citizens become active participants, placed on the same level as the administration, thus starting a project of collaboration, co-management, and sharing of choices and resources. The collaboration between the administration and citizens is founded on mutual trust, advertising, and transparency; responsibility, inclusiveness, and openness; sustainability, proportionality, and adequacy; and differentiation, informality, and civic autonomy.

Four years after the presentation of the first Regulation for shared administration of common goods, implemented first in the municipality of Bologna, the result can be considered positive as up until early 2019, 151 Italian municipalities of all sizes have adopted the Regulations.

The survey conducted in the "Labsus 2017 Report" on a sample of 113 pacts active in the first half of 2017, out of a total of 390 pacts found, shows that the Municipalities that entered into pacts are distributed throughout the country with a prevalence of central Italy, thanks mainly to the active role of the municipalities of Tuscany. In 44% of the pacts analyzed, the common goods covered by the agreement are gardens, flowerbeds, and parks, and this is evidence of widespread sensitivity to the care of public parks.

The survey also shows that more than half of the cooperation agreements have a duration not exceeding one year. This aspect, which is sometimes seen as a point of weakness, is instead the great strength: the pacts are flexible, temporary, modular tools. They live on provisional initiatives and produce changes that are not permanent. The limited duration of the agreements makes it possible to apply to the spaces that are intended to transform the destinations that a community considers more adequate over time.

Finally, experiences of active citizenship usually see associations as the main active subjects. Instead, in the experiences of collaboration agreements, single citizens are the counterpart of the municipalities in the measure of 20% of those signed. It is interesting to note that even companies stipulate partnership agreements, in the measure of 9%. These actions are not motivated by a direct or indirect economic return, but by wanting to contribute to the well-being of the community.

In addition to numerical data, sociological considerations are also worthy of note. The shared administration has as its base the social ties and the re-appropriation of the territory by citizens. The first beneficiaries of the initiative are active citizens, who can make a contribution to improve the surrounding environment, thus feeling gratified; the administrations, on the other hand, find in the citizen a new ally to realize their own institutional purpose; other citizens, seeing how active citizens carry out their activities improving the well-being of all and also creating new synergies and interpersonal relationships, are also encouraged to adhere to this type of initiative. Finally, even citizens who do not intend to carry out concrete activities benefit from improvements in the surrounding environment, which is made more usable and accessible to all.

Administrative barter

The recent global crisis increased the demand for welfare services while tax revenues decreased. Indeed, some Italian cities were able to collect less than half of the taxes due. The shift of demand toward welfare services has reduced resources available for services such as green urban areas, parks, and the maintenance of schools. Therefore, the Italian government has envisaged a possible solution. On 11 November 2014, law no. 164 article no. 24 amended the legislative decree no. 133 of "Sblocca Italia," and introduced the so-called administrative barter (*baratto amministrativo*). The first municipality that applied this instrument was the community of Invorio. After Invorio, hundreds of other municipalities have deliberated the administrative barter. The administrative barter is a new tax payment instrument that offers the option to residents in distress to pay their debts with tax authorities through community work. Citizens are not merely executors of municipality projects, but they propose their own project on urban regeneration. The administrative barter offers to municipalities the ability to accept, upon deliberation, the community work of those citizens that are unable to pay their local taxes. Community works include services such as cleaning, maintenance, beautification of green areas, roads, recovery, and reuse of common interest areas in urban and suburban areas.

The exception of the payment of local taxes due to the administrative barter may be granted only for a limited period of time. It will also depend on the type of tax that has to be paid and the activities that would be required to be done through community services. Only those residents that are not able to pay the following taxes will be able to apply for the administrative barter: Indivisible Services Tax (*Tassa sui Servizi Indivisibili – TASI*), Combined Municipal Property Tax (*Imposta Municipale Unica – IMU*), and the Waste Tax (*Tassa sui Rifiuti – TARI*). However, the selection criterion will be decided directly by the municipality based on the following requirements:

- citizen should prove their impossibility to pay taxes due to low income;
- citizens must have unpaid local taxes that have expired;
- citizens should apply for the administrative barter. Then, the application should be accepted, and citizens will be required to pay the taxes through community work.

It will be oriented toward new solutions and will help different categories of population like young people and/or pensioners who, due to the economic crisis and other factors, will be unable to pay their taxes. Moreover, priority will be given to projects submitted through civil society associations rather than individually.

This initiative was expected to deliver important social outcomes and many conferences have been organized to better understand and implement the Administrative Barter. On 15 October 2015, the first meeting on "Administrative Barter and Active Citizenship between Present and Future" was organized in the municipality of Massarosa. A second conference on "Administrative Barter and Horizontal Subsidiarity Intervention in the New Procurement Code" was held in Alseno, where more than 100 citizens participated.

Despite its positive expectations, several barriers impeded the proper implementation of administrative barter. Several local governments turned down this opportunity, as the amount of unpaid taxes was too large to give away. Others have adopted detailed regulations that enable the active participation of citizens and their associations in urban management policies. Additional obstacles were raised in the second-half of 2016 where the Court of Auditors (*Corte dei Conti*) claimed infringement of some Constitutional principles and settled strict conditions of its application. According to the Court of Auditors, the administrative barter is legitimate only if the activities are carried out by autonomous initiatives of citizens. Therefore, the tax debtors are not entitled to benefit from this administration tool. Notwithstanding, some preliminary outputs have been delivered. Citizens' participation was higher and active in small municipalities, where the proximity between the citizen and administration made it easier to implement the administrative barter. In the municipalities of Altamura, Roccasecca, and Vobarno, the first regulations on the administrative barter were approved. Meanwhile, the municipality of Massarossa granted a discount of 50% on the waste tax in exchange for road maintenance, public green space, and school assistance. In the municipality of Marcellinara, a 40% discount on the waste tax to citizens who clean and maintain green areas, playgrounds, cemeteries, and rural and outlying streets was planned (Fanin, 2017). In contrast, despite high expectations, the first results proved to be unsuccessful in medium-big cities such as Milan. The call for applications published in 2015 received only 88 applicants, obliging the municipality council to suspend this initiative. The same experience was achieved in the municipality of Leggiuno, while in the municipality of Bari only ten applications were received from which only eight were approved.

Based on the results achieved, one of the first conclusions is that simple organizational arrangements and the commitment of citizens of smaller municipalities obtained positive results because of faster communication and easier implementation, due to the proximity between the municipality and citizens. Thus, the implementation of the administrative barter cannot be considered either a success or a failure; it should consider cultural and organizational characteristics of municipalities and should not be launched as exceptional projects isolated from the municipality's context. The launch of large-scale collaboration initiatives such as administrative barter should be preceded by interventions aimed at strengthening community ties and inter-institutional collaboration, requiring resources and investments for its full potential to be realized. (Cepiku, 2017). If public policies do not acknowledge risks of collaborative arrangements, risk adverse behavior may prevent managers from adopting innovative solutions to wicked problems (Osborne & Brown, 2011). For instance, in community collaborations, there is a risk of less vocal citizens or those "willing but unable" to participate (OECD, 2011). Therefore, municipalities should put some efforts in giving voice to collaborative programs such as administrative barter.

Ad-hoc agreements between local entities and territorial associations

Many associations in Italy are organized in groups divided by neighborhoods in order to restore the original beauty of a square or a street. Part of these activities are also meetings with other citizens and merchants where the purpose of these activities is explained. Some examples of these associations include Guerrilla Gardening, Retake Movement, CleaNap, Let's Do It Movement, and Angeli Del Bello Foundation. Last May, a mass cleaning of the coasts and Sardinian beaches involving around 12,000 people from all over Europe was organized.

Currently, a new important trend is spreading in Italian regions and in particular in the region of Tuscany. Prefectures signed agreements with local authorities, other public entities, and third sector organizations to involve migrants in activities of public service in favor of the local community, setting up a fund to cover their insurance costs. Until now, more than ten municipalities have joined this initiative. The objective is to overcome the condition of inactivity of migrants during the period of permanence, which had a negative effect on the social fabric of the host country, sometimes generating attitudes of intolerance. The importance of involving them in useful activities, reactivating personal resources, creating concrete opportunities for aggregation and comparison with the local population helps prevent the risk of developing a passive behavior of benefiting from social welfare (*assistenzialismo*) and lack of confidence in the system.

The protocol agreements for voluntary activities have been promoted by the Ministry of the Interior through the circular no. 14290 of 27 November 2014 which, in the wake of the initiative experimented in Bergamo, invited the Prefects to sign agreements with local authorities to involve migrants hosted in their respective territories in voluntary activities of public utility.

The refugees and asylum seekers should take the decision to serve as a volunteer freely. The accession to the agreement involves the commitment to carry out one or more activities, individually or in groups, for the pursuit of the social, civil, and cultural aims of the organization or association to which they adhere. The activities are identified in synergy with the reference association, ensuring the necessary training; any tools, equipment, and personal protective equipment necessary to reduce any risk for one's own and others' safety; an adequate insurance coverage; and the provision of appropriate tools for the recognition of voluntary activity.

The 2017 report "Le iniziative di buona accoglienza e integrazione dei migranti in Italia. Modelli organizzativi, strumenti e azioni" of the Ministry of the Interior has considered 135 protocol agreements for voluntary activities stipulated by 53 different Prefectures, involving institutional subjects, third-sector bodies, and private social organizations (trade unions, training centers, managing bodies of the reception structures, and cultural, sporting, environmental, artistic, recreational, religious, and voluntary associations). Sometimes, voluntary activities were undertaken regardless of the signing of a specific protocol. The voluntary protocols are distributed more in the northern provinces, with peaks of 21 protocols signed in the territory of Cuneo and 17 in that of Turin.

One of the most important aspects is the people who usually benefit from voluntary activities are now activated as volunteers. This type of initiative represents for the beneficiaries a concrete opportunity for socializing, discovering the territory, and cultural exchange by promoting values such as participation, respect, and inclusion. Moreover, the contact with the community allows asylum seekers to speak Italian and improve their language skills, to be autonomous in the area, acquire specific skills, create a network of knowledge that goes beyond what is usually created in the context of host projects, and to feel recognized.

The activation of asylum seekers contributes to the implementation of various initiatives and to the achievement of the mission of the voluntary organizations in which they are involved. Finally, the active participation of asylum seekers is playing a fundamental role in raising awareness and developing a more favorable reception by the host communities. Participation and presence in varïous situations of public life can have a significant impact in changing the perception of the phenomenon.

Enti territoriali di area vasta

Local systems face different challenges inspired by the evolution of the institutional framework, which was introduced by the Delrio reform in 2014 (Law no.56/2014), and by the regional reorganization laws that, in fact, redrew boundaries and responsibilities for local governments. The Delrio law has deeply reviewed the role of provinces within the Italian system, turning them into *enti territoriali di area vasta* (inter-institutional collaboration platforms). First, it reductively redraws the provincial fundamental functions. Second, it defines metropolitan cities as authorities replacing preexisting provinces and sharing also their territorial scope. Third, the Delrio law promotes the merger of small municipalities and/or the shared exercise of their functions by their union or by an agreement among them.

Provinces have been called "intermediate bodies" for many decades. They have had the institutional mission of linking instances of municipal government with instances for regional planning. However, in spite of the introduction of reforms aimed to inspire decentralization, provinces have begun to progressively exercise more challenging functions. It is especially true by virtue of the last reform on local governance, introduced by the Delrio Law, which transformed these "intermediate bodies" into broader bodies called *enti per il governo di area vasta*. The mission regarding the territorial connection of provinces has been replaced by a more appropriate operation. It has been aimed at replacing managerial deficits, due to excessively fragmented municipalities, with a consistent action that includes the direct provision of public services to citizens at supra-municipal level (Crivello & Staricco, 2015). Consequently, the final purpose of the provincial body would be that of acting as a "hub" for a more efficient and better exercise of functions within only one wider territorial area (Pizzetti, 2014).

Four years after the Delrio reform, the reallocation process has been completed. The choice of reallocating functions seems to follow different paths in different regions. More importantly, regional laws seem to be consistently different from what has been stated in the Delrio Law. Among regions, Emilia-Romagna, through regional law no. 15/2015, has decided to create and implement a new organization, which is based on a multilevel governance model. It is characterized by sharing tasks among regions, "new provinces," the metropolitan city of Bologna, municipalities, and unions of municipalities. The reorganization of Emilia-Romagna is based on principles that establish the centrality of the region in planning and controlling. It gives the proximity government to the municipalities and their unions, and the power of governing the "vast areas" to the provinces, which also have the power of exercising functions that are normally exercised directly by the region itself.

Moreover, the regional law sets up specific coordinating tools, such as conferences and decentralized regional offices, in accordance to a model principally based on the maximum integration among the institutional levels and the valorization of inter-institutional consultation. Therefore, this model is able to create an administrative network where each level of governance – regions, provinces, municipalities, and unions of municipalities – can share part of their responsibilities on the basis of their intervention areas.

The Delrio law mainly aims to overcome the classic vision of a public system that is characterized by strong competition and weak interconnection and cooperation among bodies. Moreover, this law is really trying to accomplish and create a new model of local authorities, especially regarding the establishment and the exercise of public policies that should be based on collaboration and coordination of multilevel organizations.

However, the failure to approve the constitutional reform of 2016, which would have been the decisive step to permanently eliminate the provincial body, has led to significant problems related to the survival of the provinces: due to cuts imposed by the government, most of them are going into financial difficulties while continuing to improperly perform functions that should be transferred to municipalities, regions, and the state.

The provinces, in fact, continue to exist and represent a fundamental link in the system of Italian local autonomy, especially for the maintenance of services related to the safety and citizens' quality of life, but are subject to rules established to eliminate them. Furthermore, data released by the National Association of Italian Municipalities (ANCI) show that a total of 530 unions exists in April 2018, involving 3,097 municipalities (out of a total of 7,954 in Italy) and a population of 11,901,687. These data confirm a low propensity to the associated exercise of functions by small municipalities. The North of Italy has the highest number of unions (61.89%) with a higher concentration in the Piedmont Region (111). The problem concerns not only the intermediate level of government between municipalities and regions, but also involves the entire structure of relations that exist between the constituent bodies of the Italian Republic. For this reason, in recent times, a bill has been presented to the Senate with the purpose to restore the provinces as they were before the Delrio reform. The bill, in particular, reintroduces the direct election of president and councilors of provinces (currently voted by local administrators), giving citizens the opportunity to choose who they want to represent them, the restoration of many of the old competences, and the reintroduction of the compensations to politicians. While, in fact, the Delrio reform envisaged that the offices of president and provincial councilors were free of charge, the bill establishes a salary not higher than that of the mayor of the provincial capital for the president and fees within the limit of one-sixth of the salary of the president for the councilors. The restoration of the indemnity would be justified by the fact that the provinces, gradually emptied of funds and functions, would recover a range of competences. It can be said that the reform of Italian territorial governance is still far from finding a balance.

ReUse center in Cremona

Citizens of Cremona, a city with around 72,000 inhabitants, gather into a former market for vegetables and fruits in order to donate clothes, toys, books, and housewares in the so-called *Centro del RI-USO* on Saturday mornings. It is managed by a community group called *Amici di Emmaus*. Local government in collaboration with citizens and community implemented a local policy on waste management aiming to reuse and recycle what residents throw away. (Municipality of Cremona, 2017) It is an initiative that serves also as a European test for new ideas to promote the circular economy.

On 7 September 2007, a pilot testing project started in the neighborhoods of Boschetto and Migliaro, where orange 60-litre trash bags were distributed to families, shops, schools, and offices for the waste that cannot be recycled. The test lasted three months. There was no additional cost for citizens and there was no change to the waste tax ("Misurazione raccolta del secco", 2017 [Measurement of solid waste collection]).

The experimentation aimed to prevent and reduce the quantity of non-recyclable waste. Another important objective was to create a measuring system for non-recyclable waste to be able to identify future actions. This initiative planned to implement the so-called "punctual tariff" that was to be paid on what is actually produced, rewarding virtuous citizens.

Cremona led a three-year larger European project on waste-management strategies called *Urban Wins*, financed by the European Commission. This project was launched in July 2016 and is analyzing current strategies for waste prevention and management in 24 European cities aiming to highlight innovative plans.

Since 2014, an annual competition called *Piccoli Passi* is hosted every year by the city of Cremona. It aims to foster sustainable behavior among students and administrators. The schools are ranked and children that do best get rewards. Another part of the school's competition focuses on reducing food waste in canteens. Finally, *Tenga il resto* is another initiative of the city of Cremona where 100,000 recyclable containers were distributed to 20 restaurants' patrons trying to convince them to bring leftovers home, as a responsible behavior for the environment.

As a result of these collaborative initiatives, Cremona has increased the percentage of recycled waste collected from 53% to 72%. Furthermore, this project tends to improve understanding on what gets produced, consumed, and discarded. The outcome is not only that communities can deal with waste more efficiently but they can also prevent waste from being created in the first place. In addition, attitudes are changed through trainings for children and families on how to reduce the amount of materials they consume. In order for this initiative to be successful, a multidisciplinary and systematic approach is needed. Furthermore, to improve the quality of life a well-educated community is needed.

Conclusion

Italy faces a battle with structural weaknesses, policy-defining challenges from a rising of populist political forces, and continued EU pressure. Scarce resources, low levels of sustainability, ageing, immigration, and unemployment call for new solutions. In this process, several examples highlighted citizens and community engagement. Citizens, and community more in general, are considered as key players where the public sector struggles to deliver efficient and high-quality public services.

In this chapter, five Italian cases of collaborative governance have been analyzed with several implications. Shared administration gave the possibility to active citizens to participate in the care of common goods through new collaborative forms that were regulated by law in 2014. Its purpose was to give a new legal form to the relationship between citizens and administrators through flexible collaboration agreements. Four years after its first implementation, it can be considered a successful co-production initiative as until now 151 Italian municipalities of all sizes have adopted the regulations. Moreover, in times of fear and uncertainty, the involvement of immigrants, but not only them, in volunteering initiatives has been successfully implemented in various municipalities across Italy. Ad-hoc agreements between local entities, territorial associations, and citizens have been organized in groups, divided by neighborhoods, in order to restore the original beauty of a square or a street. ReUse Center in Cremona is another excellent example of co-production where different actors from the public sector and community get involved in activities aiming to change attitudes through training and education in order to improve the quality of life.

Although specific policy issues can be fairly solved through collaboration, collaborative governance could fail, just as market and hierarchy as collaboration arrangements are complex and difficult to manage. New types of administration have been proposed, which no longer considers the citizen merely as a recipient of the services provided by the administration. However, the collaboration between the public sector and citizens requires strong links of communication and advertising, and it should be established on mutual trust and transparency. It should promote responsibility, inclusiveness, openness, sustainability, proportionality, adequacy, differentiation, informality, and civic autonomy. The success or failure of collaborative governance can be attributed to various factors such as the nature of the problem, organizational arrangements, power, the fear of public sector in losing autonomy, commitment and costs, lack of incentives and rewards, different perspectives and varied commitment to common goals, and cultural clash. Depending on the territory, it is possible to find different tools to support initiatives, such as guidelines, regulations, and protocol agreements. These tools demonstrate the administration's commitment to the realization of a collaborative governance model. However, sometimes the administration imposes restrictions on the voluntary initiatives of citizens through strict municipal regulations. A regulation approved by the Municipality of Rome in 2017, for example, requires that citizens who want to provide their work for the occasional maintenance of public parks must submit regular applications and sign an insurance policy. This type of rule, in addition to increasing insurance costs, imposes a bureaucratic process that limits the spontaneous initiative of citizens.

Among our examples, two cases of collaborative governance have been identified that require additional efforts in order to be considered successful; those are administrative barter and *enti territoriali di area vasta* (inter-institutional collaboration platforms). Although administrative bartering was an initiative that had good intentions, it did not always lead to success. Lack of communication between municipalities and their citizens, and failure to consider legislative, cultural, and organizational characteristics of municipalities may have increased the risk of this strategic initiative to fail in large municipalities. Meanwhile, *enti territoriali di area vasta* – a form of inter-institutional collaboration – is an example of networks among metropolitan cities and municipalities that share roles and functions previously held by provinces. However, despite the fact that the law to abolish provinces was approved by the Italian Parliament in April 2014, provinces still exist and represent a fundamental link in the system of Italian local autonomy. Nevertheless, they are subject to rules and laws established to eliminate them. Consider also the difficulties in implementing the unions of municipalities: in a country characterized by the fragmentation of the municipalities, there is the need to have a disjointed and dislocated public administration on the territory, helping the territories themselves to focus on the optimal minimum size to carry out functions.

The launch of large-scale collaboration initiatives, such as administrative barter and/or *enti territoriali di area vasta*, should be preceded by interventions aimed at strengthening community ties and inter-institutional collaboration that require resources and investments for their full potential to be realized. These arrangements should not be launched as exceptional projects isolated from the municipality's context. They should acknowledge risks of collaborative arrangements, in order to avoid manager's risk adverse behavior from adopting innovative solutions to wicked problems.

In this context it is interesting to note how the role of public institutions has changed, which implies a transition from verticalization and bureaucracy to sharing and collaboration. The administration does not elaborate and put into practice responses to complex problems in solitude. It acts as an interlocutor that allows collaboration between the key actors in collaborative governance: citizens, nonprofit organizations, businesses, and public institutions. Nevertheless, it can do more: it should accelerate the spread of positive impacts for the communities and foster initiatives and processes that generate collective responses to the needs of the community itself. As did the region of Tuscany, which has developed a path with the aim of planning a regional policy on the economy of sharing and collaboration.

The initiatives, however, must always support, and never replace, the action of the public government. There is therefore a need for public institutions to equip themselves with the most appropriate tools to successfully tackle this process of change, both cultural and organizational.

References

Alford, J. (2017). Citizen co-production of public services. Meanings, processes, antecedents and consequences. In T. Klassen, D. Cepiku, & T. J. Lah (Eds.), *The Routledge handbook of global public policy and administration*. London, UK: Routledge.

Alford, J., & Hughes, O. (2008). Public value pragmatism as the next phase of public management. *The American Review of Public Administration*, 38(2), 130–148.

Altshuler, A. (1992). *Breaking through bureaucracy*. Berkeley, CA: University of California Press.

Bardach, E. (2000). *A practical guide for policy analysis: The eightfold path to more effective problem solving*. New York, NY: Chatham House Publishers/Seven Bridges Press.

Bardach, E. (2003). Creating Compendia of 'Best Practice'. *Journal of Policy Analysis and Management*, 22(4), 661–665.

Bovaird, T. (2007). Beyond engagement and participation: User and community coproduction of public services. *Public Administration Review*, 67(5), 846–860.

Bretschneider, B., Choi, Y., Nabatchi, T., & O'Leary, R. (2012). *Does public value matter for collaboration? Evidence from an experimental analysis*. Paper presented at the Creating Public Value Conference, University of Minnesota, Minneapolis, September 20–22, 2012.

Bretschneider, S., Marc-Aurele, F. J., & Wu, J. (2004). 'Best practices' research: A methodological guide for the perplexed. *Journal of Public Administration Research and Theory*, 15(2), 307–323.

Cepiku, D. (2017). Collaborative governance. In T. Klassen, D. Cepiku, & T. J. Lah (Eds.), *The Routledge handbook of global public policy and administration* (pp. 141–156). London, UK: Routledge.

Cepiku, D., & Giordano, F. (2014). Co-production in developing countries: Insights from the community health workers experience. *Public Management Review*, 16(3), 317–340.

Cepiku, D., & Meneguzzo, M. (2007). Public administration and management reform in Italy: Domestic patterns and influences from abroad. In Hill, H. (Eds.), *Current trends in public sector modernization*. Baden & Baden: German University of Administrative Sciences, Speyer.

Cepiku, D., & Meneguzzo, M. (2011). Public administration reform in Italy: A shopping-basket approach to the new public management or the new Weberianism? *International Journal of Public Administration*, 34(1–2), 19–25.

Cepiku, D., Mussari, R., & Giordano, F. (2016). Local governments managing austerity: Approaches, determinants and impact. *Public Administration*, 94(1), 223–243.

Collaborative Democracy Network. (2006). A call to scholars and teachers of public administration, public policy, planning, political science, and related fields. *Public Administration Review*, 66(s1), 168–170.

Municipality of Cremona, Misurazione raccolta del secco. (2017, August 29). [Measurement of collection of solid waste]. Retrieved from www.comune.cremona.it/node/473712

Crivello, S., & Staricco, L. (2015, May 23). La sfida metropolitana 2015 – Sedicesimo Rapporto Giorgio Rota, [The metropolitan challenge – Sixteenth Giorgio Rota Report], Turin.

De Belvis, A. G., Ferrè, F., Specchia, M. L., Valerio, L., Fattore, G., & Ricciardi, W. (2012). The financial crisis in Italy: Implications for the healthcare sector. *Health Policy*, 106(1), 10–16.

Di Mascio, F., & Natalini, A. (2015). Fiscal retrenchment in southern Europe: Changing patterns of public management in Greece, Italy, Portugal and Spain. *Public Management Review*, 17(1), 129–148.

Di Quirico, R. (2010). Italy and the global economic crisis. *Bulletin of Italian Politics*, 2(2), 3–19.

Fanin, A. (2017, July 15). Il baratto amministrativo non decolla. [The administrative barter does not take off]. *Economia Italiana*. Retrieved from www.economiaitaliana.it/it/articolo.php/Il-baratto-amministrativo-nondecolla?LT=PRIMA&ID=26512&ARCHIVIO=1

General Accounting Office. (1990). *Program evaluation and methodology division: Case study evaluations*. Washington, DC: GAO.

Gibbs, G. (2007). *Analyzing qualitative data*. Thousand Oaks, CA: Sage Publications.

Huxham, C. (1996). *Creating collaborative advantage*. Thousand Oaks, CA: Sage Publications.

Lagravinese, R. (2015). Economic crisis and rising gaps North–South: Evidence from the Italian regions. *Cambridge Journal of Regions, Economy, and Society*, 8(2), 331–342.

Myers, S. M., Smith, H. P., & Martin, L. L. (2006). Conducting best practices research in public affairs. *International Journal of Public Policy*, 1(4), 367–378.

Organization for Economic Cooperation and Development. (2011). *Together for better public services: Partnering with citizens and civil society*. Paris, France: OECD.

Organization for Economic Cooperation and Development. (2017). *Trust and public policy: How better governance can help rebuild public trust*. Paris, France: OECD.

Osborne, S. P., & Brown, L. (2011). Innovation, public policy and public services delivery in the UK. The word that would be king? *Public Administration*, 89(4), 1335–1350.

Overman, E. S., & Boyd, K. J. (1994). Best practice research and postbureaucratic reform. *Journal of Public Administration Research and Theory*, 4(1), 67–84.

Patton, M. Q. (2015, January 23). *Impact evaluation: Best practices aren't (MQP rumination #4)*. Retrieved from www.betterevaluation.org/en/blog/best_practices_arent

Patton, M. Q. (1990). *Qualitative evaluation and research methods* (2nd ed.). Newbury Park, CA: Sage Publications.

Pizzetti, F. (2014). La complessa architettura della l. n. 56 e i problemi relativi alla sua prima attuazione: Differenze e somiglianze tra città metropolitane e province, [The complex architecture of the law no. 56 and the problems related to its first implementation: Differences and similarities between metropolitan cities and provinces], Astrid, 11/2014, n. 204.

Conclusion

Coming full circle

Rick S. Kurtz

The prior chapters provide a rich mosaic of the many ways local and regional governments across the globe are tackling the challenges of economic development and community wellness. Examples like the Flint water crisis and Italy's economic meltdown illustrate just how impactful catastrophic failure can be upon a citizenry. Just as impactful are the examples of struggle and decades-long decline experienced in Windsor, Detroit, and the former East Germany (GDR). Within these chapters are also a number of examples of innovation and adaptation, ranging from social impact bonds, to South Korea's model of economic collaboration, to India's informal collaborative networks.

Old school economic development

In thinking further about these chapters, it is worthwhile to revisit where we have been, where we are now, and where we are going. Let's begin with the predecessors to Emerson and Nabatchi's (2015; Emerson, Nabatchi, & Balogh, 2012) integrative framework of collaborative governance. Certainly, for much of the past 100 years, we find many localities, and regional governments, functioned as an island unto themselves (Lee, Feiock, & Lee, 2012). Economic development for example, within the United States (U.S.), was predominantly defined through smokestack chasing. Namely, the assembling of significant financial incentive packages to lure a corporation to one's locality. Typical incentives involved basic infrastructure improvements to include street improvements, sewer, and water. Many of these took the form of government financed industrial parks and economic development zones (Turner, 2003). Typical sweeteners included tax reductions and workforce training. While industry was the traditional target, sports venues, convention centers, shopping outlet malls, and big box stores also received their fair share of economic love from local and regional governments (Bratton et al., 2018).

By the end of the 20th century, localities and regional governments were reconsidering the benefits received from their economic investments. Often times the return on investment, jobs, and boosts to the local economy simply did not materialize as hoped. News media coverage over the past 30 years is replete with examples of companies that took advantage of incentive packages and then pulled up stakes once the incentives were exhausted (Charles, 2019). New economic development models were needed. Local and regional governments had learned their lesson.[1]

The collaborative development alternative

So, why economic development collaboration? What beyond the frustration with smokestack chasing has made this the alternative method of choice for many local governments and regions on a global scale? The answer may partially be found in the roots of collaboration. One alternative to smokestack chasing is thinking and acting locally. This is sometimes called "second wave economic development" (Green-Leigh & Blakely, 2016). The second wave mandate was premised upon local governments, chambers of commerce, financial institutions, and universities partnering to develop their indigenous potential. Collaborating to incubate the economic power of local potential and entrepreneurship in their own backyard was the strategy. For example, local governments in western states partnered to move beyond their exhausted resources exploitation legacy. Outdoor recreation venues – snow sports, mountain biking, hiking, and camping –were developed, turning the likes of Vail and Aspen, Colorado into four season recreational destinations (Kurtz, 2006, 2010).

In another twist, the impetus for economic development change by the 1980s was cast through another driver of change. Namely, through the frustration an increasing number of citizens felt with the quality of government service they were receiving. Much like the 1984 Wendy's fast food advertisement, citizens wanted to know, "Where's the beef?" In political terms, this was a frustration perhaps best summed up through the pithy refrain of a U.S. President casting government as the problem, not the solution. Reagan's so-called most terrifying nine words in the English language, "I'm from the government and I'm here to help," resonated with many Americans in 1986 (AZ Quotes, n.d.). He put into words the frustration citizens were feeling post-1970s stagflation, OPEC oil embargo, jobs loss America. Nor was this frustration limited to the U.S. For example, in the United Kingdom, Margaret Thatcher was elected on a similar mandate of government no longer doing business as usual.

From this frustration emerged a number of possible solutions. The solution that resonated loudest with local and regional governments was collaborative partnerships. New public management (NPM), as it was known in the United Kingdom, Europe, New Zealand, and Australia, embraced this approach. A companion movement in the U.S. was typically referred to as "reinventing government," which was popularized by the 1993 Osborne and Gaebler publication *Reinventing Government*. This emerging movement challenged government to be more entrepreneurial, to discover new ways of achieving greater efficiency and providing improved service to citizens. By the late 1990s, local and regional governments were increasingly entering into cooperative agreements, joint arrangements with other units of government in citizen service delivery. These collaborative arrangements extended beyond the singular goal of greater efficiency. They were a recognition that no single institution had the resources or capacity to accomplish the many tasks of government, whether service delivery or facilitating robust economic development (Alford & Owens, 2008).

Reflecting on these trends, Agranoff and McGuire (2003) noted that regional and local governments were now working in a world of collaborative networks. These collaborative networks involved both vertical and horizontal partnerships. Many linked together through interdependence in formulation and implementation of service delivery. Typical of many of these collaborations was significant autonomy from top-down officialdom and red tape, instead relying upon outcomes defined and trust-based interactions as the pathway to goal achievement (Rhodes, 1997; Klijn, 2005). And while many of these partnerships were government-to-government, and public-public, a growing number were public-private collaborations.

Elaborating upon this in 2000, Savas declared that local and regional government processes had undergone a tectonic shift that was premised upon a broadening reliance on private institution partners, not government alone, to satisfy societal needs. Savas (2000, p. 4) defined this shift as public-private partnerships, commonly referred to now days as P3s. These partnerships were arrangements in which government provided activities are shifted to the private sector. This is what Osborne and Gaebler (1993), and others, referred to as the process of government doing more steering and less rowing. This entails relying upon government agency personnel, acting on behalf of elected officials, to set the goals and outcomes. Private partners, with their greater capacity and scales of efficiency, delivered the service. In practice, a number of collaborative economic development variations have emerged. Take for example, the Michigan Economic Development Corporation (MEDC). Established through state legislation, this independent government corporation works with some 100 business and government partners to facilitate economic development in communities across the state. The MEDC controls a strategic fund, providing it with monies to tactically leverage as grants and loans. The organization serves as a clearinghouse for collaborative networking, as well as providing much needed expertise.

Back to the future

When considering late 20th-century local economic development, we can certainly see threads of smokestack chasing and NPM in our case study chapters. Detroit and Windsor were the epitome of "company towns." For most of the 20th and early 21st century, their economic fortunes rose and fell with the Detroit three automakers. For these cities, romancing the smokestack was the seemingly one path to economic prosperity. However, as our first two chapters demonstrate, this strategy came at a significant cost. Relying upon the drug of automobile manufacturing largesse was a difficult habit to break. Urban blight, political corruption, out-migration, and economic decay – as well as serving as the punchline of many late-night talk show jokes – became the Detroit-Windsor legacy. Relying upon collaborative economic partnerships to somehow remedy in a timely manner – defined as a term of office until the next round of elections for some politicians – all of these economic and societal ills is asking for a lot. In spite of these seemingly insurmountable odds, our authors do call out some admirable wins. The Detroit DIA unfolding provides an example of a win-win public-private collaboration. A win for the culture and arts that many proponents say is vital to Detroit's renaissance. In similar fashion, Windsor can claim some incremental wins. From entertainment, to education, to regional health care, the city has been partnering on a regional basis to take positive steps in revitalizing the local economy.

In calling out the successes of culture, entertainment, and health care, our authors have hit upon the postulations of Richard Florida (2014). Writing about the creative class and cool cities – an often-repeated reference of former Michigan Governor Jennifer Granholm – Florida notes that the vitality of a city or region is dependent upon their ability to make themselves hospitable for members of the creative class. The creative class – for those of us over the age of 50 – is loosely defined as the late stage generation-x, millennials, and rising generation-z. Unlike their baby boomer and greatest generation elders, the creative class demands a society that is more than just a job and a house in the suburbs (Newport, 2018). These creatives want communities that are culturally stimulating. Walkable, urban cool spaces, with amenities and venues ranging from coffee shops to artisan galleries and engaging museums, to black box theaters, to dog parks. Places to easily meet, interact, and socialize with other creatives.

With this said, the question must be asked, of what value are all these creatives? What do they and their cool cities do to benefit local and regional economic development? Florida – supported through extensive and ongoing polling (Newport, 2018) – compares creatives to magnates. Creatives choose place first, and job second. They exude a confidence in their ability to find or create self-employment in their chosen cool city. Florida credits the raw collection of creative power that a concentration of creatives bring to a place. From this emerges startup enterprises invigorating the economy. Ready examples abound. Business college MBA case studies are replete with stories about how Amazon, Microsoft, Apple, and Starbucks grew from small startups into the corporate giants they are today. Their founders, nested in locales full of smart creatives, had access to a talent pool readily available to grow their businesses.

There is of course, another positive dimension to the economic synergy equation. Locales with a concentration of creatives in turn lure corporations to establish operations in the region. Consider Canadian cities like Ottawa, Toronto, and Montreal (Florida, 2014). Magnates for creatives, these cities have, in turn, become vibrant economic hubs, drawing companies to nest where the workforce they need resides. In Michigan, the MEDC (2019) is working to crack this economic development nut – this choice of place. Economic development capacity of places like Grand Rapids and Traverse City are collaborating in super-charging the cool city.

Why is this so important? A 2018 Gallup survey provides robust evidence of the pervasiveness of this lifestyle fondness. Survey data presents evidence of the overwhelming preference the creatives have for urban living. Interesting is recent survey evidence of a desire among older adults to live in, or close proximity of, large- and mid-sized cool cities. It is possible within this context that we should further consider the success of Leipzig and Dresden, in Chapter 7. Our author provides a comprehensive discussion of both the downfall and phoenix-like renaissance of these cities. The immediate years of the post-Soviet bloc collapse were not kind to East Germany. Rampant industrial decline, cold war era substandard housing and infrastructure, coupled with environmental degradation, were widespread. The resulting massive out-migration is not surprising. To place a bet in the early 1990s that Leipzig and Dresden would emerge as the robust cool cities and economic hubs they are today had all the trappings of a sucker's bet.

Today Leipzig and Dresden, just as with places like Seattle and Portland, are being overwhelmed with creative class love. The challenge for many local and regional governments – as with the MEDC through their collaborative efforts – is finding the right mix. A mix that will lure in a sufficient core of creatives to launch a new generation of cool cities. Already within the U.S. we see the emergence of this next generation of cool cities. Places like Indianapolis, Columbus, Nashville, Boise, and Denver. Certainly, in our author's case study of Leipzig and Dresden, we find some of the necessary pieces to the puzzle: collaborative partnerships, some P3s, a focus upon infrastructure, and social renewal. Renewal that also has meant, at least for a period of time, rebuilding upon a smaller more sustainable urban footprint. This is much like we see taking place through collaboration in the Flint metro area. Renewal that in Germany saw government at the federal level assume a role of facilitator, not top-down authoritarian.

This last point is important. From Osborne and Gaebler (1993) to Florida (2014), to the pages of *Governing* magazine (Charles, 2019), a frequently cited refrain is for national level government to get out of the way. Yes, to help as facilitator providing seed monies, but not as order-giver. If we are looking for parallel lessons from our chapters, we need look no further than the case studies from South Korea and Italy in Chapters 5 and 6, respectively. In the South Korea case study, we find a central government that does in fact play an active role in regional economic development collaboration. This role, however, is what might be referred to as top-down light. The central government has led in setting up a model for the creation of seven regional collaborative economic development clusters. The central government also provides financial incentives in the form of financial grants. Grant funding that has stated goals and outcomes. Primary goals being the encouragement of local and regional collaboration, and avoidance of the cutthroat competition typical of smokestack chasing. Beyond these types of stated outcomes and basic parameters, regional and local governments in collaboration with private partners have wide discretion. Success, according to our authors, has been overall positive. Contrast this with case of Italy. The post 2007–08 Great Recession years for Italy were particularly challenging. Repeated waves of financial crises – high unemployment, a dwindling tax base, and high public debt – on a national level hit the nation. Decision-makers were desperate to implement any possible remedies. Unfortunately, the solutions were a series of top-down highly prescriptive rule-bound mandates from the national government. Mandates that allowed limited flexibility in implementation at the local level. Mandates that often did not meet local needs or alternatively were challenged in court. The results were, at best, mixed.

The path forward

So, then what is the role for central governments in local and regional economic development? The literature on NPM and likewise on reinventing the corporation does identify a role for central leadership. This role comes with some caveats. Central leadership's primary task is to set outcomes. Clearly defined goals with measurable benchmarks are required. Also, there is a necessary role for leadership to provide some measure of financial support. Block grants offering significant flexibility, rather than less flexible categorical grants, are a good choice. Too many national politicians have espoused the mantra of decentralization and devolution of decision-making to regions and localities without providing any appropriate measure of financial support. This is typically not a recipe for success. What has shown success and is of relevance to local and regional economic development is the adoption of a tight-loose organizational model (Peters and Waterman, 1982, pp. 318–325). Much as we see in the economic development model utilized in South Korea, central leadership does and should have the authority to establish a set of clearly defined outcomes, coupled with a basic set of "though shall not" parameters. Basically, these are bumper stops that serve as both guideposts and measurable performance benchmarks. Within these basic parameters local and regional governments, in collaboration with their private sector partners, have the latitude to explore and adopt the best practices for their needs (Crichton et al., 2005).

However, exploring and adopting a new approach to economic development often means taking a sequence of steps risk-adverse governments have traditionally been reluctant to employ. Because with economic development exploration comes the possibility of failure, which in turn brings the wrath of an irate citizenry. Recall again from the 1980s. In the face of such risks, what are local governments to do? Three possible solutions being employed today are worthy of consideration. First among these are lessons from our chapter on informal collaborative networks in India. While we often think of smart creatives as techies clustered in the likes of Silicon Valley, or New York City's hip artisan districts, variations on the creative class are abundant on a global scale (Florida, 2014). The goal for local governments is devising means to encourage creatives entrepreneurial power in solving societal problems without relinquishing appropriate authority.

As our Indian case study in Chapter 4 readily acknowledges, informal collaborations can be chaotic and messy. However, when freed from stifling bureaucratic red tape, these networks also have the capacity to release entrepreneurial experimentation. Experimentation that often has a low-cost, low-risk threshold for government in resolving societal problems. In the case of India, our author identifies the successful role informal ride services play in relieving transportation bottlenecks in the official government licensed system. Similarly, we only need to look to the rise of Uber, Lyft, and Airbnb to see enormously successful examples of the private sector solving economic gaps in formal government regulated transportation and lodging sectors. The challenge and ultimate success, of course, is dependent upon local and regional governments' ability to legitimize these successful economic engines of entrepreneurship without smothering them through politically driven red tape and regulation.

Beyond this, Chapter 3's focus on social impact bonds (SIBs) illustrates another viable option for governments to enter into low-risk, low-cost collaborations. Local governments, as mandated, have the responsibility to identify and define societal problems. The challenge is often arriving at a low-risk, reasonable cost, effective solution. Financial issuers of SIBs bring a number of advantages to the process, not the least of which is funding that otherwise may not be available. They bring the 21st-century tools of data analytics, design thinking, and artificial intelligence to the problem (Dhasarathy, Jain, & Khan, 2019), tools that most local and regional governments lack and simply cannot afford. Likewise, SIB underwriters bring a profit-driven mindset. A mindset that gauges a problem and solutions in terms of return-on-investment (ROI). The incentive of maximizing ROI provides assurances of high quality in the due diligence SIBs issuers bring to the partnership. It is also possible for local and regional governments to move a step beyond SIBs entering into P3s. P3s – as Representative Kildee calls out in the Foreword to this book – are becoming increasingly popular as a mechanism for meeting economic goals while also addressing infrastructure needs. Local and regional governments have entered into P3s in the management of public parking garages, community centers, and sports venues (Rocca, 2017). More ambitious collaborations have included major infrastructure projects to include highway road construction and maintenance. Many of these agreements are premised upon private sector partners bearing the cost of construction, maintenance, and administration in exchange for the ability to capture a portion of the resulting revenue stream. For example, public parking and toll road fees. Colorado's E-470 toll road is an often-cited example of success.

SIBs and P3s are certainly not viewed as an economic collaboration panacea. Critics say examples of failure are readily evident. Indiana toll roads and Chicago public parking enterprises are often the targets of P3 social media rage. So much that in some localities there is significant resistance to the utilization of P3s. Does this mean there are no alternative 21st-century innovations that allow local and regional governments to be entrepreneurial? Certainly not. Our chapter authors have provided a number of examples of merit. Additionally, there is one other private sector model worthy of utilization. Namely, lean startup – failing fast. On first blush, failing fast does not read like a model local and regional governments want to have in their economic development collaborative arsenal. It smacks of unwarranted risk and citizen backlash. However, some context is necessary.

First, while the 21st-century model of failing fast comes from the writings of cutting-edge business gurus (Ries, 2011, 2017), there is a parallel local government legacy. Writing in the 20th century, Charles Lindblom (1959, 1979) spoke of the values of incrementalism in policy implementation. Lindblom noted the uncertainties of multiple means to oftentimes not well-defined problems and shifting politically driven goals. Incrementalism allowed for taking small implementation steps, experimenting in the knowledge that the path being taken may lead to a dead end. Small steps, however, meant small investment, limited risk and cost, as well as the ability to easily back away from failed experiments. Contrast this with the Pressman and Wildavsky iconic case study (1973) about the implementation of the 20th-century economic development boondoggle in Oakland, California. This classic, still widely read today, provides a cautionary case study on big economic development projects gone wildly awry.

Is incrementalism in today's fast changing 21st-century social media driven world a feasible alternative? This is where lean startup – fail fast business methods have potential merit. Best epitomized perhaps through the *New York Times* bestselling author Eric Ries' books *The Lean Startup*, and *The Startup Way* (2011, 2017). Lean startup invokes a method that has become commonplace in Silicon Valley and other technology driven startup hubs across the globe. The model is founded on the premise of building a minimally viable product, engaging in customer-focused and scientific- data analytics-testing, and then deciding whether to pivot or persevere. While it may be easy to imagine how such a method will work for a small tech startup firm, grasping its implications for local and regional government economic development may be more challenging. Think of it as incrementalism with a 21st-century twist. Writing in 2018, researchers at McKinsey and Company recommend starting small. Pick a singular project or geographic locale to prototype and test a minimally viable product. In this case, pick an economic development prototype having potentially broader collaboration power.

Drawing on some five years of extensive partnering and consulting with the corporate sector, non-government organizations (NGOs) and units of government, Ries touts the startup way methods as a practitioner proven method. A new "civic religion" for governments and NGOs to effectively navigate the uncertainties of the 21st century. This exuberance does come with a caveat. Both Ries and McKinsey & Company researchers (Corydon, Ganesan, & Lundqvist, 2016) stress the importance of scaling up, being sufficiently bold and confident in the prototyping methodology to persevere and expand the model. Such failure to implement to scale has been identified as a repeated mistake, a missed opportunity whether business or government, to reach intended goals.

Concluding thoughts

Clearly there are many opportunities to experiment and discover best practices and opportunities in local and regional government collaborative economic development. The chapters in this book set out to explain and advance our understanding of successful collaborative networks. The contributing authors have provided us with a robust set of case studies, contributing to further advancing the conceptual framework of Emerson and Nabatchi (2015). Through these chapters, we have discovered a variety of the ways in which these collaborative partnerships emerge, what makes them work when effective, and whether they are indeed achieving the intended outcomes. In assessing the performance of these collaborative regimes, we have assembled an array of evidence both positive and negative. Alone, this handful of case studies is not sufficient to make any definitive claims about what collaborative arrangements work best. What can be said, however, is that these case studies make a rich contribution to the baseline of knowledge whereby we are able to further fill in the applied and theoretical gaps Emerson and Nabatchi identify in their conceptual framework.

For those of us who are of a practitioner mindset, in need of collaborative prototypes we can turn to in the here-and-now, these case studies provide immediate opportunity. The opportunity to learn lessons from fellow practitioners. The opportunity to hold up a mirror to the collaborative economic development ventures we are contemplating. To match and align our circumstances, resources, and valued partnerships to reach intended outcomes. As Representative Kildee notes in the Foreword to this book, we have the opportunity and the need for a much more thoughtful, intentional, and holistic approach to revitalization. Solutions will be multifaceted and will only succeed through collaboration across governments, nonprofits, and private sector partnerships. Now is the time for action.

Note

1 Well, perhaps not completely. Smokestack chasing has not become extinct in the 21st century. The recent Amazon second headquarter site bidding war, or carnival as some have described it, Apple partner Foxcom's choice to set up shop in Wisconsin, and Boeing's decision to establish its corporate headquarters in Chicago were all the result of intensive smokestack chasing. Still, these examples appear to be more of the exception rather business as usual in the 21st century.

References

Agranoff, R., & McGuire, M. (2003). *Collaborative public management: New strategies for local governments*. Washington, DC: Georgetown University Press.

Alford, J., & Owens, H. (2008). Public value pragmatism as the next phase of public management. *The American Review of Public Administration*, 38, 130–148.

AZ Quotes. (n.d.). Retrieved from www.azquotes.com/quote/606434

Bratton, W. J., Eide, S., Goldsmith, S., Hendrix, M., Husock, H., Miller, J., . . . Salins, D. (2018). *Urban policy 2018*. New York, NY: The Manhattan Institute.

Charles, B. (2019). In the zone. *Governing the States and Localities*, 43–48.

Corydon, B., Ganesan, V., & Lundqvist, M. (2016). *Transforming government through digitization*. McKinsey & Company. Retrieved from www.mckinsey.com/industries/public-sector/our-insights/transforming-government-through-digitization

Crichton, M. T., Lauche, K., & Flin, R. (2005). Incident command skills in the management of an oil industry drilling incident: A case study. *Journal of Contingencies and Crisis Management*, 13(3), 116–128.

Dhasarathy, A., Jain, S., & Khan, N. (2019). *When government turns to AI: Algorithms, trade-offs, and trust*. McKinsey & Company. Retrieved from www.mckinsey.com/industries/public-sector/our-insights/when-governments-turn-to-ai-algorithms-trade-offs-and-trust

Emerson, K., & Nabatchi, T. (2015). *Collaborative governance regimes*. Washington, DC: Georgetown University Press.

Emerson, K., Nabatchi, T., & Balogh, S. (2012). An integrative framework for collaborative governance. *Journal of Public Administration Research and Theory*, 22(1), 1–29.

Florida, R. (2014). *The rise of the creative class revisited: Revised and expanded*. New York, NY: Basic Books.

Green-Leigh, N., & Blakely, E. (2016). *Planning local economic development: Theory and practice*. Los Angeles, CA: Sage.

Klijn, E. (2005). Networks and inter-organizational management: Challenging, steering, evaluation and the role of public actors in public management. In E. Ferlie, L. Lynn, & C. Pollitt (Eds.), *The Oxford handbook of public management* (pp. 257–281). Oxford: Oxford University Press.

Kurtz, R. S. (2006). The federal concessioner system: Linking policy to opportunities for local service providers. *Review of Policy Research*, 23(2), 373–386.

Kurtz, R. S. (2010). Public lands policy and economic trends in gateway communities. *Review of Policy Research*, 27(1), 77–88.

Lee, I. W., Feiock, R. C., & Lee, Y. (2012). Competitors and cooperators: A micro-level analysis of regional economic development collaboration networks. *Public Administration Review*, 72(2), 253–262.

Lindblom, C. E. (1959). The science of muddling through. *Public Administration Review*, 19(2), 79–88.

Lindblom, C. E. (1979). Still muddling, not yet through. *Public Administration Review*, 39, 517–526.

Michigan Economic Development Corporation. (2019). Retrieved from www.miplace.org/

Newport, F. (2018). Americans big on idea of living in the country. *Gallup*. Retrieved from https://news.gallup.com/poll/245249/americans-big-idea-living-country.aspx

Osborne, D., & Gaebler, T. (1993). *Reinventing government: How the entrepreneurial spirit is transforming the public sector*. New York, NY: Plume.

Peters, T., & Waterman, R. (1982). Simultaneous loose-tight properties. In T. Peters, & R. Waterman (Eds.), *In search of excellence: Lessons from America's best-run companies* (pp. 318–325). New York, NY: Harper & Row.

Pressman, L., & Wildavsky, A. (1973). *Implementation: How great expectations in Washington are dashed in Oakland*. Berkeley, CA: University of California Press.

Rhodes, R. A. (1997). From marketization to diplomacy: It's the mix that matters. *Australian Journal of Public Administration*, 56(2), 40–53.

Ries, E. (2011). *The lean startup: How today's entrepreneurs use continuous innovation to create radically successful businesses*. New York, NY: Penguin Random House.

Ries, E. (2017). *The startup way: How modern companies use entrepreneurial management to transform culture & drive long-term growth*. New York, NY: Penguin Random House.

Rocca, M. (2017). *The rising advantage of public-private partnerships*. McKinsey & Company. Retrieved from www.mckinsey.com/industries/capital-projects-and-infrastructure/our-insights/the-rising-advantage-of-public-private-partnerships

Savas, E. (2000). *Privatization and public partnerships*. New York, NY: Chatham House Publishers.

Turner, R. C. (2003). The political economy of gubernatorial smokestack chasing: Bad policy and bad politics? *State Politics & Policy Quarterly*, 3(3), 270–293.

Editor biographies

Denita Cepiku is an Associate Professor in Public Management at the University of Rome "Tor Vergata," where she teaches Business Administration and Global Public Management and serves as the coordinator of the PhD program track in Public Management and Governance. Her main research interests are in the areas of collaborative governance (network management and co-production), cutback management, and strategic performance management. Her publications have appeared in numerous academic journals and, most recently, she edited the *Routledge Handbook of Global Public Policy and Administration* in 2017. She has been board member of the International Research Society for Public Management (IRSPM) and is chair of the European Academy of Management (EURAM) Strategic Interest Group on Public Management.

So Hee Jeon is an Associate Professor and the undergraduate director of the Public and Nonprofit Administration program in the Department of Political Science and Public Administration at Central Michigan University. Her research focuses on public and nonprofit management with an emphasis on human resource management, administrative ethics, and interorganizational networks. Dr. Jeon's work has been published in various academic journals, including *Review of Public Personnel Administration*, *Public Performance & Management Review*, *Public Personnel Management*, and *International Review of Public Administration*.

David K. Jesuit is a Professor in the Department of Political Science and Public Administration at Central Michigan University and Chair of his department. He has been editor or coeditor of several academic volumes and journals, including the recently published book *Making Governance Work: Policy Making in an Era of Polarized Politics* (Routledge, 2017). Together with partners in Europe and Canada, he has taken the lead role in creating and expanding the Transnational Initiative on Governance Research and Education Network, or "TIGRE Net." This international group of scholars, students, and field specialists is dedicated to identifying the opportunities and challenges public managers confront in the global economy and to providing them with the strategies and skills necessary to overcome obstacles to domestic, cross-border, and international coordination.

Contributors

Arindam Biswas, Assistant Professor, Department of Architecture & Planning, Indian Institute of Technology – Roorkee, India.

Nebojša Čamprag, Post-Doctoral Researcher and Consortium Manager at Technical University Darmstadt, Germany.

Denita Cepiku, Associate Professor in Public Management, University of Rome – Tor Vergata, Italy.

Mohit Dev, Research Scholar, Department of Architecture & Planning, Indian Institute of Technology – Roorkee, India.

Thomas Greitens, Professor and Director of the Master of Public Administration Program, Central Michigan University.

Elona Guga, Lecturer of Management of Public Administration Reforms, University of Rome – Tor Vergata, Italy.

Robert Heuton, Adjunct Assistant Professor, Department of Political Science, University of Windsor, Canada.

Eunok Im, Assistant Professor, Department of Public Service, Kangnam University, South Korea.

So Hee Jeon, Associate Professor, Department of Political Science and Public Administration, Central Michigan University, U.S.A.

David K. Jesuit, Professor, Department of Political Science and Public Administration, Central Michigan University, U.S.A.

Dan Kildee, Member of U.S. Congress, Fifth District of Michigan.

Rick S. Kurtz, Professor of Political Science and Academic Dean, Minnesota State System, U.S.A.

Benedetta Marchese, PhD Student in Public Management and Governance, University of Rome – Tor Vergata, Italy.

Nancy Quarles, Commissioner, Oakland County, Michigan, and Lecturer, Central Michigan University, U.S.A.

Index

Note: Page numbers in *italics* and **bold** indicate Figures and Tables, respectively.

Printed in the United States
by Baker & Taylor Publisher Services